BRINGING
UP OSCAR

BRINGING UP OSCAR

The Story of the Men and Women
Who Founded the Academy

DEBRA ANN PAWLAK

PEGASUS BOOKS
NEW YORK

BRINGING UP OSCAR

Pegasus Books LLC
80 Broad Street, 5th Floor
New York, NY 10004

First Pegasus Books cloth edition January 2011

Interior design by Maria Fernandez

ISBN: 978-1-60598-137-6

10 9 8 7 8 6 5 4 3 2 1

Printed in the United States of America
Distributed by W. W. Norton & Company, Inc.

For Gogie,
who first took me to a darkened theater
and introduced me to a magical world
where anything could happen

I miss you every single day!

ACKNOWLEDGMENTS

Writing a book about 36 dynamic individuals has presented its own set of challenges. I could not have done it alone. My support team includes Alberta Asmar who never stops encouraging me on to greater things; my writer pal and research helper, Vickey Kalambakal, who knows the value of a great anecdote; my three best girls, Therese Kushnir, Carol Trana and Linda Wells, who read chapter after chapter and never once grumbled about tired, red eyes. In addition, I must also thank Bob and Barb Haberstroh who so generously let me stay in their home on Lake Michigan when I needed some quiet time to write. Many of the words in this book were written, reviewed or revised at their place.

My deepest thanks also goes to my agent, Peter Riva, and his wife, Sandra, who shared my interest in Hollywood history and took a chance on a little-known writer from Michigan. I also appreciate the efforts of my editor at Pegasus, Jessica Case, who remained upbeat, patient and understanding throughout the process.

I also want to express my gratitude to the American Heritage Center at the University of Wyoming, the London Ontario Public Library, and the Walter P. Reuther Library at Wayne State University. In addition, I want to personally thank Kevin Ball for the photos he shared from his private family collection, as well as his enthusiasm for this project. I am also grateful to the Farmington Community Library for their unending support and assistance in obtaining those hard-to-get books from all over the country whenever I needed them. My heartfelt thanks also goes out to my Facebook members who made my page, *Hollywood: Tales from Tinseltown*, so much fun to update. You all know who you are.

I also want to thank my husband, Michael, who probably didn't know what he was getting into 35 years ago; my daughter, Rachel, and her fiancé, Jon, who not only announced their engagement, but shared computer time and space whenever I visited in Denver; my son Jonathon, and his wife, Stacey, who encouraged every single page and then recently shared news of their own—the birth of our first grandchild would coincide with the publication of this book. I have a great crew and I love you all!

Last, but certainly not least, I want to thank the 36 men and women who founded the Academy of Motion Picture Arts and Sciences, and in turn, inspired me to write about them. May you and your unique contributions to the pre-eminent art form of the Twentieth Century never, ever be forgotten!

CONTENTS

——

"The Academy is the League of Nations of the Motion Picture Industry. It is our open forum where all branches can meet and discuss constructive solutions to problems with which each is confronted. In the past, we have never been able to get together on a common ground and in making this possible the Academy has conferred a great service. The producer, star, featured player, cinematographer—in fact, every individual can come into the Academy with any problem or proposal and feel that all barriers are leveled, that in this open court his voice carries the same weight as that of any other person, regardless of position and standing. There is no greater force for coordination, no greater avenue for constructive and intelligent cooperation for advancement than that offered by the Academy of Motion Picture Arts and Sciences."

(Mary Pickford, April 2, 1928)

PREFACE

- Earthquakes rattle the world killing over 200,000.
- British influenza epidemic claims 1,000 lives each week.
- One of the worst natural disasters in U.S. history affects 700,000 people as the mighty Mississippi floods.
- Dozens of children die when their school is bombed in the small farming community of Bath, Michigan.
- Yugoslavia severs its ties with Albania.
- An Italian steamer sinks off the Brazilian coast and more than 300 are lost.
- Japan faces a banking crisis.

News taken from today's headlines? Hardly. The year was 1927 and these events were sandwiched between several recessions, Prohibition, the Great Depression and two World Wars. The Roaring Twenties, much like the Twenty-First Century, were riddled with chaos. Amidst the turmoil, however, there were some remarkable achievements. The first transatlantic phone call was placed from New York to London. Inventor Philo Farnsworth transmitted the first television picture. Aviation hero Charles Lindbergh flew the first solo non-stop transatlantic flight from New York to Paris in his monoplane, *The Spirit of St. Louis*. Hollywood released its first talking picture, *The Jazz Singer* (1927) and the Academy of Motion Picture Arts and Sciences was formed.

The founders of the motion picture industry were dynamic individuals each with a vision for entertainment's future, who knew they were on to something revolutionary. They believed that a simple white sheet, which hung from the ceiling as a screen, could evolve into the premier art form of the Twentieth Century and then some.

Movies, however, didn't just magically appear on the silver screen nor was Hollywood shaped by the wave of a wand. It took determined 'collaboration'—a word the motion picture industry still bats around today—by talented individuals who weren't afraid to dream big. Early filmmakers faced obstacles similar to the financial and social challenges that impact our Twenty-First Century entrepreneurs. So what made these Twentieth Century pioneers stand apart and succeed? Dedication, tenacity, passion and their refusal to give up—qualities that forward thinkers everywhere must embrace today.

With the popularity of silent movies on the downswing and an astonishing new technology offering sound, 1920s Hollywood needed to keep the motion picture momentum going. A relatively new industry recently racked by mysterious murders and drug-related scandals, the key players had no rules to go by and made them up as they went along.

What the business really needed was one united front where competitive factions could come together to resolve disputes, discuss industry-wide challenges and promote the film community's positive side. MGM's headman, Louis B. Mayer, had an idea. Over dinner at his house, one Sunday evening in early January 1927, Mayer discussed his plan with guests actor Conrad Nagel, director Fred Niblo and the man in charge of censorship, Fred Beetson.

The three men agreed with Mayer's concept of one organized group overseeing the film industry. Days later, they presented their plan to 32 filmmaking giants at the Ambassador Hotel in Los Angeles. Everyone present approved. Together, this team of 36 unique and distinctive Hollywood professionals founded the Academy of Motion Picture Arts and Sciences. Their golden child, however, was not yet a gleam in anyone's eyes.

He hasn't changed much since making his public debut back in 1929. His height remains a steady 13½ inches. Like most of us, however, he has gained a pound or two over the years. He even picked up a nickname. Glamorous women have slept with him; powerful men have fondled him. Now, as the little man moves closer to membership in the centenarian club, he shows no signs of aging. Recognized around the world, he is the ultimate symbol of success, Hollywood-style. But what is his story? Where did he come from? Who was responsible for this legendary icon?

The founders included the following actors, producers, writers, directors, technicians and lawyers who saw an opportunity and took it:

Joseph Arthur Ball	Richard Barthelmess	Fred W. Beetson
Charles H. Christie	George W. Cohen	Cecil B. DeMille
Douglas Fairbanks	Joseph W. Farnham	Cedric Gibbons
Benjamin F. Glazer	Sid Grauman	Milton E. Hoffman
Jack Holt	Henry King	Jesse L. Lasky
M.C. Levee	Frank Lloyd	Harold Lloyd
Edwin J. Loeb	Jeanie Macpherson	Louis B. Mayer
Bess Meredyth	Conrad Nagel	Fred Niblo
Mary Pickford	Roy J. Pomeroy	Harry Rapf
Joseph M. Schenck	Milton Sills	John M. Stahl
Irving G. Thalberg	Raoul Walsh	Harry M. Warner
Jack L. Warner	Carey Wilson	Frank E. Woods

The group didn't waste time. Within two months, they elected officers. Douglas Fairbanks was the first president, along with Vice President Fred Niblo, Treasurer M.C. Levee and Secretary Frank E. Woods. The following May, the State of California recognized the group as a non-profit corporation. Later that month, the Academy hosted its first official banquet at the Biltmore Hotel in downtown Los Angeles. Of the 300 guests invited, 231 paid a $100 fee and joined the newly formed organization with its five main branches: Producers, Actors, Directors, Writers and Technicians.

One of the Academy's responsibilities was to publicly recognize outstanding achievements in film—kind of like tooting your own horn—and the Academy Awards were born. MGM art director Cedric Gibbons sketched a sleek statuette depicting a knight perched upon a reel of film and clutching a sword. Sculptor George Stanley created the molds. The Award of Merit, as it was known back then, was 13½ inches tall and weighed almost seven pounds.

With little glitz or glamour and absolutely no suspense (winners had been announced three months earlier), the first award ceremony quietly took place on May 16, 1929 in the Blossom Room of Hollywood's Roosevelt Hotel—minus the red carpet. Tickets were ten dollars each. The room was simply decorated with Chinese lanterns. Candles topped each table along with candy replicas of the award itself. If you didn't win one—you could at least eat one.

Before dinner, there was an hour of dancing. Afterward, Academy President Douglas Fairbanks presented the following twelve awards including two each for Best Picture and Best Director:

Best Picture (Production): *Wings*

Best Picture (Artistic Quality of Production): *Sunrise*

Best Actor: Emil Jennings (*The Way of All Flesh, The Last Command*)

Best Actress: Janet Gaynor (*Seventh Heaven, Street Angel, Sunrise*)

Best Director (Drama): Frank Borzage (*Seventh Heaven*)

Best Director (Comedy): Lewis Milestone (*Two Arabian Nights*)

Best Writing (Original story): Ben Hecht (*Underworld*)

Best Writing (Adaptation): Benjamin F. Glazer (*Seventh Heaven*)

Best Writing (Title Cards): Joseph W. Farnham (*Fair Co-Ed,
Laugh Clown Laugh, Telling the World*)
Best Cinematography: Charles Rosher/Karl Struss (*Sunrise*)
Best Engineering Effects: Roy J. Pomeroy (*Wings*)
Art Direction: William Cameron Menzies (*The Dove, The Tempest*)

This was the first and only year the Academy simultaneously recognized two best pictures and the only time winners were acknowledged for more than one movie. It also marked the one occasion that a silent film reached best picture status. Two special awards were also given that night: one to Charlie Chaplin for writing, acting, directing and producing *The Circus* (1928) and one to Warner Bros. for producing *The Jazz Singer* (1927). By honoring this talking picture, the Academy officially acknowledged the beginning of a new era in film.

Eventually, the Academy's Award of Merit got its famous nickname. No one knows for sure where it came from, but credit is often given to Margaret Herrick, an Academy librarian and executive director. According to Hollywood lore, she thought the statuette looked like her Uncle Oscar and the name stuck.

So just how did these 36 movers and shakers from around the world, with varying educational levels and a wide range of unrelated experiences, end up in the same room together in early 1927?

A healthy mix of strong conviction, a little sweat, and a whole lot of chutzpah.

BRINGING UP OSCAR

Part One

YOU OUGHTA BE
IN PICTURES!

Chapter One

THE FLICKERS

Once upon a time, before any director ever yelled "CUT!," there was a sleepy little place just outside of Los Angeles with a few ranches and farms scattered here and there. It wasn't yet a town and it didn't have a name, but locals could claim miles of dirt roads and plenty of dust. That all began to change in 1886 when realtor Harvey Henderson Wilcox, along with his wife, Daeida, purchased a 120-acre property on the outskirts of the City of Angels at a cost of $150 per acre.

Soon after, Daeida, on a train trip back east, met a woman who talked about her residence that she had christened "Hollywood." Daeida liked the sound of it so much that she adopted the name for her newly acquired west coast property.

Crops and cattle, however, weren't quite what the Wilcoxes had in mind. They registered a map of their subdivided land with the county recorder on February 1, 1887—the first official document to carry the name Hollywood. They sold sizeable lots to wealthy folks who wanted to spend their winters in California. It wasn't long before large, fashionable Victorian and Queen Anne style homes lined the main street known as Prospect Avenue.

The town became official in 1897 when Hollywood's first post office opened inside the Sackett Hotel. The wooden building was located at Prospect Avenue and Cahuenga. It took another six years before the village was incorporated into a city. The eight-member team who comprised the Hollywood Board of Trustees made up all the rules. Back then, liquor was illegal unless it had something to do with a doctor's prescription. Bicycles were banned from the sidewalks. Cowboys could drive cattle, horses or mules through the city streets, but only in small herds of 200 or less. Hogs and sheep were different—competent men could herd more than 2,000 at a time, as long as the animals were supervised. Fireworks were also taboo.

But it wasn't the illicit hooch or the unruly livestock or the forbidden pyrotechnics that caused the city's biggest headache. It was water—there just wasn't enough of it. By 1910, the situation was so serious residents voted for annexation to the City of Angels, which at that time had enough water for everyone. Before the annexation was official, however, Hollywood's Board of Trustees slipped in a few final changes—like renaming Prospect Avenue to Hollywood Boulevard.

As the first decade of the Twentieth Century came to a close, Hollywood, as well as the rest of the world, poised on a precipice of change. Horseless carriages, flying machines and telephones were just a few of the cutting edge inventions that were slowly reshaping daily life. A newfangled form of noiseless entertainment, affectionately referred to as "flickers," was also taking hold.

Early flickers were brief—hovering right around ten minutes. They consisted of one reel of film—some made for laughs, some for excitement, but all meant to entertain. These one-reelers were often shown on a simple white sheet that hung from the ceiling of a church basement, vaudeville theater or town hall. Sometimes department stores also hosted flickers if the owners wanted to earn extra income after hours. There were even some tent-carrying exhibitors who took their show on the road. For a nickel or a dime, patrons could witness a little action. Before long, entrepreneurs like Sid Grauman, Harry Warner and Louis B. Mayer realized that presenting flickers might well turn into a lucrative business.

Sidney Patrick Grauman's journey to Hollywood began in Indianapolis, Indiana where he was born to Rosa Goldsmith and her husband, David Grauman, in 1879 on St. Patrick's Day—hence his middle name. From Indianapolis, the Graumans trekked across the country touring with vaudeville and minstrel shows. Grauman once claimed: "I went to a hundred schools, and I never got out of the fifth grade." The first time he put on a show, the ten-year-old was simply trying to rescue a friend's birthday party from boredom. Much to everyone's delight, he rounded up the guests and asked them to perform.

In 1898, as the Alaskan gold rush fever spiked, the elder Grauman took his son to the Yukon hoping to strike it rich. Panning for gold didn't quite work out, but there, in the rugged terrain, young Grauman found his calling. The following year, father David was forced to leave Alaska and his son behind due to an illness in the family. Before he left, however, he gave the boy $250. Grauman gambled it away in no time. Now alone and needing money, the resourceful child bought newspapers for eighteen cents each and then sold them to the miners for a dollar. He also arranged for some entertainment—usually boxing matches or other talent when he could find it. He even persuaded budding novelist Jack London to help him sell tickets. (Years later, Grauman took an uncredited part of a poker player in the 1935 movie version of Jack London's famous book *Call of The Wild*.) Grauman soon realized that entertainment was a commodity everyone wanted. Better yet, they were willing to pay for it.

The younger Grauman left Alaska in 1900 traveling south to San Francisco where he once again teamed up with his father. It was there that they discovered moving pictures at the Cinemagraph Theater, San Francisco's first movie house. Sid Grauman was so impressed with the place, he took a job there selling tickets. His boss gave him fair warning: "Don't let even the wind get by without a ticket!"

Before long, he and his father financed a theater of their own, The Unique, located on Market Street. They set up hundreds of kitchen chairs along with a piano and held fifteen shows daily—a blend of live performances and single reel films. Actors took their meals onstage right in front of the audience to avoid disrupting the schedule. Even then, Grauman had an eye for talent, hiring movie-mogul-to-be Jesse L. Lasky to play the cornet and future movie star Al Jolson to sing.

The Unique Theater was so successful that the Graumans built a second cinema, The Lyceum. The two theaters were popular venues among the locals until the devastating earthquake of 1906 shook things up. The theaters along with most of the city were flattened, and what remained standing was severely damaged. Never one to give in, Sid Grauman believed that, in the midst of tragedy, entertainment was more important than ever. Just days after the earthquake, he raised a large tent, which had been used for revival meetings, where The Unique once stood. Under the big top, he installed old church pews. Holding 3,000 people, Grauman's National Theater brought movies back to San Francisco with a banner proclaiming: "Nothing to fall on you except canvas!"

Each day, thousands of people came to the makeshift theater seeking short-term relief from their troubles. The soft-sided cinema remained in continuous operation for the next two years. To the locals, Grauman was a hero. He even received a commendation from the city for aiding public morale during the disaster. Sid Grauman always had a knack for endearing himself to the people who surrounded him and he certainly knew how to put on a helluva show.

While the Graumans were searching for Alaskan gold, Harry Warner was fixing shoes and selling bicycles in Ohio. Born on December 12, 1881 in Krasnashiltz, Poland—at the time a Russian province—Warner's parents, Benjamin and Pearl Wonskolaser, named their first son Hirsch Moses. Benjamin, a cobbler, found it hard to live and support his family under the unrelenting threat of overbearing Cossacks. He made a difficult decision and left for America without his family hoping life might be better there. Taking the new last name of Warner, he arrived in Baltimore and opened a shoe repair shop. One year later, he had saved enough money to send for his family. That's when Hirsch Moses, newly arrived in America, became Harry Morris Warner.

As the Warner family grew, cobbling shoes no longer provided a steady enough income. Benjamin went on the road attempting to sell pots and pans while Pearl and Harry minded the shoe shop. The traveling peddler business didn't live up to Benjamin's financial expectations so he made another daring move. He left the shoe business behind, packed up his family and, with a horse and a wagon, headed north to Canada. There, he found fur trappers willing to trade their pelts for supplies. What should have been a prosperous business turned into a disaster when a dishonest partner stole all the furs, leaving the hardworking Warners destitute. They had no choice but to return to Baltimore and once again fix shoes.

By now, fifteen-year-old Harry and his twelve-year-old brother Abe had become pretty good cobblers themselves. With two sons to work with, Benjamin decided to leave Baltimore in 1896 and try his luck in Youngstown, Ohio. The shoe business was good, but with nine children to care for (including four-year-old Jack who was born in London, Ontario, Canada in 1892 during the fur-trading days), the Warners needed more. They expanded their business to include groceries and meat. At long last, the tide of instability turned and the family's finances improved. In 1899, Harry and Abe ventured out with their very own bicycle shop.

In 1904, the Warner Brothers, Harry, Abe and now Sam, had a chance to buy a projector. Dazzled by the possibilities that moving pictures might offer, they pooled their resources. Even their father contributed after pawning his watch and faithful old horse. The projector came with one reel of film, *The Great Train Robbery* (1903), a groundbreaking western by early filmmaker Edwin S. Porter.

Within 800 feet of film, Porter sequenced together several scenes that told a complete and true story in ten minutes. He included a daring robbery, a thrilling chase and a gripping shoot-out—still staples of all good westerns. Porter even incorporated a revolutionary closeup of a six-shooter that appeared to fire straight into the shocked audience. Paying patrons flocked to see all the action and for the first time it was apparent to the Warners that these moving pictures might just have some big business potential. Harry and his two siblings temporarily rented an empty store in Niles, Ohio and played to sell-out crowds making $300 the first week the film rolled, which is the equivalent of more than $7,000 today.

While Harry tried to find a more permanent place to house their burgeoning business, brothers Sam and Abe went on the road. They traveled around Pennsylvania and Ohio until the reel of film literally wore out. Back home, Harry sold the bicycle shop when he found a former penny arcade in Newcastle to rent long-term. They built a stand for the projector and then painted the opposite wall white. All they needed now were seats. No problem. The innovative brothers visited the funeral parlor next door where they persuaded the undertaker to loan them 99 chairs. The Cascade Theater held its first showing on May 28, 1905.

While Harry took care of the business, Abe and Sam manned the projector and carefully handled the nitrate films. Younger brother Jack was brought in to sing and recite poetry in between showings, which guaranteed the audience's quick exit making room for the next group. Their venture was a huge success, but Harry was always thinking.

Renting movies one at a time from the actual filmmakers was expensive and finding good movies was even harder. Abe Warner described what happened next:

> One day a man came around and told us he was getting twenty representative theater owners to pay him a hundred dollars each for ten weeks' supply of films—twenty reels. Well, we gave him the hundred dollars each and got our films. It was a good plan and it worked.

Everyone was satisfied, you see, and at the end of ten weeks the man still had his twenty reels of film that he could take to another territory and begin all over again.

Harry soon realized that more money could be made renting movies than showing them. He sent Abe and Sam to New York instructing them to buy films—as many as they could. There, the two brothers met Marcus Loew who owned several successful movie theaters. Loew never rented films, he bought them and once he was done running the reels, he simply stored them in trunks. For $500, Loew sold three trunks filled with film to the Warners.

The brothers' next stop was Pittsburgh where they opened The Duquesne Amusement Supply Company, the first official film exchange, or distribution center, in the country. Harry, now married to a woman named Rea Ellen Levinson, stayed in Newcastle to run the theater while Abe and Sam manned the exchange. A bitterly disappointed Jack was sent back to his father's house in Youngstown to help mind the family store. He desperately wanted to be with his brothers, especially Sam, but Harry gave the orders—something Jack resented for all of his days.

Harry, however, had good business sense and knew what he was doing. The exchange was so successful, bringing in about $2500 weekly, that Harry sold The Cascade in 1909. He then opened a second exchange in Norfolk, Virginia and this time gave a happy Jack the position of Sam's assistant while Abe remained in Pittsburgh. The Warner Brothers, with Harry at the helm and Jack bringing up the rear, were finally on track to a future with unlimited potential.

Like the Warner family, Jacob and Sarah Meir were originally from Russia where they were married in 1874. The Jewish couple had three children, Yetta, Ida and their first-born son Lazar. Later in life, when Lazar turned into Louis (pronounced the French way "Louie"), he would claim that his birthday was July 4, 1885, but his father reported it as July 12, 1884. Either way, the boy grew to be his mother's favorite.

By 1886, the Meirs were one of many Jewish families who left their homeland to escape the oppressive Russians after they had enacted a series of severely anti-Semitic laws including the forced conscription of at least one boy from every Jewish family. The Meirs fled to England and then to Ireland before finally coming to America and settling in Long Island. There, Jacob, a small man with a big temper, worked as a peddler/ junk dealer for the next few years and Americanized the family name to Mayer. In New York, the couple had two more sons, Rubin and Gershon. Moving from the east coast, the Mayers migrated to St. John, New Brunswick near the Bay of Fundy. The exact reason why they headed north is unclear. Some say that Jacob's temper got him into a spot of trouble with the law. Crossing the border may have been his version of the "get out of jail free" card.

Once in Canada, Jacob continued collecting and selling unwanted items. He even salvaged shipwrecked objects that found their way to shore. Eventually, the Mayers became Canadian citizens and Lazar, now using the name Louis, attended school. He also helped his father in the scrap business, by collecting bits and pieces of metal. By 1899, young Louis Mayer was doing a lot of Jacob's legwork. Then the boy got arrested for running a business without a license. As it turned out, Louis wasn't even old enough to hold a license. Upon hearing that the lad was simply trying to support his family, the judge assigned to the case helped Jacob obtain a license and legally hire his son so that everything was on the up and up. In his down time, Jacob's eldest son escaped the daily drudgery by visiting the local theater—a place he found fascinating.

In early 1904, as Sid Grauman was opening up a movie theater in San Francisco and Harry Warner was acquiring his first projector, Mayer left his father and struck out on his own. He traveled to Boston where he met bookkeeper Margaret Shenberg, three years his senior and the daughter of a kosher butcher/cantor. The couple married on June 14, 1904 and Louis, like his father, went into the junk business. Their first daughter, Edith, was born the following year. Shortly after, the young family moved to Brooklyn where a second daughter, Irene, joined them in 1907—a momentous year for the Mayers.

Intrigued by flickers and the fact that patrons were willing to part with a nickel to see one, Mayer changed professions. He found an empty, run-down theater called The Gem in Haverhill, Massachusetts. Years later, Mayer recalled: "What I saw in front of me wasn't that dingy theater. I saw what it could become, and I convinced Margaret that I knew what I was doing."

With financial help from his siblings, he leased the place. It took several weeks and a lot of elbow grease to clean up the 600-seat theater, but Mayer opened it on Thanksgiving Day in 1907 with a mix of motion pictures and live vaudeville acts. Renamed The Orpheum Theater, Mayer declared that his establishment had only "high class film" and "refined amusement." He also picked up a middle name—Bert—a common thing for immigrants to do in those days. He must have liked the way it sounded and later admitted that he enjoyed being called "L.B."

The first actual feature shown in the updated theater was a film by Pathé called *The Passion Play* (1903). This biblical movie covered the entire life of Christ in about 27 scenes beginning with the angel's appearance to the Virgin Mary and ending with Christ's ascension into heaven. Mayer's biggest concern was whether the audience would sit through such a long film—two reels worth instead of one. He needn't have worried. Coinciding with Christmas and accompanied by a series of religious slides and hymns, the show was a holiday hit. Crowd-pleasing seemed to come natural for the man who once sold junk.

With Margaret keeping the books and Mayer in charge of everything else, the theater flourished. He even took a chance and doubled, sometimes tripled general ticket prices to 10 or 15 cents. Moviegoers were not deterred by the increases and Mayer's theater evolved into a local hotspot. After a weeklong closure due to further remodeling in 1908, he reopened the theater as The New Orpheum and was finally able to move his family into a nicer home.

To ensure the continued success of his business, Mayer hobnobbed with Haverhill's upper echelon. His name appeared in the paper. He spoke to civic groups assuring them that movies were not immoral, but wholesome family entertainment to be enjoyed not feared. In the process of selling himself and his theater, he also captured a spot in the city's social registrar. Louis B. Mayer was in his element—a celebrated member of the community who ran the show.

By 1908, about 8,000 neighborhood movie theaters had opened throughout the country. That equated to a sharp rise in patrons, who could now go see a show whenever they wanted to, which also meant a huge demand for new films. Multiple film production companies popped up around the nation, but the most successful ones were located on the east coast—primarily New York and New Jersey—not far from America's very first movie studio built by inventor Thomas Edison on the grounds of his laboratory in West Orange, New Jersey. New York provided the big city backdrop while New Jersey offered more scenic locations for filming. Situated within the same proximity, early filmmakers traveled between both to make movies that required the hustle and bustle of a sophisticated metropolis and/or the serenity of a picturesque countryside.

Several of the larger film companies such as The Edison Manufacturing Company in New Jersey and The American Mutoscope Company along with the American Vitagraph Company in New York were embroiled in a number of heated legal battles involving patents. The underlying issue was control of the film process itself. No one wanted to back down; they knew that film was here to stay. The long drawn-out fight finally ended when they all joined together forming The Motion Picture Patents Company (MPPC), or "The Trust"—a fancy name for a movie monopoly.

The Trust permitted only certain producers to make films with approved equipment while The Eastman Kodak Company only sold film to Trust members. All other filmmakers were considered renegades and their movies illegal. In addition, the MPPC was not above using violence to get their point across, foreshadowing the years of mobsters and hired goons that were to come—not the best circumstances for creativity to flourish.

A few venturous souls headed west taking their production companies with them. California with its fair weather, sparkling sun and magnificent landscapes had a certain appeal—especially for flickers shot outdoors. The thousands of miles that distanced the west and east coasts, and the bitter corporate rivalries, didn't seem so bad either.

As for that sleepy little town called Hollywood, it was about to wake up with a bang.

Chapter Two

WELCOME TO HOLLYWOOD!

The first American movie studio traces back to inventor Thomas Edison and West Orange, New Jersey. Located on the grounds where his laboratory stood, "The Revolving Photograph Building," formally known as The Kinetographic Theater, opened in early 1893 for film production. The structure itself was nothing to brag about and certainly not user-friendly. The odd-shaped building was completely covered with black tar paper on the outside and painted black on the inside. This dismal venue caused some members of Edison's staff to dub the place "The Black Maria"—a slang term of the period that referred to a police paddy wagon, also black and uninviting.

Pronounced "muh-rye-uh," the working studio sat upon large rollers and had a hinged roof that opened to the sun through a series of ropes, pulleys and weights. As the angle of sunlight shifted throughout the day, the entire building also rotated ensuring that there was always enough light for filming. Early flickers made at The Black Maria included such simple actions as sneezing and kissing—not on the same reel, of course. Edison also hired circus performers, vaudeville acts and sparsely costumed dancers, who jumped, gyrated and jiggled their way around the stage while a large wooden camera called a Kinetograph caught all the action. Filming even included a couple of boxing matches, the second of which was fought inside the studio on September 7, 1894. Boxing Champion James J. Corbett knocked out his opponent Peter Courtney in front of the camera.

As flickers grew in popularity, other production companies began to surface, mostly in New York and New Jersey. Then the complicated patent problems emerged. With their work negatively impacted, some early filmmakers, like David Horsley, took their business elsewhere. Prior to Horsley's move, several film companies, including The Selig Polyscope Company, set up shop in the Los Angeles area. Other companies, such as Biograph and its pioneer producer/director D. W. Griffith, sent units out west to take advantage of the mild weather and spectacular scenery. Until Horsley, however, none of them had established a permanent studio in Hollywood.

Horsley originally founded the Centaur Film Manufacturing Company in Bayonne, New Jersey along with partner Charles Gorman in 1907. They chose the name "Centaur" because it referred to the mythological creature who was half-man half-horse. After four years of struggling under the thumb of The Trust, Horsley knew that survival in the business meant relocation. He thought Florida would work, but one of his directors, Al Christie, disagreed. He suggested California. Two fair-minded businessmen, they flipped a coin. Christie won.

Packing up and heading west, The Centaur Film Manufacturing Company became The Nestor Motion Picture Company. Nestor of Gerenia was another figure from mythology—the Greek king of Pylos who led his people to victory during the Trojan War. In 1911, Horsley's outfit became the first motion picture studio to take up permanent residence in the boondocks of Hollywood. He housed his fledgling film company in the former

Blondeau Tavern on the corner of Sunset and Gower. For $30 a month, he rented not only the pub, but also the stables and carriage house. The tavern garden served as his back lot. With a weekly budget of $1200, the company averaged three films every seven days—a comedy, a western and an "eastern" or drama. Al Christie was in charge of the comedies and also served as overall manager for the company.

Christie wrote his movies at night and filmed them during the day using a stopwatch. When the time was up, they were done and the reels sent back east for processing. No one on the set had a chance to look at them before they were printed and distributed. Christie shared his stage sets and actors with the other directors, Tom Rickotta and Milton Fahrney. Everyone took his turn at filming on different days throughout the week.

By 1912, The Nestor Motion Picture Company was doing business with Universal Films. Three years later, the two companies merged with Christie taking charge of the comedy department. Being an independent spirit, however, Christie wanted to strike out on his own. In 1915, he returned to the Sunset and Gower location asking big brother Charles to join him there.

The Christie Brothers hailed from Canada. Their father, Scotland-born George Wiseman Christie, was a police constable in London, Ontario. He had a daughter, Anne, from his first wife, Mary Reynolds, who died at an early age. George took a second wife, Mary Ann Jarvis, and the couple had a son, Charles, born on April 13, 1880. Younger brother Alfred joined the family in late 1881. The following year, the Christies were plunged into despair when George unexpectedly died of consumption, an old term for pulmonary tuberculosis. Mary was forced to fend for herself and her children, including stepdaughter Anne, so she took in boarders. Many of her guests worked in the theater, which made an impression on young Al.

He spent much of his time at The London Ontario Opera House watching the performers—particularly the comedians who intrigued him. He even started suggesting ways the comics could get more laughs from the audience. Those who were receptive to his ideas tipped him. Others told him to get lost. Eventually, he took on the position of opera house stage manager before moving to New York where he also worked in the theater until David Horsley hired him to direct films.

The elder and more serious-minded Christie brother, Charles, remained in Canada and became a railroad man. He worked for the Grand Trunk Railroad in the passenger department and eventually moved on to advertising in their Ontario Division. He also married Edna Durand, the daughter of Canadian architect George F. Durand and his wife Sarah Parker, on October 15, 1902. The next year, Christie left the Grand Trunk to become a salesman before moving on to run a large department store in Ontario where he stayed until Al beckoned him to Hollywood.

In 1915, Christie stopped minding the store when he joined younger brother Al at Sunset and Gower. Together, they established The Christie Film Company, which specialized in comedies. Fun-loving Al oversaw production while Charles, with his knack for business, took care of the books. Based on a good word from Horsley, Universal agreed to distribute their pictures. The two brothers stayed away from slapstick and produced situational comedies, such as *Seminary Scandal* (1916) starring comedienne Billie Rhodes. This short with the titillating title told the story of a young boy who dressed as a girl in order to be with his lady love when she went away to boarding school where boys weren't allowed. Explained Al Christie:

> We were more concerned with storylines than sheer slapstick, and I don't think we would have been nearly so successful if we had tried to copy Sennett. He was the master of slapstick. He dressed his people up in odd-looking clothing that no normal person would be seen dead in outside the studio. We dressed ours in street clothes and gave them funny situations that were, in our eyes, much more acceptable to the more sophisticated audiences. . . .

The brothers were spot on. Moviegoers delighted in their storylines and proved it at the box office with high ticket sales. Now independent producers, The Christie Film Company turned the men into big-time filmmakers and their mother helped. She joined her sons in California and to cut overhead, she often loaned them her furniture. For example, if a scene required a table and chairs, she sent her dining room set to the studio—as long as her boys promised they'd have it back to her in time for dinner.

While business was on the upswing, Charles suffered a personal setback. His wife, Edna, developed an ulcer requiring surgery. As a result of the operation, she died on July 16, 1918. The childless couple had been married almost sixteen years. Charles never took another spouse.

As for the movies, The Christie Film Company was so successful that the brothers increased their production capacity and purchased new equipment—the latest technology had to offer. They even established a fan mail department where secretaries answered letters written to their popular players by enthusiastic moviegoers. Each actor had his or her own unique stationery and was required to personally sign every letter written on their behalf. An autographed picture usually accompanied each response. It may have been a lot of bother, but the innovative Christie Brothers believed it helped business.

This same department also created a movie magazine called *Film Follies* so that fans could keep up with their favorite players along with the film company's latest news. First published in 1919, the magazine proved very popular and had a successful run for more than a decade. While Al kept everyone laughing, Charles went to the bank and the Christie Brothers morphed into movie moguls.

While the Christies established themselves at Sunset and Gower, other production companies followed suit. Former Biograph director Mack Sennett set up The Keystone Pictures Studio near Los Angeles. Carl Laemmle, head of The Universal Film Manufacturing Company of New York, opened a studio right across the street from The Nestor Motion Picture Company.

New York theatrical producer and booking agent Jesse L. Lasky organized the Jesse L. Lasky Feature Play Company, which also settled in Hollywood at Selma and Vine.

Born in San Francisco on September 13, 1880 to Isaac Lasky, a shoe-store proprietor and his wife, Sarah Platt, Jesse Louis Lasky was one of the few early filmmakers native to California. His grandparents immigrated to the United States from Germany. In the mid-1800s, they journeyed across the country in a covered wagon until they reached Sacramento.

As a youngster, Lasky's family moved from San Francisco to San Jose where he loved to fly fish with his father. He also spent time playing the cornet on the family's front porch. It was his hope that band leader John Philip Sousa would march down his street, hear the music and be so impressed that he would have no choice but to make room for Lasky in his famous ensemble. Sousa never got to Lasky's house. Instead, Isaac fell ill and lost his business. The family moved back to San Francisco where Lasky's father passed away. With part of the insurance settlement, the family invested $500 in a machine that was supposed to make maple syrup. The venture was a scam and the two men who sold them the contraption took the money and ran.

Next, Lasky rushed off to Alaska hoping to strike gold, as did so many other young men during the late nineteenth century. Like Sid Grauman, however, he found that gold could be elusive. He purchased what he thought was a gold mine near Nome. As it turned out, the con man that sold him the property had just 'salted' it with gold dust when Lasky wasn't looking. Now totally broke, he took a job playing his cornet in an Alaskan bar called The Sourdough Saloon. Musically inclined from childhood, he continued honing his skill and was now adept at playing. From The Yukon, he traveled to Hawaii where he once again played his cornet—this time with the Royal Hawaiian Band and the only non-islander in the group.

In 1901, Lasky returned home to reconnect with his younger sister Blanche, an accomplished cornetist herself. The two formed a brother-sister act and hit the vaudeville circuit blowing their dueling horns. After several years of performing and traveling together, the pair grew tired of life on the road and Lasky turned to the business side of vaudeville. Like other early movie pioneers, he also had a knack for discovering talent. He became a booking agent in New York where he found jobs for various acts while Blanche stayed home with her mother—not uncommon for a young, single woman at that time.

Three years later, while vacationing in the Adirondacks, Lasky met artist, poet and accomplished pianist Bessie Mona Ginzberg of Boston. Despite a disastrous date where the slender, dark-haired Bessie toppled out of their canoe and into a local lake, she married him on December 11, 1909. With a little help from Bessie, sister Blanche also found herself a mate—glove salesman Samuel Goldfish who later changed his name to Goldwyn.

Goldfish cut a fine figure. He'd come a long way since his early days in Poland where he was known as Schmuel Gelbfisz. Penniless, he had walked across Europe finally stopping in England where he took the name Samuel Goldfish. He eventually immigrated to the United States by way of Canada. Goldfish found work at a glove factory in Gloversville located in upstate New York. At the time, Gloversville, as the name would imply, was the hub of American glove manufacturing with multiple factories churning out all sorts of hand wear for both men and women.

Goldfish worked hard and eventually became a successful salesman for the Elite Glove Company. Always looking sharp, he wore only the best suits with accessories to match—all the way down to the sheen cast by his dapper shoes. He never carried a wallet or change in his pocket. It was important to steer clear of any noticeable bulges that might disrupt his flawless facade. With his eye-catching wardrobe, he traveled from city to city throughout New England and upstate New York peddling gloves of every kind. The chic image he created for himself worked. He made sales earning about $15,000 each year—and women noticed him. Goldfish, however, was fond of his boss's niece—Bessie Ginzberg.

Much to Goldfish's disappointment, Ginzberg chose the young entertainment entrepreneur, Lasky. After they were wed, Bessie invited Goldfish to dinner where she introduced him to her new sister-in-law, Blanche. Theirs may not have been a match made in heaven, but a matter of two people who were unhappy with the single life. Goldfish soon married into the family and tired of the glove business. He wanted to try something new and the idea of flickers excited him, but he needed a partner. Who better than Blanche's brother, a man already established in show business? To Goldfish's dismay, Lasky didn't share his enthusiasm. He had reservations about endorsing a new medium that might rival the theater. Lasky offered another idea. He thought they should corner the tamale market in New York: "I know a business that would be wonderful—tamales. They make them in San Francisco. In the east, you never hear about them."

Goldfish, however, wouldn't let go of his dream and tamales did not seem like a rewarding alternative. Helping his cause was the huge financial loss that Lasky took in 1911 when his private venture, the Folies Bergère, didn't pan out. The elaborate restaurant/cabaret that Lasky built near Times Square was modeled after the famed French nightclub of the same name. Despite featuring the seductive Mae West, his establishment folded after a disappointing five months due to a lack of paying customers. The failed enterprise cost Lasky more than $100,000. All the while, Goldfish continued pestering his brother-in-law about the movies.

Following the Folies Bergère fiasco, Lasky bought the rights to an operetta called *California*. He needed someone to adapt it for the vaudeville stage. Accomplished playwright William DeMille, who had written *The Warrens of Virginia*, was at the top of his list. He visited the office of agent Beatrice DeMille to request her eldest son for the job, but Beatrice had other ideas. William was busy so she insisted that Lasky use her younger son Cecil who, with a wife and young daughter to care for, needed the work.

Cecil Blount DeMille was born on August 12, 1881 in Ashfield, Massachusetts, and was named after his grandmothers, Cecilia Wolff and Margaret Blount Hoyt. The second son of Henry Churchill DeMille and his British-born wife, actress Matilda Beatrice Samuel, Cecil had an older brother, William. Little sister Agnes followed in 1891. Henry, whose family came to America in 1658, was of Dutch descent, while Beatrice had a Jewish heritage. A former actor, Henry taught school, worked as a lay reader in his Episcopalian church and wrote plays on the side.

In the evenings, Henry would read the bible to his sons—one chapter from the Old Testament and one from the New. He followed the scripture readings with classic literature written by celebrated novelists such as Victor Hugo and William Thackeray. Eventually, Henry teamed up with legendary theater producer and playwright David Belasco and earned enough money penning plays to quit his day job. On the verge of a promising writing career, Henry caught typhoid fever and died on February 10, 1893 at the age of thirty-nine. Two years later, the DeMilles were once again shaken by loss when four-year-old Agnes died from spinal meningitis.

Now the sole provider for two young sons, Beatrice went to work. She became a playwright herself in addition to opening an agency with an office on Broadway. She also established a school called The Henry C. DeMille School for Girls adjacent to the historic family home, Pamlico, in Pompton, New Jersey. The house was named after the Pamlico River, which ran near Henry's boyhood home in Washington, North Carolina.

At fifteen, Cecil went to military school in Chester, Pennsylvania. A shrewd woman, Beatrice managed a trade-off—Cecil's tuition requirements were met by allowing the headmaster's daughter to attend the DeMille school at no charge. Cecil, however, was more intrigued with military life than military school. In 1898, The Spanish-American War fired him up. Determined to fight, he left the educational institution for the army, but his tender age was against him. The Army sent him packing—he was too young to enlist. Instead, he entered the New York American Academy of Dramatic Arts, an unlikely substitute, but considering both his parents' theatrical background, it was no surprise that

DeMille chose to act upon his rejection from the Army. He talked about his early years on stage: "Kind-hearted publicists who have written about me have sometimes said that I became an actor in order to learn production. The facts are more elemental. I became an actor in order to eat."

While working in the play *Hearts Are Trumps*, DeMille met actress Constance Adams—eight years his senior and the daughter of New Jersey State Judge Frederick Adams. The couple married at the Judge's home in East Orange on August 16, 1902. That very same year, Beatrice welcomed a new pupil to her school at the request of socially prominent architect Stanford White. The teenage girl, Evelyn Nesbit, was also White's lover at the time.

Despite a relatively uneventful term at school, several years later, Nesbit was embroiled in White's scandalous murder. Before marrying the wealthy Henry Thaw of Pittsburgh, she ended her relationship with the architect. Her new husband, however, could not get over the fact that his wife had had an affair before their marriage. The unstable Thaw eventually snapped and shot White at the Madison Square Garden Theater in front of a large crowd. Thaw's ensuing trial revealed a myriad of sexual escapades that included some unusual physical activity involving White and a certain red velvet swing. After such blazing headlines involving a former student, enrollment at the DeMille school declined, and Beatrice was forced to close the establishment and concentrate on her agency where she now represented several clients including writers Mary Roberts Rinehart and Avery Hopwood, as well as both of her sons. Playwright William was by far the more successful brother. That's when Beatrice paired the skeptical Lasky with her youngest boy who in addition to his wife, Constance, now had a young daughter, Cecilia, to support.

Despite Lasky's initial misgivings about Cecil's inexperience, DeMille adapted *California* for the stage and it was a hit both critically and financially. The two men continued their collaboration on several more plays. In the process, they found that they actually liked each other and a long-lasting friendship began. Lasky enjoyed his success while DeMille, unhappy in his brother's shadow, grew restless. And lurking in the background was Samuel Goldfish—still talking up the potential of movies every chance he got.

Goldfish finally persuaded Lasky, who was once again encouraged by the success of the *California* play, to create a new film company, which included attorney Arthur Friend as secretary. They called their new business the Jesse L. Lasky Feature Play Company. Even Lasky conceded to Sam that this sounded much better than Lasky's Hot Tamales. Now, with Lasky's name and financial expertise at the helm and Goldfish ready to sell their goods, all they needed was a director—someone to make the films and manage their creative output. After D.W. Griffith, who had recently directed the gang drama, *The Musketeers of Pig Alley* (1912), turned them down because of their inadequate financing, Lasky and Goldfish met DeMille for lunch to discuss their business venture. Instead, DeMille made a startling announcement:

> Jesse, I'm pulling out. Broadway's all right for you—you're doing well. But I can't live on the royalties I'm getting, my debts are piling up, and I want to chuck the whole thing. Besides, there's a revolution going on in Mexico and I'm going down and get in on it—maybe write about it. That's what I need—a stimulating and colorful change of scene.

According to Lasky, DeMille's proclamation pushed him over the edge. He did not want his good friend to wander so far off. Lasky impulsively offered DeMille the position of director-general in his new film company, and DeMille accepted on the spot. It was an offer he could not refuse. Now all they had to do was figure out how to make a movie. DeMille, eager to learn the nuances of film versus live theater, went to the Bronx where he visited the Edison studios for a day. There, he watched a scene being filmed. A frightened young girl climbed over a wall and ran down a road where she met a man. The two characters then engaged in an animated conversation, and that was that. Cut. Over and out. DeMille told Lasky and Goldfish: ". . . If that's pictures, we can make the best pictures ever made!"

The group then bought the rights to a play called *The Squaw Man* written by Edwin Milton Royle. Goldfish, ever the salesman, sold hundreds of prints throughout the east coast before the movie was even made. The leading roles went to Broadway actor Dustin Farnum and his girlfriend, actress Winifred Kingston, who came as a package deal. Cameraman Alfredo Gandolfi and experienced Edison director Oscar Apfel also joined the troupe. With DeMille in charge, the group headed to Flagstaff, Arizona in 1913. After all, they would be making a western and Flagstaff would provide an authentic setting. Once they arrived, however, their target city didn't measure up to DeMille's expectations. The next time Lasky heard from his director-general was when he received the following wire:

> Flagstaff no good for our purposes. Have proceeded to California. Want authority to rent barn in place called Hollywood for $75 a month. Regards to Sam. Cecil

His words sent Lasky and Goldfish into an uproar. They thought their movie was being filmed in Flagstaff, but DeMille had taken it upon himself to move the entire company to Hollywood—a place they had never even heard of. After much debate, they cautiously wired DeMille back:

> Authorize you to rent barn, but on month-to-month basis. Don't make any long commitment. Regards. Jesse and Sam.

As president of the company, Lasky left for California to check the place out. Arriving in Los Angeles, he called for a taxi and asked to be driven to Hollywood. The cabbie didn't know how to get there. He stopped at the elegant Alexandria Hotel for directions.

After cruising along several miles worth of dirt roads, the taxi driver dropped Lasky off at the Hollywood Hotel, which was situated on

Hollywood Boulevard between Highland and Orchid Avenues. Once inside, Lasky introduced himself as the head of the Jesse L. Lasky Feature Play Company and asked where his studio was located. The hotel clerk had no idea. Lasky then asked the clerk if he knew Cecil B. DeMille. The clerk had never heard of DeMille either. He did remember, however, that there were some movie folks working out of a barn about six blocks down near some pepper trees in the middle of an orange grove.

Lasky followed the clerk's directions and sure enough, he found the barn where DeMille greeted him with a grin: "Welcome to Hollywood, Jesse!"

Chapter Three

TEAM BIOGRAPH

When inventor William Kennedy Laurie Dickson, who helped develop the Kinetoscope, became disenchanted with his boss, Thomas Edison, Dickson designed the Mutoscope. To simulate motion, Dickson's new machine quickly flipped a series of still photos, while the Kinetoscope relied on a single strip of film moved at a very specific rate. One machine was no better than the other, but the changes were just subtle enough to allow Dickson and his three business partners to establish their own New York film company in 1895—The American Mutoscope Company. The following year, this same group also came up with a machine that projected images on a screen. They called it the Biograph and it rivaled Edison's Vitascope, which also utilized the projection method. In 1899, almost fifteen years before Jesse Lasky entered the film business, Dickson's outfit was officially renamed The American Mutoscope and Biograph Company to clearly identify the two types of films they manufactured.

Because of the differences in its equipment, the new company did not fall prey to Edison's otherwise wide reach. Instead, it was so successful over the next nine years that they even had international partners who produced and distributed their films around the world and also used their technology. Their heady achievements were mostly credited to a thirty-something former stage player who happened by the studio looking for work in 1908 shortly after the more sophisticated Biograph had completely taken over the Mutoscope. This young actor/writer who went by the stage name Lawrence Griffith joined the team now simply known as The Biograph Company where he continued acting and writing.

Lawrence Griffith was, in reality, Kentucky-born David Wark Griffith, the son of Lieutenant Colonel Jacob Wark Griffith who had once served in the Confederate Army and his wife, Mary Oglesby. He arrived at the Griffith farm on January 22, 1875—one of their seven children. Jacob, or "Roarin' Jake" as he was sometimes known, suffered a serious stomach wound during the Civil War. That, however, didn't deter his keenness for drinking, but for "Roarin' Jake," mixing alcohol with a bad stomach turned toxic. After treating himself to pickles followed by a good swig of whiskey, he died in 1882.

Mary and her children ran the farm until 1890 when she moved them all to Louisville. Young David took odd jobs in an effort to help his family with finances. He worked as an elevator operator, a bookstore clerk and a newspaper reporter. Eventually, he was taken with the theater and became an actor, but he never hit the big time. Instead, he toured with several traveling companies and met his first wife, actress Linda Arvidson, in San Francisco. After the couple married in Boston, they moved to New York in 1906 where Griffith tried his hand at playwriting. Despite having one produced play, he was unable to scrape together a living. In 1908, he hired in at The Biograph Company as an actor and writer, and from there his luck would change.

Three months after he joined Biograph, the company needed a director so Griffith was promoted to the job. He accepted on the contingency that he could return to acting if his directorial abilities were found lacking. He needn't have worried. While he was a mediocre actor, in the director's chair, Griffith and his handpicked teammates saw art where others saw novelty. His cutting edge one-reelers catapulted Biograph into the proverbial spotlight and set the course for future films.

In addition to his directing duties, he hired several new players including Florence Lawrence and Jeanie Macpherson. At the time, actors were not given on-screen credit for their roles because film companies believed that anonymous actors remained low-paid actors. An otherwise nameless face, Florence Lawrence, originally with Vitagraph, grew into one of Biograph's most popular players and movie fans simply dubbed her "The Biograph Girl." Lawrence eventually left Biograph for The Independent Motion Picture Company under the imaginative direction of producer Carl Laemmle who openly identified her through a rigged publicity stunt. Laemmle gave Florence all the credit she deserved once she joined his company and as a result, Florence Lawrence became a household name and the silver screen's very first movie star.

Jeanie Macpherson, however, wasn't content with working in front of the camera—or keeping her feet on the ground. Red-haired and dark-eyed, Jeanie Culbertson Macpherson was born on May 18, 1887 into Boston's high society. Her father, the Canadian-born John Sinclair Macpherson, was of Scottish descent. Her mother, Evangeline Claire Tomlinson, was a Michigan girl with French roots. Macpherson's paternal grandfather moved his entire household including servants, teachers and his very own Presbyterian minister from Scotland to America. S.J. Tomlinson, her maternal grandfather, ran a Michigan newspaper. As a young girl, Macpherson also acquired a colorful stepfather resulting from her mother's second marriage in October 1895 to Chicago's very own "Barley King," Henry Joseph O'Neill.

Once a wealthy man, O'Neill lost his fortune in bad barley investments just before the turn of the century. He claimed that he owed $500,000 to various debtors, but had only $5,000 in assets. He also told the courts that $50,000 of the total amount owed was incurred jointly by him and his wife. The extravagant Evangeline was not about to pay up so she took Jeanie and fled to Montreal. There, she checked into the swanky Windsor Hotel. Her plan was to board a Dominion Line steamer headed to Liverpool and get away from it all—via first class passage. Instead of sailing the next morning, however, Evangeline was arrested. Officials seized all eight of her traveling trunks and took note of her property totaling more than $8,000 in lace, linen, jewelry and silverware. She was released after posting $800 in bail money.

By 1901, the O'Neills had resolved their credit issues and Jeanie was being schooled in Paris. Upon returning home, she attended Chicago's Kenwood Institute. Passionate about music, she pursued a career in the opera and also studied dance under the famed Russian-born ballet great Theodore Kosloff. From the Chicago stage, she traveled to New York where she worked in the theater before joining Griffith at Biograph. A quick wit who welcomed a challenge, Macpherson once told *Photoplay* magazine's Alice Martin about her first visit to Griffith's office:

> Mr. Griffith wasn't in. His assistant was. I told him my stage experience.
>
> He ignored it, scorned it. "We want to know what you can do before a camera," he said.
>
> I said, "If you get me on my Scotch Day, I can't do anything, but if you get me on my French day, I can do [Italian] parts."

According to Macpherson, Griffith quickly hired her to work in his motion pictures. He cast the twenty-one-year-old in her first film, a crime drama called *The Fatal Hour* (1908) where she shared screen time with Griffith himself, his wife Linda Arvidson and future Keystone Kop creator Mack Sennett. Over the next few years, Macpherson made more than 100 films at Biograph, dozens of them with an up and coming young actress named Mary Pickford.

Mary Pickford's given name was Gladys Louise Smith when she was born on April 8, 1892 in Toronto, Canada. Around 1890, her mother, the hardworking Charlotte Hennessey, had married John Charles Smith, an unreliable man who could down a drink but couldn't keep a job, as was the issue with so many men in those days, despite the proclivity of temperance societies. Charlotte was the daughter of Catherine Faeley who, as a young girl, traveled with her family from Ireland to Canada. In Quebec, Catherine met her husband, Irishman John Pickford Hennessey who, in a Freudian twist, also liked a drink. Charlotte's husband, John Charles, was one of twelve children belonging to Sarah and Joseph Smith. The elder Smith was originally from Liverpool, but moved to Canada at an early age. After Gladys's birth, Charlotte and John Charles had two more children, Lottie followed by John, better known as Jack.

Around the time that Jack was born, John Charles, no longer interested in his wife and children, left them. Desperate to hold on to her good name, Charlotte declared herself a widow. Ironically by the time Gladys turned six, John Charles actually died of a head injury that he suffered while working on a steamer, bequeathing Charlotte an honest claim to widowhood. Alone with three small children and an ailing mother, Charlotte took in sewing and boarders to help pay the bills. Gladys, always in tune with her mother, took her role as the eldest child very seriously—especially after a local doctor offered to adopt her to ease the number of mouths Charlotte had to feed. When she realized that she would have to leave her mother and her siblings in order to gain financial stability, Gladys refused to go through with the adoption out of sheer stubbornness and a firm resolve to somehow take care of her family. Pickford later recalled:

A determination was born in me the day of our visit to Dr. Smith [no relation] that nothing could crush; I must try to take my father's place in some mysterious way, and prevent anything from breaking up my family.

One of Charlotte's boarders worked at the nearby Princess Theater. When he suggested that Gladys and Lottie work for him for extra pocket money, Charlotte turned him down. She didn't want her children exposed to those sinners who called themselves actors, but after a visit to the theater, Charlotte softened. Most of the cast and crew were "regular," hardworking folks like them, just doing the best they could. The Smith family sorely needed money and once she met the players in person, she found that these sinners were no worse than any other sinners she had known.

The two Smith sisters debuted in *The Silver King* written by Henry Arthur Jones at Toronto's Princess Theater in January 1900 while Charlotte played the organ. Young Gladys tested her acting chops by playing Ned, the main character's son. As the dainty child stood in front of the audience earning money for her family, a spirited ambition and dogged drive enveloped her. Mature for her age and feeling responsible for her mother and siblings, Gladys embraced the challenge of being the family's main breadwinner and she never looked back.

For the next several years, the Smiths joined touring companies that played throughout Canada and the United States. By the time she was nine, Gladys took on starring roles such as Little Eva in Harriet Beecher Stowe's classic *Uncle Tom's Cabin*. Life on the road was often difficult. The nicer hotels wouldn't rent to "theatricals." The Smiths often stayed in rundown rooms, took their meals in train stations, sometimes scrounging for food and huddling under newspapers for warmth.

In between jobs, they stayed in New York where Gladys, still feeling responsible for the well-being of her family, hoped to find permanent work in the city's theater district. It was no easy task and fifteen-year-old Gladys promised herself that if acting didn't work out, she would soon trade in the stage for needle and thread. Besides acting, sewing was all she knew how to do, and in her mind, it was the only alternative she had to support her family.

Before she invested in a sewing machine, however, Gladys set her sights on meeting notable Broadway producer David Belasco. She tried for several weeks to get his attention through letters of introduction and personal visits to his casting office. Nothing worked. Out of ideas, the determined young girl made a drastic move. She approached the maid of popular theater actress Blanche Bates begging her to intercede on her behalf. In turn, the maid pleaded with Bates to help the young actress. At the maid's urgings, Bates gave Gladys permission to use her name—sight unseen. Gladys then marched into Belasco's office and told his staff that Bates had sent her. Belasco finally agreed to meet the persistent young girl.

A nervous Gladys introduced herself to the legendary producer. He was amused by her youth and tenacity, but thought that the name "Gladys Smith" didn't suit her. Belasco asked what other names might be in her family. She rattled off a few, but when she got to "Pickford," he stopped her. She then told him that her baptismal name was Marie. On the spot, Belasco re-christened her Mary Pickford. He also cast her in his production of *The Warrens of Virginia* written by none other than William C. DeMille.

The play ran on Broadway from December 1907 through May 1908, after which Pickford joined the touring company. Her steady income, most of which she turned over to Charlotte, ended when the play finally folded in March 1909. Out of work and still feeling responsible for her family, Pickford reluctantly considered a new and far less familiar medium—the movies. Charlotte suggested The Biograph Company and Pickford, who almost always listened to her mother, agreed to give it a try. By this point, D.W. Griffith was making a name for himself as the Biograph director and had been known to hire stage actresses in the past. Convincing herself that this was only a temporary job, Pickford entered the Biograph studio where she encountered Griffith for the first time.

Pickford prided herself on her professional acting experience, but her stage credentials didn't impress Griffith. He eyed her up and down wondering how she might come across on film. There was only one way to find out and Griffith himself prepared her for a screen test. She felt nervous and quite awkward in front of the camera until one of the actors, Owen Moore, asked: "Who's the dame?"

Pickford's acting came to a sudden halt as she bellowed: "How dare you, sir, insult me? I'll have you understand I'm a perfectly respectable young girl, and don't you dare call me a bad name!" Griffith lost his patience and scolded her for disrupting the film, but by the time Pickford completed the screen test, her scrappiness had won him over. A calmer Griffith invited her to return to Biograph the next day. Still skeptical of the movie business and embarrassed by her faux pas, Pickford agreed to come back, but deep down wondered what Griffith might really be after. She was also pretty certain that her work at Biograph would be as insignificant as a mite of dust in a windstorm and every bit as temporary.

The next day, Griffith cast an unenthusiastic Pickford as an extra in a Florence Lawrence comedy called *Her First Biscuits* (1909). The seventeen-year-old didn't stay in the background for long. She was just warming up and like the dutiful daughter she was, she kept her unconventional family fed, clothed and protected. She also kept them close to her, still craving the comfort of their shielding presence. Soon the ambitious young actress, now comfortable in the new film medium, stepped out of the crowd and into the lead roles. By the end of 1909, Florence Lawrence had left Biograph for producer Carl Laemmle's Independent Motion Picture Company and Pickford was popular enough with moviegoers to inherit her title, "The Biograph Girl."

The following January, Griffith took a Biograph acting company to California to finish filming scenes for *The Newlyweds* (1910). The story, about a young girl who falls in love and then runs away with a Native American boy, took place on a California ranch. The rough New York winter wasn't quite the atmosphere he was looking for so Griffith chose to complete his film in Los Angeles where the outdoor scenery would be more authentic. He also wanted to check out the area hoping that Biograph would set up a permanent studio on the sun-filled west coast.

Back east, early films were often made on city rooftops where sunlight could be captured at its brightest. The summer months worked fine, but the dark dismal winters made filming difficult if not downright impossible. To escape the inclement weather and to continue working, some film companies headed west on a seasonal basis. In California, they found everything they might want—the city, the country, the sea, the mountains and the fair weather, particularly the almost constant sunshine.

Now starring in *The Newlyweds*, Pickford joined Griffith and his gang as they headed west. Her brother, Jack, was not part of the crew, but at the last minute Charlotte put him on the train as it slowly pulled out of the station. He had no luggage, just an order from his mother to look after his big sister. A disappointed Jeanie Macpherson was not invited on the road trip and cried as her coworkers left without her.

Once in Los Angeles, Griffith rented a loft to store equipment as well as a vacant lot located at Grand Avenue and Washington Street to be used for outdoor filming. Pickford described their working studio:

> Our stage consisted of an acre of ground, fenced in, and a large wooden platform, hung with cotton shades that were pulled on wires overhead. On a windy day our clothes and curtains on the set would flap loudly in the breeze. Studios were all on open lots—roofless and without walls, which explains the origin of the term "on the lot" . . .

In many of those early films, windblown actors can be seen standing amidst flapping tablecloths and waving draperies in what was supposed to be an interior scene. Some things, like the elements, just couldn't be helped, but it was all taken in stride. Perfection wasn't part of those early budgets.

The next one-reeler that Griffith shot on the west coast was called *In Old California* (1910). It was a period picture starring Marion Leonard as a Spanish senorita and the first movie to be entirely filmed along the country roads of Hollywood. The locals were curious about the camera-toting crews that suddenly appeared in their midst. As upstanding citizens, however, they also feared that sharing their small town with these dubious movie-types might very well lead to no good. Their qualms made little difference as filmmakers eventually outnumbered them, and the money they spent in the town while filming soon silenced any misgivings.

Three months and over 20 films later, Griffith's troupe returned to New York. By now, Pickford's sweet, and still very girlish, face framed by curls was popular with the public although no one knew her name. She was also secretly seeing actor Owen Moore who, like Florence Lawrence, had left Biograph to work for Carl Laemmle where he was given on-screen credit. Handsome and sophisticated, Owen Moore was five years older than Pickford. The eighteen-year-old admired him and, infatuated with his worldly ways, overlooked two things: Charlotte's disapproval and Moore's frequent bouts with the bottle.

Laemmle had been after Pickford for quite some time. He even offered her a raise in salary and on-screen credit for her performances. The thought of working with Moore again didn't hurt either so, at the end of 1910, Pickford gave in. She left Biograph for Laemmle's company and on January 7, 1911, she secretly married Moore. Professionally, Pickford's star was rising. Personally, she soon discovered that Charlotte was right— running off with Moore had been a ghastly blunder.

Later that same year, Jeanie Macpherson also split from Biograph while her mother was back in bankruptcy court. This time in New York for $1,570 worth of debt attributed to dressmaking, dental work, lingerie and china. While Evangeline once again focused on her finances, her daughter went to work for director Oscar Apfel at Biograph's rival, the Edison Company. Later, when Apfel joined DeMille on his trek to Hollywood with the Jesse L. Lasky Feature Play Company, Macpherson got to thinking: maybe heading west would be good for her career, too.

Despite the loss of Pickford and Macpherson, 1911 had good points for Griffith. Biograph consented to opening a permanent studio in California and Griffith found his right-hand man, journalist Frank E. Woods.

Frank Emerson Woods and his twin sister, Carrie, were born in Linesville, a tiny western Pennsylvania town (less than one square mile in size) near the Ohio border, in 1860. Their father, James, was a bookkeeper. The twins joined older brother Arthur, who became a physician before carving out his own niche in Hollywood as a research director for the movies.

The younger Woods, who always liked to write, began his journalism career in high school before moving on to start his own newspaper in Erie, Pennsylvania. In 1890, he married West Virginia-born Nancy Ellen Anderson who often went by the name of Ella. By 1907, Woods was in New York and employed by *The Dramatic Mirror* as a salesman and writer. He frequently wrote about the emerging film business and as early as 1908 began reviewing movies—often credited as the first journalist to do so.

Woods took his job quite seriously and believed that filmmakers must take their responsibilities just as seriously—the ability to forever change the world was in their hands. He saw the film medium as a new art form—unique to the Twentieth Century. He panned movies that lacked depth and at the same time praised those films that reached a new level of sophistication. He once wrote on a hopeful note: "Motion pictures are at last gaining recognition as an institution of immense value to mankind." Remaining anonymous, he signed his column "The Spectator."

Woods reviewed the good with the bad and where he saw bad, he figured he could do better. He penned several scenarios for Biograph, which ended up under Griffith's direction. By 1911, the two men were collaborating together nearly full time.

In addition to his responsibilities as screenwriter and story editor, Woods also acted as production manager and publicist. Forever a gentleman when it came to the ladies, around the men Woods enjoyed a good story—the bawdier the better. Now in his early fifties, he was older than most of the people he worked with. His gray hair along with his ever-present horn-rimmed glasses commanded respect from the younger players. Actress Lillian Gish described him: "Frank Woods, a kindly white-haired man whom we all called 'Daddy' Woods, was not only head of the story department but also judge in all our disputes."

As a father figure, "Daddy" Woods' word was almost always final. Woods was also the man who initially grasped the concept of writing specifically for the movies, versus adapting from the theater or just creating random stories. Before he went to work for Griffith, films were written haphazardly with little or no attention paid to story structure or continuity. As for the details, there weren't any. Woods changed all that with his new way of thinking. He once explained:

> . . . The makers of the picture have assumed that because *they* understood the meaning of every action, the spectators should also understand, forgetting that the spectators will view the picture for the first time. The moment a spectator becomes confused and loses the sense of what he is seeing on the screen, his interest is gone . . . While he is wondering "What are they talking about now?" or "Who is the chap in the long coat?" or "How did he get from the house in the woods?" the film is being reeled off merrily and the spectator has lost the thread of the story. . . . The average spectator is none too alert. . . .

Taking all that into consideration, Woods set the standard of excellence for scenario writing. Together, he and Griffith brought films to a new level of sophistication during and especially after their Biograph years. By 1913, Griffith no longer wanted to make one-reelers, but Biograph wasn't interested in making features. It would cost too much, take too long and audiences might get fidgety if they had to sit still for more than ten minutes—not to mention the dreaded discomfort of eyestrain due to the still relatively primitive technology that did not include sound. Griffith disagreed. He was anxious to film longer and more complex movies so he and Biograph parted ways.

During his tenure with Biograph, Griffith was responsible for hundreds of films and made movie history by using close-ups, panoramic shots and editing multiple scenes that, once joined together in the final cut, conveyed a story. He also had an eye for talent. He brought in individuals like Jeanie Macpherson, Mary Pickford and Frank Emerson Woods and gave them their start in the business. All of them, including Griffith himself, would soon land in Hollywood where they would not just make movies, but shape an entire industry as well as an art form.

Chapter Four

THE SCRIBES

Before there were screenplays, there were photoplays. In 1913, authors J. Berg Esenwein and Arthur Leeds defined a photoplay: ". . . a story told largely in pantomime by players, whose words are suggested by their actions, assisted by certain descriptive words thrown on the screen, and the whole produced by a moving-picture machine."

Action was the key ingredient with a smattering of suspense tossed in for good measure. Explanatory words were used sparingly. The sharper the photoplay, the less need for narrative and dialogue. The most important rule concerned the spectator—don't confuse or lose him. There was no time to recapture a bewildered viewer's enthusiasm in the ten minutes it would take to view a short, or a one-reeler.

Once the carefully crafted photoplay was typed and ready for submission to the filmmakers, it was called a script. This script contained the following elements:

- Synopsis—A brief summary or outline of the story, which always included the names of the characters. A well-written synopsis was key as it compelled the reader to continue on. The reader would certainly reject a poorly penned synopsis long before he reached "The End."
- Cast of Characters—A listing of the characters noting which specific scenes they appeared in. This let the director/producer know if he could cast a player in two or more parts. For example, the same actor who was cast as a policeman in scene 3 could also play a butcher in scenes 5 and 6—great for budget purposes.
- Scenario/Continuity—A series of actions that tell a story. Each scene must be clearly identified as an interior/exterior shot along with any necessary elements that may need to be inserted such as newspaper headlines, letters or telegrams. With no time to waste, action should always begin promptly.
- Scene-Plot—A simple listing of the scenes to help the director/producer determine at a glance how many and what type of shots would be needed to complete the movie. The scene-plot was an optional component of the photoplay, but strongly recommended. Any director worth his salt appreciated this extra effort.

Rules were also established for photoplay formatting. In order to be seriously considered by filmmakers, photoplays had to be typewritten in black ink on opaque white paper (standard size of 8½ by 11 inches). Nothing irritated a filmmaker more than seeing page two through flimsy paper while trying to read page one. A smart writer always made at least one carbon copy to keep—just in case the original was lost and he had to retype it. The photoplay pages could be folded no more than twice in order to fit into a standard-size envelope. Never, ever roll the pages into tube-form. That would surely scream amateur.

Early photoplaywrights, or scenarists, like Frank Woods, set these precedents. Woods continued working with Griffith who, after leaving Biograph, joined the Mutual Film Company at the urgings of its president, former insurance man Harry E. Aitken. With the promise of making longer movies, Griffith sought more challenging stories. When Woods approached him about filming *The Clansman*, both a novel and a play, written by southern clergyman Thomas Dixon, the Civil War story struck a chord in the Kentucky-born Griffith. Griffith convinced Aitken to finance the film and Woods was given the task of writing a feature-length photoplay based on *The Clansman*. The still-controversial movie would be known as *Birth of a Nation* (1915).

Before the actual filming began, Griffith and Woods moved to California where the Mutual Film Company opened a studio in Edendale. While Woods was preparing the script, he was also working to protect authors' rights to ensure adequate pay and credit for their screen work. In 1914, he and several other early scenarists such as Anita Loos, Russell E. Smith and Hettie Gray Baker founded The Photoplay Author's League (PAL), a forerunner of today's Screenwriter's Guild of America. The group, with Woods as its first president, even backed an amendment to the copyright law to include the registration of unpublished photoplays. They also published a monthly bulletin called *The Script* to keep members informed of their activities, as well as general industry news.

Following Woods' example was another Biograph alumna, Bess Meredyth. Born Helen Elizabeth MacGlashan in Buffalo, New York on February 12, 1890, Bess was the youngest of three children. Her father, Andrew Fuller MacGlashan, was the son of a Scottish Presbyterian minister. Her mother, Julia Ginther, was a Roman Catholic whose family was originally from Alsace-Lorraine. Julia's brother was a priest and when she married a Presbyterian, her family promptly disowned her.

Bess' siblings were considerably older—William by twelve years and Viola by ten. Because of the age difference, Bess grew up more or less as an only child. She spent most of her time alone, becoming an avid reader. She also discovered that she had a flair for music and learned to play the piano. Unable to afford piano lessons for his youngest daughter, Andrew thought Bess would get the musical attention she needed free of charge in Detroit where his sister, Martha MacGlashan Woodward, resided.

In 1900, the ten-year-old child moved in with her Aunt Martha. Martha, the widow of a distinguished Michigan soldier and surgeon, Dr. Charles Meredyth Woodward, lived with her four spinster daughters—Martha, Elizabeth, Emma and Agnes. The Woodwards were tunefully inclined with Emma and Agnes, both teachers of music. Agnes, however, was fonder of whistling than piano playing. She put together a ladies' group, which she christened The Agnes Woodward Whistling Chorus—even Viola signed up. Agnes took them on tour in their own yellow bus. She went on to greater whistling heights when she moved to Los Angeles in 1909 and founded The California School of Artistic Whistling—the only one of its kind in the country.

After one year in Detroit, Bess had had enough of her female relatives and their warbling. She returned to Buffalo where she continued reading and playing piano. She also tried her hand at something new—writing. By the time she was twelve, she believed that her stories were good enough for publication so she approached a local newspaper editor with her work. Impressed by her gumption, he hired her to write a daily column for one dollar each.

The lively Bess grew into an impulsive teenager. When an acquaintance dared her to marry one of the football players on her high school team, the fifteen-year-old complied. Since the bride and groom were both underage, all stunned parents involved hastened to have the marriage annulled before too much damage was done. Later, Bess put romance on hold and her musical talents to use by playing piano for nearby vaudeville theaters.

Intrigued by the flickers, Bess left vaudeville for New York where she found work as an actress at the Biograph Company with D.W. Griffith in 1911. She also changed her last name to Meredyth—something she borrowed from her Michigan days and her late Uncle Charles. In addition to her acting responsibilities, she began writing scenarios to earn extra money and left her less-profitable musical skills by the wayside. Meredyth's life paused momentarily when doctors misdiagnosed her with tuberculosis. They advised her that moving to a warmer climate would be good for her health. Naturally, she chose California where other moviemakers were migrating. In addition to improving her physical well-being, she might also find more work.

Once on the west coast, the tuberculosis scare turned out to be nothing more. Her health no longer in jeopardy, she began working for the Universal Film Manufacturing Company where she made many films including a series of popular one-reelers known as *Bess The Detectress*. In these comedies, she starred as Bessie Pinkerton Holmes, a lady private eye who experienced the many perils and adventures of a female crime fighter. She also continued to develop scenarios much like Jeanie Macpherson who by now was also directing and writing at Universal in addition to acting. Despite being left behind on the original sojourn out west, she had truly come into her own.

During this time, Meredyth was seeing Canadian actor Wilfred Lucas. The couple had previously met in New York when they both worked for Biograph. Lucas, who had two sons from a previous marriage, hailed from Ontario, where he was born on January 30, 1871. After graduating from the University of Montreal, he spent over twenty years on the stage. His distinguished acting career made him a good fit in front of the camera. Despite their nineteen-year age difference, Meredyth and Lucas married in Philadelphia in 1917. She then gave up acting to become a full-time photoplaywright—a decision she never regretted.

One of Meredyth's future writing partners was scenarist Carey Wilson. The animated Wilson was born in Philadelphia on May 19, 1889 to Anna

Margaret Rapp and her husband, William Trego Wilson, whose Scottish ancestors migrated first to Ireland and then to the colonies during the 1700s where they settled in Pennsylvania. His sister, Helen, was older by four years. Always energetic, *New York Times* journalist Theodore Strauss once described him:

> . . . Mr. Wilson is as close to being a human spark-plug as we have met in a month of Sundays. He has a stream of talk that for sheer volume and torrential force probably hasn't been equaled since the Johnstown flood. He twists his words a little in delivery, like a billiard player putting English on a ball. Without scientific backing, we'd say that Mr. Wilson in two hours of conversation expands energy equivalent to a ten-hour day with a pick and shovel. . . .

After finishing school in Philadelphia, Wilson accepted a brief stint clerking at an extermination company, but soon decided that insects and vermin weren't for him. His attention turned to flickers. By 1911, he had learned how to run a film projector and within two years began his career as a film salesman for the newly formed Jesse L. Lasky Feature Play Company in New York. From there, he worked for the Fox Film Corporation as a general manager and foreign agent that allowed him to travel extensively to intriguing places like China and Australia. After leaving Fox, he took a managerial position with Peerless Productions, a state-of-the-art studio located in Fort Lee, New Jersey. In addition to his official duties, Wilson thought he'd try his hand at writing photoplays.

According to Wilson, he had a knack for words and earned a quick $2,000 for the sale of a single photoplay. Within ten days, he penned three more stories and sold them for $3,000, $4,000 and $5,000, respectively. Feeling lucky, he quit his day job and purchased two things—a Stutz Bearcat roadster just for fun and a typewriter so he could get down to business. Three-hundred-and-sixty-five days later and armed with 85 unsold photoplays, Wilson had neither car nor typewriter—just some cast-off newspapers stuffed inside his clothes for warmth as he slept in the subway station.

Now looking for steady employment, he happened to run into Samuel Goldfish who remembered Wilson from his sales days with Lasky. After hearing Wilson's unfortunate tale, Goldfish, who had been let go from his brother-in-law's company once Adolph Zukor took charge, was now running the Goldwyn Pictures Corporation. Goldfish asked Wilson if he happened to have a photoplay about the South Seas. Wilson assured Goldfish that he had just the thing. He then rushed off to a friend's office, borrowed a typewriter and banged out his made-to-order story. Goldfish liked the script well enough to give Wilson $400 along with a three-month contract for more. Rushing back to the subway station to tell his jobless cohorts the good news, he was robbed. Penniless, but with his contract in hand, he headed to California where he joined forces with Goldwyn's other popular photoplaywrights June Mathis, Ralph Block and Paul Bern.

During his tenure with Goldwyn, he was recognized as one of the screen's leading scenarists. He even had advice for beginners:

> . . . Characterization in pictures is becoming more and more important. It is not sufficient that a story shall merely classify its principals by name and occupation, as amateurs generally do.
>
> It is absolutely essential that movie characters be endowed with as much humanity, as much individuality and personality as are the people whom you meet in every-day life and feel you know well. Failure to do this is fatal.

But Carey Wilson had not yet reached the top of his game. That would come later by way of an adolescent actor named Mickey Rooney and a French prophet from the Middle Ages known as Nostradamus.

Besides teaming up with Meredyth, Wilson would eventually work with another writer, Benjamin Floyer Glazer, who was an expert at translation. Born in Ireland, at Newry, County Down, a suburb of Belfast, on May 7, 1887, his parents, Reuben and Rebecca, were originally from Russia. Reuben, who sometimes used the name Robert, was a picture frame maker while Rebecca bore eight children. The three eldest, Martha, Morris and Edith came along in Russia with Benjamin and Bessie following in Ireland. The Glazers immigrated to the United States in the fall of 1889 where their three youngest children, Eugene, Herbert and Rose, were born in Philadelphia.

Known to his family and friends as Barney, Glazer attended the University of Pennsylvania Law School and passed the bar in 1906. He remained in Philadelphia where he practiced law for several years and married a local girl, Alice Pulaski. Of Polish and German descent, she was the daughter of Frank and Rachael Pulaski. Alice's brother, Jack, was a well-known reporter and drama critic for *Variety*. Originally hired in the publication's early days by founder Sime Sullivan, Jack remained with *Variety* for more than thirty years.

Glazer himself preferred the pen to the legal life. He, too, became a newspaperman writing for *The Philadelphia Press*, but ultimately made his name by adapting foreign plays into English. As early as 1912, he traveled to St. Ives, a picturesque seaside village in Cornwall, where he spent the summer translating *Der Meister* originally written by Viennese playwright Hermann Bahr. Glazer's version, *The Master*, debuted on the American stage in 1916. The play starred theater actor Arnold Daly. Glazer, with his usual wit, described his search for just the right performer:

> One actor who had left his fiftieth birthday behind him, decided that the title role was too old for him. Another invited me down to his country home to rewrite the play under his direction. A third was afraid that he was too short to play the part; whether in talent or in stature he did not specify. A fourth contended that it was a subordinate role because it failed to enlist the sympathy of the audience. . . .

Glazer's biggest hit came five years later with his adaptation of *Liliom*, first penned by Hungarian dramatist Franz Molnar. Critics gave Glazer high marks for preserving the original spirit of the story and capturing the Hungarian terms with similar English slang. The play was so popular that Metro Pictures based a movie on it called *A Trip to Paradise* (1921) giving Glazer the first of his many on-screen credits. He and Alice soon left the east coast behind in exchange for the Hollywood hills where, at the stroke of Glazer's pen, the legendary love affair of Garbo and Gilbert waited to ignite.

But scenarists like Frank Woods, Bess Meredyth, Carey Wilson and Benjamin Glazer weren't the only film scribes who took their jobs seriously. Title writers were another dynamic group who carved their niche in the world of silent celluloid. Specializing in subtitles, these professional penmen had the power to enhance a good movie, save a bad one, or make an awful film even worse.

Title cards or intertitles were comprised of printed text that once filmed were then edited into the midst of a movie's action. They were developed to assist the audience in understanding the characters' conversations, move the story along and provide additional narrative information for clarity purposes. A clever intertitle inserted at the proper place and time was sure to stir up an emotional tear or elicit a hardy guffaw from the audience. Some moviegoers, however, grumbled that they didn't patronize flickers in order to read.

Title writer Gerald Duffy had a not-so-unique problem with one intertitle he worked on for Mary Pickford's movie *Through the Back Door* (1921). It was up to him to convey to the audience that the action was taking place in a New York hotel where Mary *might be* eloping and her mother *might be* considering a divorce. Seventeen words later, he came up with the following:

If it were not for New York hotels where would elopers, divorcees, and red-plush furniture go?

Title writing was a challenge for any wordsmith and the work soon became specialized. Each title card had to be short, to the point and inserted exactly between the right frames. Too many words meant there wouldn't be enough time to read them; not specific enough and they caused confusion; timed too late or too early, they made no sense. As films became longer and storylines more involved, the need for well-written title cards grew even more essential. According to Frank Woods:

> The sub-title should be in complete harmony with the story and should never divert interest from the story. It should never be obtrusive. It should be there only because it belongs there. Therefore all sub-titles should be couched in language that harmonizes with the story. Every word should be weighed. Nothing should ever shock the spectator out of his interest in the picture by its incongruity, extravagance or inanity. Too much in a sub-title is as bad as too little—like seasoning in a pudding. The function of the sub-title is to supplement and correct the action of the picture, to cover lapses in the continuity, and to supply the finer shades of meaning which the actor has been unable to express in pantomime.

Famous for his razor-sharp sub-titles, Joseph White Farnham, one of Hollywood's elite 'Titular Bishops', was a man of few words—just enough to fit on those fleeting title cards. Before he became one of filmdom's most revered writers, however, he was a military man. Born in New Haven, Connecticut on December 2, 1884, his father, George Frederick Farnham, was a clothing salesman. His mother, Anna, was born in New York to German immigrants who settled in America during the 1850s. Farnham also had an older sister, Lois.

In 1911, he began his writing career as a columnist at the *New York Morning Telegram* using the pen name Gordon Trent. Eventually, he became the advertising manager of the newspaper's newly formed picture section. From news writing, he went to the All-Star Feature Corporation where he worked as a publicity director and manager. While working for the film company, Farnham gave actor Dustin Farnum his first movie role in *Soldiers of Fortune* (1914), as well as actress Dorothy Dalton her first screen appearance in *Pierre of the Plains* (1914). Farnham also managed the first film starring stage great Ethel Barrymore.

After his stint with the All-Star Feature Corporation, he joined the Connecticut Coast Artillery Corps. Two years before the United States entered into The Great War, Lieutenant Farnham received orders sending him to France where fighting had begun. He was assigned to work on war pictures in conjunction with the Carnegie Peace Foundation due to his filmmaking experience.

Just before leaving the States, he secretly married his sweetheart, Alma Rose LeCourt, daughter of Emil and Rose Lowenthal, on February 6, 1915. Alma, born in South Orange, New Jersey in 1888, was a prize-winning horsewoman. She competed not only in New York and Maine, but also in Paris and Budapest. She had planned to study art in Italy upon retiring from her equestrian career, but World War I hampered her lessons. The young couple kept their marriage under wraps for more than a year.

After military life, Farnham found work at the Frohman Amusement Corporation owned by brothers Gustave and Daniel Frohman. There, Farnham was in charge of production and sales. Originally, the Frohman Brothers numbered three and were well-known New York theatrical producers. They founded their film company intending to make movies based on various plays that they owned. Charles, the youngest brother, was lost at sea on May 7, 1915 when a German U-boat torpedoed the luxury liner on which he was a passenger. The *RMS Lusitania* went down taking 1,198 victims with her including the fifty-eight-year-old Frohman. The headline news stunned the world and ushered in America's involvement in World War I, but for the Frohmans, the tragedy morphed into a very personal disaster. Despite their loss, remaining brothers Gustave and Daniel continued running the film company after their brother's death, perhaps as a way of memorializing his life and years of hard work.

While taking care of business at the Frohman Amusement Corporation, Farnham was also elected president of the Screen Club—the early filmmakers' version of New York's prestigious Lambs' and Friars' Clubs. Unfortunately, the Screen Club, a once-prominent group, founded by actor/director King Baggot in 1911, was now floundering. The three prior club presidents were successful movie men, but not such good business managers. Trying to keep up with the Lambs and the Friars, their excessive spending on fancy offices and lavish parties left the organization in financial shambles. Nor did it help when many influential members deserted New York for Hollywood.

Farnham, a charter member and officer of the Screen Club, was a well-respected businessman throughout the fledgling film industry. The monumental task of salvaging the group was left to him, but even he couldn't work miracles. The final blow came when former landlords sued the club for unpaid rent. The short-lived but extravagant-prone association came to an end and Farnham joined the defectors leaving New York for Hollywood.

By 1918, he wrote his first intertitles for the film *Once to Every Man* (1918) starring Jack Sherrill, a popular player who also worked for the Frohmans. As Farnham continued composing title cards, he soon realized that he was good at putting complicated ideas into brief phrases or sentences. More significantly, he grasped their importance. Farnham once discussed the art of writing title cards:

> Many people believe that writing titles is an easy task. They are badly mistaken. . . . Look down the [theater] row in which you are seated and you will find, especially at the beginning of a picture, that various people like various kinds of subtitles. You may like something subtle but the man next to you would fail to understand anything like that and prefers broad humor. The next person in the same row may like irony, the next satire, the next sarcasm. Every one of these people must be considered by the picture producer—and must be catered to. . . .
>
> Most successful title writers try to give a variety of titles to each picture. He appeals to every type of audience and he picks out a few

surefire ones that can't help but set everybody laughing. If he baffled you continuously with titles you would not like it. If he made them too difficult to understand you would be attending a guessing contest instead of being entertained . . .

While Farnham was on his way to being ordained one of Hollywood's nine exalted Titular Bishops, Bess Meredyth, Carey Wilson and Benjamin Glazer were honing their own writing skills preparing for a future when movies would talk. D.W. Griffith and Frank Woods teamed up with Keystone Cop creator Mack Sennett and producer Thomas Ince to form Triangle Films along with Harry Aitken and his brother, Roy.

Despite its cutting edge techniques and epic imagery, the release of Griffith's *Birth of a Nation* (1915) caused rioting in several major cities, including Philadelphia and Boston, due to its racial overtones. Other places like Chicago and Denver banned the Civil War story entirely. For the first time, a movie was more than just a romp across the screen. Flickers had been replaced with thought-provoking imagery and a story that made people think stirring up real emotion beyond a fleeting feeling of entertainment. *Birth of a Nation* roused fervor over film and people across the country were finally paying attention to this new medium.

Chapter Five

THE SILENT TYPES

W hile *Birth of a Nation* (1915) was making headlines, curious words like "aviation," "automobile" and "income tax" tip-toed into daily conversation. Names such as Woodrow Wilson, Henry Ford and Pancho Villa captured the headlines. The Panama Canal opened for business and the Boston Red Sox gained a new starting pitcher—Babe Ruth. Mexico fought its own bloody Civil War as the Ford Motor Company produced its one-millionth car. After more than 300 years in the driver's seat, Russia's House of Romanov, with a little help from their detractors, was self-destructing. Major unrest loomed across Europe and the world was an intimidating place sliding into the modern era faster than anyone realized.

Ordinary citizens, however, had more immediate concerns like earning a living, feeding their families and avoiding the constant threat of deadly diseases such as influenza, polio and tuberculosis. They needed a break from their daily routines and worries—a moment to catch their breath.

For a paltry sum, films provided that temporary distraction. Moviegoers knew that purchasing a show ticket meant procuring an escape, no matter how brief, and they gladly welcomed each getaway. As actor Milton Sills once explained in a 1927 article he wrote titled *The Actor's Part*:

> The motion picture enables the spectators to live vicariously the more brilliant, interesting, adventurous, romantic, successful, or comic lives of the shadow figures before them on the screen. . . . Here are men and women of the kind they would like to be; here is the kind of conduct they would elect to make theirs if they could. . . . The film offers them a . . . made-to-order reverie . . .

Sills also believed that attending a movie beat downing drinks at the corner saloon no matter how you looked at it, and no doubt many abandoned children and saloon-widowed wives agreed. An intellectual, Sills did not take kindly to fools. A well-educated philosopher, he certainly understood the concept of movie actors and why the public was so drawn to them. The players, with their on-screen antics, difficulties and lifestyles, were the focal point of the audience's experience. Embraced by average movie fans, these thespians, who were once shunned by their contemporaries, suddenly became extraordinary heroes, magnificent lovers and captivating clowns. Milton Sills, himself a popular actor, knew what he was talking about.

Milton George Gustavus Sills hailed from Chicago's upper echelon. Born on January 12, 1882, he was the first son of successful mineral dealer William Henry Sills and his banking heiress wife Josephine Antoinette Troost. Younger brother Clarence William joined the family seven years later in 1889. Sills recalled that as a youngster, he enjoyed the usual pastimes—shooting marbles, spinning tops and brandishing a baseball bat. Although he classified himself as a "lazy student," in reality Sills was no slouch. After graduating from Hyde Park High School in 1899, he received a one-year scholarship to college, an extremely rare thing in those days.

He studied calculus, psychology and philosophy at the University of Chicago where he also joined the prestigious Delta Kappa Epsilon fraternity. He spoke four languages—French, German, Italian and Russian, which allowed him to read the classics by masters such as Tolstoy the way they were originally written. In addition, Sills was a member of the university's drama club—just for the fun of it.

After earning his Bachelor of Arts degree, he remained at the school working as a researcher and then as a professor fully intending to obtain his doctorate. He also penned articles for local publications to make extra money. His scholarly life took an unexpected turn, however, when he crossed paths with Scottish-born theater actor Donald Robertson who happened to visit the university in 1905. There to guest-lecture on Norwegian playwright Henrik Ibsen, Robertson met Professor Sills. He thought that the prof and his handsome looks might well be appreciated on the stage.

Behaving totally out of character, the serious Sills abruptly abandoned the intellectual life for the not-so-cerebral footlights. He had been bitten by the stage bug. He joined Robertson's professional touring troupe and three years later found himself in New York where he was an instant success. Several noted producers such as David Belasco and Charles Frohman all wanted to hire him. For the next six years, Sills worked steadily on Broadway and also toured with several key theatrical companies.

While working in *The Servant in the House*, a play written by British lawyer Charles Rann Kennedy, he met costar Gladys Wynne, an English player. Her sister, Edith, was a famous stage actress, as well as Kennedy's wife. Gladys became more than just a professional counterpart. After taking Sills home to make sure her father approved, she married him in London on May 6, 1910. The couple had one child, a daughter named Dorothy Gardine whom Sills affectionately referred to as "My Kiddie."

By 1914, Sills was still working on stage, but thought he could do better and itched for a change. Looking for something different, he gladly accepted producer William A. Brady's offer to work in the movies. He took on the brief role of Corthell in a film called *The Pit* (1914), which was based on a novel by Frank Norris. At thirty-two years old, Sills once again met success head-on—this time on-screen. Handsome in a classic way, Sills went on to work as a leading man much to moviegoers' delight. After making several films with Brady, Sills struck out on his own. For the next ten years, he did something no other major movie actor dared to do—he freelanced.

Disassociating himself with any one company, Sills maintained his popularity and worked continuously for most of the major studios. He made one successful film after the other starring opposite such big names as Geraldine Farrar, Lois Wilson and Enid Bennett. He even appeared with famed ballroom dancer Irene Castle in a fifteen-part serial called *Patria* (1917). Although he claimed to like Castle, he often referred to the serial as "penance" for his many sins. Perhaps the serious Sills found *Patria* a bit brainless.

In light of this new success and popularity, he chose not to return to the stage, but still preferred New York to California. Sills kept an apartment near Columbia University where he spent as much time as he could in between pictures. *Photoplay* magazine reporter Alison Smith visited him there and was most impressed by his overwhelming collection of multilingual books:

> The walls are literally lined with books from floor to ceiling. It is the type of library that has been lovingly gathered together instead of being ordered by the square foot through a conscientious interior decorator. The books are obviously in daily contact with the life of their owner . . . This library dominates the room; you feel that all the rest was built about it and that the whole belongs to a scholar and a gentleman . . .

Sills was also an active member of both the Lambs' and Friars' Clubs. Known throughout the industry for his keen intelligence, Sills enjoyed a good game of chess, classical music and some serious gardening. Tall and stately, he was often pictured in a pensive moment wearing a well-turned suit and sporting a pipe that Sherlock Holmes would envy. A man with vision, Sills always had a lot on his mind. He once spoke to a group of Harvard business students:

> . . . For the survival of the industry, it is necessary today, to draft men of finer intelligence and cultural background, of greater energy, of greater business power, and of greater poetic creativeness. . . . Personally, I look forward to the day when . . . schools of motion picture technique may be developed, from which we may draw our cameramen, our directors, our supervisors, our writers. . . .

As an actor, the upstanding Sills was a fan favorite who commanded respect both on-screen and off. A true scholar and a genuine gentleman, he brought brainpower and sophistication to the movies proving that highbrow could be just as entertaining as its country cousin, slapstick, which by and large still dominated the movie scene at the time.

While Milton Sills continued his studies and polished his smooth persona, western star Jack Holt was building his brawn. The fifth of six children, Charles John Holt was named after his father, an Episcopalian minister. His mother, Frances Marshall, was the great-granddaughter of Virginian John Curtis Marshall who after serving as a captain in the Revolutionary War was appointed the fourth Chief Justice of the Supreme Court by second U.S. President John Adams in 1801. For the next 34 years, Marshall molded the Supreme Court into the authoritative and influential branch of government that exists today.

Like his great-great-grandfather, Holt often claimed to be from Virginia. Unlike Marshall, however, he wasn't really born there. Holt spent many years of his youth in Winchester, but he was actually born in Fordham, New York on May 31, 1888. Given Holt's penchant for horses and range riders, Winchester just sounded like a better place for a cowpoke to come from.

After attending New York's historic Trinity Preparatory School, sixteen-year-old Holt enrolled in the Virginia Military Institute located in Lexington, giving himself a bit of that Virginia pedigree. His first year there went by with little fuss, but during his second year, Holt outraged the school's faculty and students when he festooned a statue of George Washington with orange and green paint. His prank cost him one year's suspension. When he was finally forgiven and taken back into the fold, he got serious and, without further incident, earned a degree in civil engineering. Holt then returned to New York where he found work with the Pennsylvania Railroad supervising laborers in a tunnel underneath the Hudson River. A restless man, it didn't take long before boredom caught up with him.

Holt didn't want to spend the rest of his life on the rails or under the ground, but he couldn't decide where to go next. He was drawn to the excitement generated by Alaska, as well as the unique opportunities offered by the developing Panama Canal Zone. Undecided, Holt flipped a coin and Alaska prevailed. He took an engineering job with the Donahue Exploration Company who had copper interests in the frigid territory. Before long, however, Holt found that the business of engineering just wasn't exciting enough. With adventure on his mind, he struck out on his own. For the next six years, he traveled throughout the Yukon working as a gold prospector, fur trapper and even a postman who delivered the mail across hundreds of miles championing a dog-pulled sled.

When Holt finally tired of mushing, he traveled to Oregon where he pitched a tent in the middle of a friend's fruit orchard. Soon working with cowboys, he rekindled his youthful fondness for horses and became an expert rider. In 1913, his wanderlust took him to San Rafael, California, near San Francisco. While looking for work, he spotted a movie crew filming near the Russian River. The filmmakers needed a stuntman brave enough to tumble down the steep riverbank and into the water—on a horse. The fearless Holt stepped up and did such a fine job that the director gave him a bit part in the early western, *Salomy Jane* (1914).

Holt followed the crew back to Hollywood where he continued working as a stuntman, extra and occasional villain. His square jaw, striking looks and tough muscular build, however, were well suited for heroes. The Ford Brothers, directors John and Francis, soon noticed him. They cast him in several films including *His Majesty Dick Turpin* (1916) and *Born of the People* (1916). He even worked with Milton Sills and Irene Castle in that serial *Patria*—though unlike Sills, Holt never once mentioned penance.

In between movies, Holt met divorcée and single mother Margaret Helen Wood. She was the daughter of Henry Stanley Wood who owned the American Hoist and Derrick Company located in St. Paul, Minnesota. The international business was responsible for manufacturing construction equipment some of which was used for building the Panama Canal, as well as the development of Mount Rushmore. Holt married Margaret on December 6, 1916 and took in her young daughter, Imogene, from her previous marriage. The Holts also had two children of their own, Charles John III born on February 5, 1919 and Elizabeth Marshall born November 10, 1920.

The always-reliable Holt worked steadily, but it was his supporting role as the wicked Lord Raa in *The Woman Thou Gavest Me* (1919) that grabbed moviegoers' attention. By 1922, he was so popular that when the drug-addicted matinée idol Wallace Reid could no longer work, Holt replaced him as John Webster in *Nobody's Money* (1923). Starring roles in comedies and dramas continued, but the brawny actor finally came into his own when he returned to the western genre with some assistance from novelist Zane Grey.

Grey's best-selling book, *Riders of the Purple Sage*, published in 1912, was one of the first novels set in the old West. In 1918, Hollywood produced the film version under the direction of Frank Lloyd. Grey continued churning out western novels and Hollywood continued adapting them for the silver screen. In 1924, with Grey's blessing, Holt was cast as cowboy hero Adam Larey in *Wanderer of the Wasteland*. The following year Holt made five movies, three of them Zane Grey westerns—*The Thundering Herd*, *The Light of Western Stars*, and *Wild Horse Mesa*. A skilled horseman and passionate polo player off-screen, Holt handled his own riding stunts and always wowed the crowd with his agility. Moviegoers couldn't get enough of this strapping plainsman who was always fearless and frank.

Sometimes his work followed him home as Barbara Miller reported in the *L.A. Times* on April 26, 1925:

> . . . The other day at the studio [Holt] was called off the set to answer a frantic phone call from home telling him that two Indians were there in a taxicab and the nurse had no idea what to do with them.
>
> So Holt had them come over, for they are members of the Arapahoe tribe who took part in *The Thundering Herd*—Chief-Goes-In-The-Lodge and Lone Buck, come to see their friend "Big Buffalo," the name given Holt when he was taken into the tribe. The venerables are appearing in the prologue at [Sid] Grauman's Egyptian [Theater] under the direction of Colonel Tim McCoy.

Amidst all the electrifying drama and exhilarating action supplied by the brainy Milton Sills, the brawny Jack Holt and others of their ilk, film fans still couldn't resist a genuine, belly-rattling guffaw at the end of a tough week. They also knew who to count on for an entertaining, light-hearted delivery—Charlie Chaplin with his twirling cane, Buster Keaton with his stone face, Fatty Arbuckle with his pie-throwing and fan favorite Harold Lloyd with his infamous horn-rimmed glasses.

Harold Clayton Lloyd was born in the tiny town of Burchard, Nebraska (.2 square miles) on April 20, 1893 in a small frame cottage. Five years younger than his older brother, Gaylord, he was the second son of James Darsie "Foxy" Lloyd and Sarah Elizabeth "Lizzie" Fraser, a milliner. The Lloyds moved from city to city throughout Nebraska and Colorado because Foxy couldn't keep a job. He was too busy chasing grandiose get-rich-quick schemes that never seemed to materialize. Among his enterprises, Foxy had a go at taking photographs, clerking in a shoe store and selling sewing machines.

The youngest Lloyd was stage-struck from an early age. By the time he was 12, he was performing in local theaters. As a teen, he left the boards to take a short-lived turn at boxing. Although he relished the audience's attention, he didn't appreciate the punches so he quickly left the ring and returned to the stage. Eventually, Lizzie grew tired of following Foxy from place to place so she divorced him in 1910. Her seventeen-year-old son chose to stay with his father.

In 1911, the elder Lloyd won a $6,000 settlement (split 50/50 with his lawyer) for an earlier motor vehicle accident in Nebraska. He decided to use the money to benefit his son. Lloyd later explained:

> . . . I didn't know whether to go to New York, the Mecca of show business, or to California, where I would be accepted in the stock company. We actually tossed a coin and California won. . . .

The two men moved to San Diego where Foxy ran a pool hall and lunch counter while his son finished high school and made his film debut as an Indian in *The Old Monk's Tale* (1913). Young Lloyd then moved to Los Angeles where he worked for producer Mack Sennett in a number of Keystone comedies. He was also employed as an extra at Universal where he met future filmmaker, and former Alaskan adventurer, Hal Roach. After receiving an inheritance, Roach, along with partner Dan Linthicum, established their own studio, Rolin Film Company, in Culver City, California. Lloyd joined him there to play a character named Willie Work in a series of shorts. Willie, similar to Chaplin, with his baggy pants, scruffy hat and cat mustache, wasn't exactly a crowd pleaser.

Lloyd then developed a more popular character, Lonesome Luke, another pale imitation of Chaplin's Little Tramp. Luke's ill-fitting clothes were too tight, unlike Chaplin's oversized outfits. Like the Tramp, Luke also sported a mustache and large clumsy shoes, which he wore on the wrong feet. Between 1916 and 1917, Lloyd and Roach made over 100 films depicting Luke and his leading lady, teenage actress Bebe Daniels, in various predicaments. Lloyd later recalled:

Whatever the plot, the picture always ended with 200 feet of chase. I was pursued by dogs, sheriffs, angry housewives, circus tigers, motor cars, baby carriages, wild bulls, trolleys, locomotives and, of course, legions of cops.

As popular as he was, Lloyd thought he could do better. Keeping Daniels as his costar, as well as off-screen romantic partner, he got rid of the mustache and donned a simple two-button suit topped by a dapper straw boater. His only distinguishing feature was a pair of black horn-rimmed glasses minus the lenses. Inspired by a theater actor with a similar pair, Lloyd visited an optical shop in Los Angeles where he found just the right ones. He filmed using those glasses until they practically fell apart and then ordered another 20 identical pairs. Still, sentiment prevailed and Lloyd once admitted to wearing that original pair in the first scene of each of his subsequent films. Although he never wore them off-screen, the spectacles became his trademark.

He referred to his new creation as "The Glasses Character" or "The Boy" and described him as a "quiet, normal, boyish, clean, sympathetic, not impossible to romance" kind of guy. Lloyd was the first to bring an ordinary Joe to the silver screen. With his average, everyday guise, "The Boy" could have been anyone—a neighbor, a brother, a coworker or classmate. Naïve and unsuspecting, trouble found him everywhere he went. Enthusiastic moviegoers couldn't wait to see what outrageous predicament he encountered next as he tried romancing his sweetheart.

Beginning with *Over the Fence* (1917), Lloyd and Daniels so charmed the audience with their early romantic comedies that Lloyd eventually stopped making Lonesome Luke films altogether to concentrate on "The Boy." His success allowed Roach to buy out Lithicum and change the name of his film company to Hal Roach Studios.

Two years later, "The Boy" and "The Girl," still a Hollywood couple, were filming two-reelers. Lloyd talked about his real-life romance with Daniels in his 1928 autobiography, *An American Comedy*:

> From the time we made the three pictures at San Diego in 1915, she and I had been pretty constant companions, one of our chief bonds of interest, a mutual love for dancing. For a year or two before the war, dancing for cups was a craze in the picture colony. Bebe and I won twenty cups or more in competition against Wally and Dorothy Reid, Gloria Swanson and Wallace Beery and many other movie couples . . .

The dark-haired Daniels eventually grew tired of playing in comedies. She had always wanted a more serious acting career. Once her contract with Hal Roach ended in 1919, she left Lloyd both on-screen and off to work with Cecil B. DeMille who was still directing movies for the Famous Players-Lasky Corporation. Now, with his popularity on the upswing, Lloyd and "The Boy" both needed a new leading lady. Enter Mildred Hillary Davis.

Roach recommended the petite blonde Philadelphian, often called "Mid," to Lloyd. After seeing her on-screen, Lloyd thought that she looked like a "big French doll." In addition to Davis, Roach hired her younger brother, Jack, to play one of The Little Rascals in the *Our Gang* comedies. Lloyd and Davis filmed their first feature together, *From Hand to Mouth* (1919), as "The Boy" and "The Girl." Her youthful innocence complemented his unsuspecting naïvety and audiences fancied their wacky adventures.

But the job also had its hazards. Posing for publicity pictures on August 24, 1919, the "prop" bomb he held for the camera suddenly exploded leaving Lloyd badly burned and blind. The freak accident blew off his thumb and index finger on his right hand. Doctors believed his recovery impossible, but nine months later, Lloyd surprised them all. His vision returned. His wounds healed. He donned a specially made glove to disguise his disfigured hand and went back to the studio to film *Haunted Spooks* (1920) with Davis. For the most part, audiences remained unaware of his permanent disability and that's the way he liked it. Lloyd was afraid if the truth about his damaged hand leaked out, he would gain audience sympathy and forever lose their laughter.

Over the next four years, Lloyd and Davis transitioned into five-reelers. They made a total of 15 movies together including several classics such as *Grandma's Boy* (1922), *Doctor Jack* (1922) and Lloyd's most famous film, *Safety Last* (1923).

Inspired by real-life building scaler Bill Strothers, Lloyd created and filmed the classic scene where "The Boy" climbed a tall building in an effort to reach his ladylove who was waiting on the roof. Before he made it to the top, however, he was forced to grab the hands of a clock mounted to the building. Holding on to save himself from falling, he dangled over a busy city street. The rest of the story was written around this one scene because Lloyd never used a screenplay—at least until the talkies came along. "The Boy's" unorthodox antics not only made the film audiences laugh out loud, but also made them hold their collective breath in suspense. How would their favorite son ever get out of this one?

For Lloyd and Davis, their on-screen antics ironically ended with *Safety Last*, their final film together. He married his costar on February 10, 1923 effectively ending his tenure as one of Hollywood's most eligible bachelors, as well as her career in filmmaking. The Lloyds had daughter Gloria the following year. Lloyd also parted on friendly terms with Roach to start his own production company, the Harold Lloyd Corporation. Wanting to keep things in the family, he brought in father Foxy as treasurer and brother Gaylord as casting director. Lloyd was quickly becoming one of the most influential and highly paid stars in Hollywood.

With Milton Sills supporting modern-day dramas, Jack Holt disarming the Wild West and Harold Lloyd discovering that "The Boy" really can get "The Girl," distinct film genres were evolving. Motion pictures were getting longer, but moviegoers didn't seem to mind the extra time it took to watch a film. Plots were growing more complex, but audiences were up to the challenge. Worries over eyestrain and brain drain slowly dissipated as box office revenues continued to climb.

Chapter Six

THE IDOLS

The word "matinée" is derived from the French word "matin" meaning "morning." A matinée originally referred to a live theatrical performance, which took place during daylight hours—usually the afternoon. Well-to-do women, who picked up the moniker "matinée girls," mostly attended these performances. During the daytime, male escorts weren't required and wealthy ladies accompanied by other wealthy ladies thoroughly enjoyed their "girls only" outings. Critics claimed that these women came to the theater just to ogle their favorite leading men like the handsome Irish actor James O'Neill, father of playwright Eugene O'Neill.

The elder O'Neill was a popular performer during the 1870s and 1880s. His dashing roles, such as Edmond Dantés in *The Count of Monte Cristo*, which he played thousands of times, so endeared him to the ladies that a reporter once dubbed him "the patron saint of the matinée girls." Yet being idolized by these girls wasn't exactly a compliment. The actor's talent wasn't always recognized—just his good looks.

With the evolution of movies, matinée idols could also be found on the silver screen. Handsome faces such as Wallace Reid, Rudolph Valentino and John Barrymore became some of Hollywood's most popular leading men lionized by female fans. There were some prerequisites, of course. Matinee idols were two parts handsome and one part charming with a dash of debonair thrown in. They also possessed a keen sense of humor seasoned with a little pizzazz. Always smooth, alluring and fearless, they handled adversity the way they handled their women—with competence and a cool demeanor—even as the storyline turned against them. Heroes, lovers and good sons to their mothers, matinée idols oozed sex appeal, but their exclusive club had a limited membership.

Take Douglas Fairbanks, for example. He thoroughly enjoyed being Douglas Fairbanks. With a whirl of motion and an ever-present suntan, he delighted in the throngs of fans who greeted him around the world. Fairbanks lived large much like the way he made movies. His brother-in-law, Jack Pickford, however, didn't buy into that famous Fairbanks charm. He once told reporter Adela Rogers St. Johns that: "[Douglas] was always on. . . . He was always acting!" Well, not quite always. In the beginning, he was just the youngest son of an absentee father and a devoted mother.

When New York-born Ella Adelaide Marsh met wealthy and handsome John Fairbanks, she was enchanted. The couple married and in 1873 had a son, also named John. That same year, the elder John died from tuberculosis and his family lost his fortune. Ella hired Hezekiah Charles Ulman, her late husband's friend and prominent New York lawyer, for legal assistance, but she couldn't recoup any of John's assets. Destitute, she took her young son to Georgia and moved in with her sister's family.

In Georgia, she met and married Judge Edward Wilcox who turned out to be an abusive alcoholic and a bad connubial choice. Despite her new husband's shortcomings, Ella gave birth to another son, Norris. Soon after, she'd had enough and called upon Ulman's services once more— this time for a divorce. With Ulman's help, Ella dissolved her marriage while growing increasingly fond of her attorney.

Ulman, or H. Charles, as he preferred to be called, was born in Pennsylvania and served in the Union Army where he rose to the rank of captain during the Civil War. Rumor had it that he was Jewish and already wed, but Ella paid no mind to rumors. Besides, she was pregnant with Ulman's child so the couple, along with John, Jr., rushed off to Colorado where they wed on September 7, 1881. Ulman claimed he headed west to make his fortune in the gold and silver mines, but he was most likely trying to keep his New York family far away from his new frontier family. Little Norris, left behind with an aunt, was never in the western picture, but Ella's third son, Robert Paine Ulman, was born on March 2, 1882 in Denver.

Ella, who was used to the finer things in life, wasn't happy in the Wild West. Her husband was often absent and like so many others, he much preferred the bottle to domesticity. Despite Ulman's heavy drinking and his habitual disappearing acts, Ella managed to have one more boy—Douglas Elton who arrived on May 23, 1883. Ulman's bad habits were not conducive to family life, but when he was home, he liked to attend the theater often taking young Douglas with him. As a result, Ulman unwittingly taught his son two valuable lessons—alcohol shattered lives and the stage offered escape.

By the time Douglas was five, Ulman had left his family and returned to New York where he worked on the 1888 presidential campaign of Benjamin Harrison. Ella took in borders to make ends meet. She went back to being a Fairbanks and changed Robert's and Douglas' last name to match hers. John, the eldest who was always a Fairbanks, worked while the younger boys attended school.

Douglas was not the most studious child—he much preferred amusing his fellow pupils with acrobatic antics and shenanigans like walking on his hands. Ella enrolled him in a local acting school hoping to put his entertainment skills to good use. After being expelled from East Denver High School, Fairbanks joined a touring theatrical company. By 1902, he found himself in New York hoping to join the ranks of the celebrated Barrymores and 'the Divine' Sarah Bernhardt. His dedicated mother was not far behind.

It didn't happen overnight, but Fairbanks made a name for himself on Broadway in *The Man of the Hour* (1906). Once the show closed in New York, the troupe took it on the road. One of their stops was Boston where the twenty-five-year-old Fairbanks met nineteen-year-old Beth Sully, a starry-eyed matinée girl from the upper crust. Although Fairbanks' mother approved of the match, the Sullys did not. Wealthy businessman Dan Sully liked his daughter's beau, but taking a thespian into the family was not in his plan. He made Fairbanks a proposition—if the actor wanted to marry Beth, Fairbanks would have to give up the theater and help run the family business—the Buchanan Soap Company.

After a lavish wedding and a European honeymoon, Fairbanks kept his word and went to work for Sully's soap company. The theater, however, kept calling. By August 1908, soap selling was a memory and he was back on the stage where his popularity grew. It was a good choice, since the soap company soon folded and Fairbanks now had a family to support. The couple's only child, Douglas Fairbanks, Jr., was born on December 9, 1909.

Fairbanks Senior loved the spotlight and the spotlight loved him. Audiences couldn't get enough of his physical action and daring. When he joined ranks with the legendary showman George M. Cohan and his partner, Sam Harris, Fairbanks' career reached a new high. Theater critic Percy Hammond described Fairbanks in the 1913 play *Hawthorne of the USA*:

> Bounding, sprinting, diving, hurdling, he arrived in the last act in time to say "I love you" to the slim princess, as the curtain fell. Meantime Hawthorne, impersonated by Mr. Fairbanks, had also smashed the bank at Monte Carlo, arrested a regicide, escaped from jail, harangued a mob, acted as king for a few minutes, and had introduced slang and chewing gum into the Balkans. In one scene he pinched the Secretary of War, upset much of the army and kicked a seditious prince in the chest before jumping off a balcony for the second time in the act. It makes one breathless to write about it.

The stage, however, was a bit confining for someone with Fairbanks' exuberance. In order to reach his full potential, he needed the unlimited expanse that movies offered. He just didn't know it yet. Most legitimate theatrical performers in the early 1900s looked down upon the flickers— Fairbanks included. No real actor would ever leave the stage for such nonsense. Or would he?

In 1914, the Triangle Film Company, whose partners included film-makers D.W. Griffith, Mack Sennett and Thomas Ince, offered Fairbanks a chance to make a motion picture. His wife thought that acting in a movie would hurt his stage career, as well as their social standing, but his mother encouraged him to grab the opportunity. He was torn, but Ella's blessing and the offer of $2,000 per week helped change his mind. Due to prior theatrical commitments, however, Fairbanks had to postpone his motion picture work until the summer of 1915—after the release of Griffith's groundbreaking film, *Birth of a Nation* (1915). That film's success eased some of Fairbanks' apprehensions about the legitimacy of movies and his upcoming career shift.

Leaving his wife and son in New York, he rode the rails to Hollywood. Upon his arrival, Griffith was not impressed with Fairbanks or his physical maneuvers. He thought the actor had a head like a cantaloupe and that he'd be better off joining Mack Sennett's Keystone Kops. Before Griffith relegated the energetic theater actor to slapstick, however, he cast Fairbanks in a comedy called *The Lamb* (1915). The final cut greatly disappointed Griffith. In his eyes, Fairbanks and his frolics just weren't movie material, but even the master got things wrong on occasion. To everyone's surprise, the film was a hit after its September 23, 1915 debut at New York's Knickerbocker Theater. Fairbanks' vitality, charisma and comedic timing excited audiences who had never seen anyone like him. The Triangle Film Company suddenly reconsidered their original position—maybe this Fairbanks fellow had something to offer after all.

Several weeks later, actress Elsie Janis invited the Fairbanks to her home in Yonkers. Also present were actor Owen Moore and his actress-wife,

Mary Pickford, who was growing tired of Moore's alcoholic habits. When Fairbanks met Pickford, in true Fairbanks style, he swept her off her feet—literally. That day as the group of five meandered around Janis' property, they came upon a rather wide stream. Janis and Fairbanks nimbly skipped over some stones to the opposite bank. Moore clumsily followed. Mrs. Fairbanks was not so adventurous—she turned back. Pickford gave it a try, but soon perched atop a log, hesitant. As everyone watched, Fairbanks took matters, and Pickford, into his own hands. He picked her up and whisked her to the other side. His chivalrous gesture marked the beginning of their fabled romance even though they wouldn't see each other again until the following year.

With his movie career on the rise, Fairbanks took his family to California while Pickford stayed in New York. By 1916, Fairbanks had made over a dozen films for Triangle along with a name for himself in the motion picture industry. For the next several years, thirty-something Fairbanks was cast as the contemporary, yet adventurous, fun-loving all-American boy.

To moviegoers, a Fairbanks film guaranteed a good time charged with eye-popping action. While dominating the screen, he always saved the innocent girl from the evil cad in between a cache of stunts. Fairbanks once discussed his second film *Double Trouble* (1915): ". . . I ran a car off a cliff, had six rounds with a pro pugilist, jumped off an Atlantic liner, fought six gunmen at once and leapt off a speeding train."

With success, however, came sorrow. Late in 1916, Fairbanks was summoned to New York where his beloved mother, Ella, unexpectedly died of pneumonia. Her death hit Fairbanks hard, but he kept his emotions in check until after the funeral. Pickford, who cherished her own mother, sent him a sympathy note. Fairbanks then came calling and the couple took a drive through Central Park where he suddenly stopped the car and sobbed, for once letting his guard down. Pickford was deeply moved. She also noticed that the clock in the car had stopped. They believed it was Ella giving them a nod from beyond. The term "by the clock" became their mantra. Pickford soon left New York and went west to join Fairbanks permanently.

One year after Douglas Fairbanks filmed *The Lamb* (1915) for Triangle Films, theater actor Richard Semler Barthelmess made his first movie, *War Brides* (1916). Barthelmess was named after his paternal grandfather, a doctor who migrated to the United States from Bavaria in 1852. Barthelmess was born in New York near Central Park West on May 9, 1895. His father, Alfred, was a successful businessman and former member of the National Guard. One year later, Alfred died at the age of 35 leaving his wife, Caroline, to care for herself and her baby.

In addition to taking in boarders, Caroline worked in the theater under the last name of Harris. Growing up watching his mother perform onstage, Barthelmess thought he'd follow in her footsteps. After graduating from high school, he joined a summer touring company and traveled throughout Canada. That fall, he attended Hartford, Connecticut's Trinity College, but never earned his degree. Instead, his mother's good friend, the Russian-born actress Alla Nazimova, gave him a small role in her movie *War Brides*. The film's director, Herbert Brenon, was impressed enough to offer Barthelmess a one-year contract at $50 per week. Even with a degree, the young man knew he'd never get a better offer. Trinity College was history.

For the next three years, Barthelmess worked in almost two dozen films. Leading man status eluded him until 1919, when D.W. Griffith cast him opposite actress Lillian Gish in *Broken Blossoms* (1919). Aided by a little make-up and a tight rubber band hidden under his cap, Barthelmess plays young Asian missionary Cheng Huan, living in England. He takes in Lucy Burrows, a battered twelve-year-old London girl (played by the adult Gish) who is repeatedly beaten by her prizefighter father. Gentle and caring, Huan provides her with a safe place to stay until her racist father finds her with the Oriental man and ultimately kills her. Devastated over her death, Huan shoots her evil father, takes the child's body back to his room and then kills himself. The drama catapulted Barthelmess from bit player to matinée idol making him one of the silver screen's most popular bachelors.

It's no wonder public concern turned to panic when it was reported that he and over thirty others disappeared along with D.W. Griffith onboard the 60-foot yacht, *Grey Duck*, in December 1919. The group set sail from Miami where they had been filming and headed for Nassau. A hurricane-like storm blew near the Florida coast interrupting their journey, which normally should have taken about twelve hours. When the yacht did not reach port in Nassau, it was feared that the *Grey Duck* and her illustrious guests might have been lost at sea.

Seaplanes laden with supplies went looking for them during daylight hours with no luck. Even Secretary of the Navy Josephus Daniels, sent ships to search the waters, but to no avail. A few days later, the yacht wobbled in to the Nassau port. Lacking communication, they had found safe harbor at Whale Key where they had waited out the storm. According to the *New York Times*, a wireless message sent to the *Miami Herald* reported:

Grey Duck arrived late today driven by a heavy gale. D.W. Griffith and party safe, but three days without food, and little water. Two of the party were swept overboard, but were rescued. The boat nearly capsized twice in the Northwest channel. The pilot was injured and others were forced to take their turns at the wheel, while the helpless boat drifted far from her course . . .

In later years, however, Barthelmess explained that although the disappearance was definitely not a publicity stunt, he was not onboard the *Grey Duck* when the incident occurred, but safe in Miami with his mother. They later joined the group in Nassau once the weather cleared.

Six months after the seafaring adventure, Barthelmess dropped his bachelor status when he married actress Mary Hay Caldwell, whom he had met while working on *Way Down East* (1920). D.W. Griffith brought her into the picture because of her resemblance to actress Clarine Seymour who died unexpectedly before filming was finished. The eighteen-year-old Texas dancer was also a Ziegfeld girl and the daughter of Brigadier General Frank Merrill Caldwell. Although she found some success onstage, her movie career ended after only four films.

For Barthelmess, *Way Down East* paired him up once again with Lillian Gish and secured his place in movie history. He will forever be remembered as the brave Galahad who saved the freezing Gish from those raging rapids. Clad in a raccoon coat, our hero jumps from ice floe to ice floe trying to reach the maiden in distress as the fast-moving current carries her toward a perilous waterfall where certain death awaits her.

That famous scene was filmed at White River Junction in Vermont where the ice was so thick it had to be sawed and dynamited to create the necessary floes. Gish herself decided that letting her hair and hand drag along in the icy water would add to the excitement. It took three weeks for Griffith to get the shots exactly as he wanted. Barthelmess later recalled:

> Not once, but twenty times a day, Lillian floated down on a cake of ice, and I made my way to her stepping from one cake to another, to rescue her. I had on a heavy fur coat, and if I had slipped, or if one of the cakes had cracked and let me through, my chances would not have been good. . . . I would not make that picture again for any money that a producer would be willing to pay for it.

It took the wise Gish to remind him that they weren't doing it for the money.

Two years after Douglas Fairbanks and Richard Barthelmess made their motion picture debut, Conrad Nagel made his first film. He played Laurie Laurence in *Little Women* (1918), which was based on Louisa May Alcott's classic novel of the same name. Nagel was born into a musical household in Keokuk, Iowa on March 16, 1897. His father, Frank, was a noted pianist as well as a composer and conductor. Nagel's mother, Frances Murphy, was a singer. Both parents encouraged their son's interest in the theater.

Nagel attended Highland Park College in Des Moines where his father had been named Dean of the Music Department. Dean Nagel was so well respected in his field that the school also honored him with a doctorate degree in music. As a student, the younger Nagel appeared in school plays and was a member of the glee club. He also liked sports and belonged to both the football and track teams. Nagel studied under the well-known dramatic reader Edna Means who was the Dean of the Oratory Department.

After graduating in 1914 with a degree in the School of Oratory, he took on a few odd jobs—bricklayer, hotel key clerk and telephone operator. The call of the boards was stronger, however, and he soon joined the local Princess Stock Company where he appeared onstage with future movie star Fay Bainter. The Princess, which was built in 1909, was one of the first theaters to boast air conditioning—blasting air that skimmed across ice blocks. Nagel eventually left the theatrical company for vaudeville before breaking into Broadway. His successful stage career was temporarily interrupted during World War I when he served in the U.S. Navy on board the *U.S.S. Seattle* under Rear Admiral Albert Cleaves.

The *Seattle* was primarily used for transporting American troops to the European front. On her first trip out, her helm jammed and she veered off course. Crewmembers blew the whistle to warn other nearby ships. Once the armored cruiser regained her position, several seamen noticed an enemy submarine in the water near her bow. As it turned out, two German U-boats had been covertly following the American ship, fully intending to attack. The submarines dashed off when they heard the whistle blowing thinking they had been detected. The *Seattle* continued escorting troops without incident for the duration of the war.

After his stint in the service, Nagel began working in films. He also married his sweetheart Ruth Emily Helms in June 1919. The newlyweds took a month-long honeymoon in Maine. The following year their daughter, Ruth Margaret, was born.

Standing six feet tall, with blond hair and blue eyes, Nagel's matinée idol status was soon guaranteed. His breakout role came in *The Fighting*

Chance (1920) when he starred opposite former model turned actress Anna Q. Nilsson. The Swedish-born beauty was a veteran moviemaker whose first film, *Molly Pitcher,* was released in 1911. In *The Fighting Chance,* Nilsson is rich girl Sylvia Landis who falls in love with heavy drinker Stephen Siward played by Nagel. Landis leaves him for a wealthy but unscrupulous man. In the end, however, she returns to her first love and in true Hollywood fashion, straightens him out. Nagel's wife also had a role in this film—the only movie she ever made.

Nagel became so popular, in fact, that he rarely had a day off. Filming back-to-back pictures for months at a time, the actor was only allowed an occasional Sunday for himself. The *L.A. Times* reported:

> He started his vacationless period seven months ago when he played Paul in . . . *Three Weeks* (1924). The day following the last scene of that production he entrained for New York to appear in *The Rejected Woman* (1924). Before he had finished his role he received a wire to return immediately to [Hollywood] to commence work in another picture so the final week of *The Rejected Woman* was a period of night and day work. He boarded the Twentieth Century Limited with makeup on, having worked until immediately before train time.
>
> Nagel was sent for to commence work in . . . *Tess of the D'Urbervbilles* (1924). Photography had started before he arrived so he went directly from the station to the studio . . .

Tess' production schedule was changed allowing Nagel to complete his scenes in just a few weeks so that he could begin filming another movie the very next day. He was then slotted for yet another picture eight weeks later. Some matinée idols didn't get much rest.

No matter what the critics might have written, those matinée girls sure knew how to pick 'em.

Chapter Seven

CALLING THE SHOTS

S ometimes flamboyant, sometimes eccentric and almost always colorful with ambition on their sleeve, early film directors took charge of their productions whether they knew what they were doing or not. Most were men with the exception of one or two determined ladies such as Dorothy Arzner and Lois Weber. Some directors, like many of their actors, came from theatrical backgrounds, while others drew upon military experience that enabled them to bark orders with authority. A few were simply actors or writers plucked from the ranks of their respective studios when necessity dictated.

One of the earliest film directors, Allan Dwan, was originally a scenarist for a Chicago film company. In 1911, his superiors sent him to California in search of a missing film crew. He located the group in San Juan Capistrano—their director had gone on a binge and disappeared. Not knowing what else to do, the troop was simply waiting for their wayward leader's return. Dwan wired the bosses back east, explained the situation and recommended they disband the film. They countered by telling him to direct it. Dwan later recalled: ". . . I got the company together and told them either I direct or you're out of work and they said you're the best damn director we ever saw."

Most early film companies had their own stable of directors—sometimes up to a dozen. Movies were usually filmed next to each other inside the studio. Rehearsal for a western might be underway while a comedy wrapped up right behind it. At the same time, mood music for a drama might be playing just a few feet over. Sets were simultaneously built while others were torn down. The chaotic environment was anything but quiet. Directors took to using megaphones so they could be heard above the ongoing din.

Amidst the hubbub, it wasn't unusual for those early one-reelers to be churned out at a rate of one per week per director who had to be good at multi-tasking. While still filming their current production, they had to prepare for the next one in order to maintain their quota. After studying the selected photoplay, the director chose a cast, approved costumes, ordered sets and developed the scene-by-scene filming schedule. He was also responsible for finding offsite locations to accommodate exterior shots where megaphones were even more helpful. Many of these film-makers drove fast cars allowing them to quickly travel from place to place. Later on, several of them took to the skies searching for locations from the air. Regardless of how they did it, the prep work had to be done before the camera even started to roll.

Once the sets were built, the costumes sewn and the make-up applied, the director then went about filming his movie one scene at a time—almost always out of sequence. For budget purposes, all scenes with the same background were completed before moving on to the next scenes, which required different settings. An efficient director would keep a list of all backgrounds along with associated scene numbers to maintain the tight schedule. This saved the company from tearing down and rebuilding sets, as well as traveling more than once to the same place—a very cost-effective use of time, materials and people.

Filming out of sequence, however, often caused problems with continuity, another thing the director was responsible for maintaining. If a player pins her hair up when she leaves the house, she mustn't wear it down for the exterior shot in the front yard. Spectators would surely notice the difference and frown upon the director's sloppy methods, and the overall reception to the film would suffer.

Before filming each scene, the director stood behind the camera and rehearsed his players. According to author Austin C. Lescarboura who wrote *Behind the Motion Picture Screen* in 1919:

> Once the director is satisfied with the way his players interpret a scene he calls for the lights (if the scene is in the studio) and gives the order to the cameraman to film the action. At the command "Action! Camera! Go!" the players start work as if electrified, while the cameraman cranks away. . . .

At the sound of that famous order, "Cut!," the cameraman immediately stopped cranking the camera and called out the number of film feet used for the current scene. With only 1,000 feet per reel, scenes often had to be reshot at a slower or faster pace to ensure they were completed at the appropriate length. Timing was everything.

Once all scenes were filmed, the director began the editing process. He cut away unnecessary footage, inserted title cards and closeups, as well as blended scenes together to effectively tell his story. Nitrate or not, unused footage was often stored for possible use in a future picture—either his own or another director employed by the studio.

As the motion picture industry evolved from ten-minute silent flickers to full-length features with sound, the best directors, such as Cecil B. DeMille, naturally rose to the top of their field where they remained making high-quality films for several decades. Although their filming methods may have differed, all were creative storytellers who knew how to spin an entertaining yarn. And when it came to embellishing a tale, director Raoul Walsh was hard to top. Mixing a little fabricated fiction with the truth often created a helluva story no matter which version Walsh decided to go with. It's no wonder he found his way to the megaphone and stayed for over fifty years.

Raoul Walsh's father, Thomas, was born in England and came to the United States as a child in 1872. He established himself in New York as a successful men's clothing designer. In 1886, he married Elizabeth Brough, and on March 11, 1887, Albert Edward (later known as Raoul) was born. The wealthy and socially prominent New York couple had two more children, George in 1889 and Alice in 1891. Elizabeth was an attractive woman who often entertained at home. As a young boy, Walsh remembered hobnobbing with the likes of theater actor Edwin Booth, writer Mark Twain and boxing champ John L. Sullivan.

After his high school graduation, Walsh briefly attended college, but dropped out when cancer claimed his mother. According to Walsh, his life of adventures began when he and his uncle sailed to Cuba. His sea legs were shaken, however, when their schooner tangled with a hurricane. After floating aimlessly for three days, they were towed into Veracruz. While in Mexico, Walsh learned to break horses, as well as a few rope tricks. He also bragged about a scorching, south of the border love affair he had with a Mexican general's mistress that almost cost him his life. After narrowly escaping that fiasco, Walsh dashed off to Texas where he tried his hand at roping and riding steers. From the Lone Star state, he traveled by rail to Butte, Montana—at that time a frontier mining town.

Totally broke due to a bad poker bet, Walsh became an undertaker's assistant. He claimed he was never paid for his mortuary duties; therefore, he quit and went to work for a local physician assisting with surgeries and administering anesthetics. Walsh professed he may have killed a patient, but the good doctor assured him that the man didn't have much of a chance anyway. When the doctor unexpectedly died from "lung trouble," Walsh's career in medicine was over. He bolted back to Texas where he broke horses for the U.S. Cavalry in San Antonio.

A traveling theatrical troupe happened to be in the area. They needed someone to ride a horse onstage as it walked on a treadmill. The producer approached Walsh who was recuperating from a recent knee injury. By now, an excellent rider, Walsh took the job, and made his horseman debut in *The Clansman*, which later became the infamous film *Birth of a Nation*. Stage-struck after sailing, cowpoking, undertaking and operating, Walsh finally found something to stick with.

With some stage experience behind him, he returned to New York in 1909 and took acting jobs both in the theater and the movies. He also studied with family friend and popular playwright Paul Armstrong. According to Walsh, it was Armstrong who suggested he drop the names "Edward Albert" and try the more colorful "Raoul." Like Mary Pickford and other stars of the time, Walsh too claimed that "Raoul" was his official baptismal name. Completely random or not, the name fit and he made good use of it.

The idea of switching from actor to director came to him as he worked on a period film that required him to ride a horse down the middle of a street. Describing the director in charge as a "roughneck," Walsh later recalled the incident:

> . . . I got off the horse and looked back. I saw that I'd been riding between two trolley tracks. So I told the guy, I said, "Say, they didn't have any trolley tracks in—." He said, "Who the hell is directing this picture, you or me?" That's about when I decided I'd have to become a director. . . .

Before he actually took over that megaphone, however, Walsh joined D.W. Griffith and his Biograph team. He played in multiple one-reelers alongside several big names like Mary Pickford and Lionel Barrymore who entered the studio by way of the alley so none of his theatrical counterparts would see him. When Griffith left Biograph, he took Walsh with him to Hollywood and in between acting assignments put him to work as an assistant director.

According to Walsh, one of his many shining moments came in 1914 when Griffith decided to make a movie about the Mexican General, Pancho Villa. In one of several versions Walsh liked to tell, Griffith sent him to Mexico in search of the real revolutionary. After making contact with one of Villa's men, Walsh says he was blindfolded and taken to a run-down building somewhere in Juarez where he met the General and spoke with him through an interpreter:

> I thought to myself, I'd better start off good with this bum. . . . "Tell the General that the press in America say he is a bandit. I'm going to make a picture of the General to show that he is a great hero and the savior of the Mexican people." Well that went over and I knew I was in. . . . "eighty million people would see the picture of the General. And the story that I'm going to tell of the General . . ." And now I'm thinking like hell—what the hell story was it? I had thought of three of them on the way out on the train. . . .

Although his story is sometimes disputed, Walsh maintained that he not only persuaded the General to cooperate, but to play himself in the movie, *The Life of General Villa* (1914). In turn, Walsh took on the role of Villa as a younger man—the only detail that remained constant regardless of which tale he told.

Impressed with Walsh, Griffith assigned him to work on the battle scenes for *Birth of a Nation* (1915) while also playing the part of John Wilkes Booth. He did such a fine job that Griffith finally gave him his own films to direct.

Other studios took note of the young man's accomplishments and the following year, the Fox Company, a new studio back in New York, offered him a contract at $400 a week. Walsh's first film for Fox was also one of the first feature length gangster films, *The Regeneration* (1915). One pivotal scene in this movie involved a fire that erupted on a crowded riverboat. While filming on the Hudson River, the action was so realistic that the fire department arrived along with the police who dragged Walsh to jail for causing such a ruckus.

By 1916, Walsh was an established director at Fox now earning $1,000 each week and working with such exotic screen sirens as Theda Bara. That same year, he secretly married petite actress Miriam Cooper—one of the players he worked with under Griffith. Cooper, who was less than five feet tall, also appeared in *Birth of a Nation*. She was a fearless actress and preferred doing her own stunt work, which must have made quite an impression on the adventure-loving Walsh. The couple couldn't have children of their own and eventually adopted two boys, John and Robert.

One year later, Walsh made one of his most important films, *The Honor System* (1917)—the first of many edgy dramas that he brought to the screen. Shot on location at the Arizona State Penitentiary, the movie explored issues concerning penal reform. Walsh even spent a few nights in the clink just to get the feel of it. Starring Milton Sills, Miriam Cooper and featuring George Walsh, the director's younger brother, the film was a commercial and critical success defining Walsh as a major filmmaker and proving that he had ability outside of acting. During *The Honor System's* premiere, a real convict spoke to the audience about reformation efforts. Right after his speech, he fled toward the Canadian border and disappeared.

Joining Walsh at Fox was another young director, Frank William George Lloyd. Lloyd, the youngest of seven children, was born in Scotland on February 2, 1886 to a family that lived just outside of Glasgow. His father, Edmund, originally from Wales, was a steamship engineer who encouraged his son's love for the sea—something that was apparent in many of Lloyd's films. His Scottish mother, Jane, preferred the theater. As a teen, Lloyd went to London where he performed in various musical comedies and operettas throughout England. In January 1909, he set sail on the *R.M.S. Empress of Ireland*—the same ill-fated ship that sank five years later in the St. Lawrence Seaway after colliding with another vessel. The accident claimed 1,024 lives making it Canada's worst maritime disaster.

While in Canada, Lloyd worked installing telegraph lines before returning to the stage where he met and married singer Alma Haller. The couple came to America and Lloyd worked on the West coast in vaudeville. In 1913, a fellow actor at the Century Theater in Los Angeles introduced him to Universal Studios founder Carl Laemmle. Laemmle hired Lloyd as an actor and for the next two years he appeared in dozens of films starting out as an extra and working his way into more significant roles. The Lloyds also had a daughter named Alma born on April 3, 1914.

Eventually, Lloyd was asked to direct his first motion picture. He wanted a raise, but the company heads countered his request by offering him an extra $25 a week for every reel of film he completed. During his first week on the new job, he turned in two reels and earned an extra $50 on top of his normal $60 salary making him the highest paid member of the group. He also wrote many of his own photoplays and showed his innovative side with *The Gentleman from Indiana* (1915) featuring popular player Dustin Farnum. The *New York Times* reported on October 3, 1915:

> Director Frank Lloyd will introduce a novelty by staging a genuine rainstorm at night in the street with lights inside the store windows and the water streaming down the panes. This is a secret effect, which Lloyd has never made public before. . . .

Lloyd joined the Fox Film Corporation in 1916 where he continued writing and directing with some success, but it was not until he collaborated with author Charles Dickens that he scored a major hit. Feeling that it might be better to film Dickens' classic novel *A Tale of Two Cities* than one of his own original stories, Lloyd went to great lengths to capture the saga with all of its historical details. As a result, one reviewer declared that with these seven reels of film, Lloyd "earned himself a place in the hall of fame of directors."

He followed up with several more classic tales such as Victor Hugo's *Les Miserables* (1917), which clocked in at ten reels and another popular

Dickens tale, *Oliver Twist* (1922), starring child actor Jackie Coogan in the title role along with the versatile Lon Chaney as Fagin. In between, Lloyd wrote and directed many of his own photoplays, and still found time for a classic western, *Riders of the Purple Sage* (1918), based on the Zane Grey novel.

By 1921, Lloyd was head of his own production company and searching for film locations by air. He enjoyed a relaxing round of golf, duck hunting, trout fishing and a good dinner at Musso and Frank. Lloyd also belonged to the Motion Pictures Directors' Association, which was founded in 1915 by a small group of film directors including one of his closest friends, the Irish-born William Desmond Taylor who ultimately ended up more famous for his murder than his movies.

Amidst a whirl of missing love letters, and a notorious silk negligee, a suspect list comprised of superstars and an intriguing butler, Henry Peavey, who probably didn't do it, forty-nine-year-old Taylor was shot in the back in his own home on February 1, 1922. The ensuing investigation revealed that the director's name was actually William Cunningham Deane-Tanner. Investigators also found that he had been married, but deserted his wife and daughter years before in New York.

Multiple suspects were questioned, but no arrests were made and no charges ever filed. Silent film comedienne Mabel Normand was the last person believed to have seen Taylor alive. Rumors of a heated argument and scandalous affair between the two pretty much ended her filmmaking days. Letters found in Taylor's home also alluded to an affair with the young screen actress Mary Miles Minter whose career was all but destroyed after the incident. In addition, Minter's mother, Charlotte Shelby, made the suspect list because she owned a gun that fired similar bullets used in the murder. Her motive? Jealousy and/or disapproval over her daughter's alleged relationship with Taylor.

As drug-related buzz and the hint of homosexuality also surfaced, Taylor was given a military funeral planned by the director's association. Frank Lloyd, ever a loyal friend, was a pallbearer. Almost one hundred years later, theories about the mysterious murder continue to emerge and the case remains unsolved.

While Taylor's murder investigation dragged along, Lloyd continued delivering popular films with a passion for accuracy. Known for his dry wit and eye for detail, he firmly believed in getting things right:

> We spend hours discussing how a flag is hung in a certain country, in order to get it absolutely correct, because if we don't some observing, fault-finding person is apt to notice that it is wrong and criticize us for it. The result of the whole thing is that as nearly as possible these little things which are characteristic of other lands, or other times, are correct, and the fan is absorbing, without knowing it, perhaps, the knowledge it has taken us so much pains to dig up.

Like Frank Lloyd, movie director John Malcolm Stahl also began his stage career as a teenager. Born in New York on January 21, 1886, his father was a successful businessman. Stahl quit school and ran away from home to join a touring theatrical company. For the next fourteen years, he played in theaters throughout the country and when he wasn't performing on stage, he took his turn at directing.

By 1914, Stahl was back in New York directing his first movie. *The Boy and The Law* (1914) starred youth advocate Judge Willis Brown and the young Canadian musical prodigy William Eckstein as themselves. Over the next several years, Stahl worked for various New York film companies sharpening his skills. He wrote as well as directed many of his films. His first major release was *Suspicion* (1918) featuring Boston-born Warren Cook, a popular silent screen character actor. In between films, Stahl married his wife, Irene, and by 1920, the couple had moved to Hollywood where he worked for producer Louis B. Mayer.

Stahl was a Mayer favorite due to the morally upright and emotion-packed films he created. Known for his personal dramatics, Stahl usually wore a coat draped over his shoulders and almost always leaned on a walking stick. If he wanted to speak to someone, he just "hooked" them in with his cane. According to screenwriter Sheridan Gibney:

> [Stahl] was trying to imitate David Belasco. He thought he was a magician—hypnotizing everybody. . . . He amused people. But he did have a way of getting what he wanted.

Stahl's assistant, Margaret Booth, had been a film "patcher" with D.W. Griffith. There, she learned the mechanics of splicing and editing film. It was Stahl, however, who showed her how to cut film for dramatic impact and timing. She admitted that Stahl was a perfectionist and often a difficult taskmaster, but always credited him for her legendary success in the cutting room.

After his popular film *The Child Thou Gavest Me* (1921), featuring a young Lewis Stone, was released, Stahl shared his thoughts on current filmmaking:

> We are at the stage in pictures where everything depends on character. This is not a new thing. In fact, it has always been the prevailing factor in drama. . . . Only by making your situation and your plot grow out of your people can you really succeed in making your drama real.

Best known for his emotionally charged melodramas, Stahl was also a man with a plan—or at least a director who thought ahead. Before filming, he pre-rehearsed every scene with miniature sets and characters made of cardboard. Based on these pre-rehearsals, Stahl would take detailed notes concerning camera angles and actors' movements making any necessary changes to the miniatures before completing the actual set construction. Working out the kinks beforehand was a cost-effective method of ensuring that the filming itself would run smoothly.

One journalist in the *Los Angeles Times* believed that Stahl's success was largely due to the "mature" characters and storylines he presented rather than the youthful "flapperism" that seemed to prevail on-screen. His greatest films, however, were destined for sound unlike Fred Niblo who scored multiple blockbuster epics under the silent system.

When Fred Niblo deserted the boards and joined the ranks of Walsh, Lloyd and Stahl, Hollywood hit the jackpot. Not only did they gain a fine director with a polished stage presence, but also a man of wit combined with a little zigzag. He even had leadership experience resulting from his tenure as head of The White Rats.

Born Frederick Liedtke in York, Nebraska on January 6, 1874, he was the third of four children including eldest sister Clara, older brother Otto and little sister Vesta who debuted five years later. Fred was named after his German-born father who was a Union Captain during the Civil War and wounded in Gettysburg. He also held the office of Nebraska State Auditor in 1879. Fred's mother, Annette, hailed from France and spoke several languages. According to one of Fred's children, the couple had a rocky marriage and divorced in 1881.

Young Fred eventually traveled to New York where William Niblo hired the lad to work at his theatrical establishment, Niblo Gardens. Fred took to both the stage and the name, replacing Liedtke with Niblo for the rest of his life. By 1897, he was performing in musicals, dramas and comedies under his new name. He also appeared in minstrel and vaudeville shows where, known for his monologues, he was dubbed "The American Humorist." He then joined George M. Cohan's company as a manager and performer working closely with the famous foursome—George, his older sister, Josephine, and their parents, Jeremiah and Helen. Taking things a little further, Niblo also joined the family when he married Josephine in 1901. Their son, Fred, Jr., was born two years later.

The three Niblos traveled around the world performing throughout Europe. They visited such exotic places as Africa, Russia, Egypt and Rome snapping dramatic photographs and filming the unusual sites. One of the earliest entertainers to present travelogues, Niblo dazzled audience members with what became known as his "zigzag talks"—vagabond stories highlighted by never-before-seen visual aids. While introducing the amazed spectators to other parts of the world, he also made sure they had a good laugh:

> All the Americans who travel abroad go to Scotland in the summer. In fact, Scotland is full of Americans in the summer, just as the Americans over here are full of Scotch in the winter. . . . Next I visited . . . the Eternal City. Talk about theaters. The world's greatest theater was there. The monster Coliseum, where in the days of Nero a hundred thousand people gathered and the actors were the gladiators, fighting with the wild animals. Actors don't fight with wild animals these days; they fight with their managers. . . .

In between shows and travel, he also found time to head up an early actors' union known as The White Rats of America. This organization was founded in 1900 by a group of theatrical performers who came together to protect themselves against unfair wages and treatment. They borrowed their name from a similar British group known as The Water Rats. The membership even had a theme song called "The Emblem," which touted their unity and reminded anyone who listened that "rats" spelled backwards is "star!"

By 1912, Niblo gave up his New York existence. Josephine was in poor health so the family sailed to Australia where they stayed for three years working and hoping her well-being would improve. Once back home, Niblo dabbled in the movies while Josephine grew weaker and finally succumbed to a bad heart in 1916 at the age of forty. Now a widower and single parent, Niblo returned to Australia where he reconnected with Aussie actress Enid Bennett whom he had met during a previous stay. He married her in 1918 and, after more than twenty years on the stage, Niblo took a permanent leap into films. Employed by the Thomas H. Ince Corporation, he directed *The Marriage Ring* (1918) starring his new wife.

Already well known and liked in the entertainment community, Niblo continued directing, but was often called upon to emcee various banquets, premieres, openings and dedications held in the movie colony. His easy stage style made him one of Hollywood's favorite hosts and he remained adept at working a crowd no matter how rich and famous they were. Movies came and parties went until 1920. That's when Douglas Fairbanks summoned Niblo to his United Artists' kingdom where Hollywood history was about to change with a capital "Z."

Fred Niblo wasn't the only director who had Civil War ties. Born in Christiansburg, Virginia on January 24, 1888, Henry Edmondson King was the grandson of a Confederate soldier who served under General Lee. His father, John, was a farmer and railroad attorney. After graduating from public school, King enrolled in Roanoke College. While still a student, he performed in blackface and found he liked the stage. He greatly disappointed many more conservative family members by joining the Empire Stock Company instead of the Methodist ministry, which they deemed a much more respectable occupation. His choice even caused a huge rift between his mother and aunt as he once explained:

> By this time my father was dead and my mother and aunt had become mortal enemies, because my aunt had said that she was glad to see my dad dead, so he wouldn't be able to see me in the theater. . . . As long as she lived, my mother was my greatest booster.

As a result, King toured around the country with several traveling troops working in theater, vaudeville, burlesque and even the circus. He never considered the movies because of his blue eyes. He thought they wouldn't photograph well in the black and white format. That all changed when he went to an interview at the Lubin Company with actress Pearl White. While there, King was assured that due to advancing technology, blue eyes were no longer a problem on-screen, as the shading color contrast on the film was now sharper than it had ever been. By 1913, King was filming shorts beginning with A False Friend featuring actress Dorothy Davenport.

From Lubin, King moved on to the Balboa Amusement Company located in Long Beach, California. In addition to his acting duties, he began writing photoplays and providing suggestions about the filming itself. He came up with an idea to take several short shots— eight or ten frames long—to cover a brawl. The montage had never been done before and King had to show the film editor how to put it all together.

In 1915, King married actress Gypsy Abbott in Fort Worth, Texas. As a result, he gained not just a wife, but stepdaughter Ruth as well. That same year he also got his chance at directing in *The Brand of Man* (1915), but it wasn't until he teamed up with child star Baby Marie Osborne in *Little Mary Sunshine* (1916) that he commanded attention. As director and star, he not only cornered the box office, but praise from the critics as well. After several "Baby" vehicles, King moved on to the American Film Manufacturing Company in Niles, California where he concentrated on directing. He worked with another young leading lady, Mary Miles Minter, and western star William Russell.

Two years later, King went to work for Thomas Ince and had his first major hit, *23½ Hours Leave* (1919)—a comedy about soldiers who, just before heading to the battlefields of France, were granted furloughs. Despite his success, the studio manager fired King for going over budget. When Ince got wind of it, he fired the studio manager. King continued studio hopping until 1921 when he, along with matinée idol Richard Barthelmess and New York attorney Charles H. Duell founded their own company, Inspiration Pictures.

Inspiration's film *Tol'able David* (1921) starred Barthelmess and was filmed near Christiansburg, Virginia, King's birthplace. Based on a short story by author Joseph Hergesheimer, the plot centers on country boy David Kinemon who, after many tribulations, is forced to avenge his family and thereby become a man. The movie was an international hit and even won awards such as *Photoplay* magazine's Gold Medal. Henry King's status was elevated to director extraordinaire.

Like Frank Lloyd, King was also a pilot and preferred scouting locations by air and like most of his contemporaries, he dressed in the familiar military style. The austere riding boots and britches commanded authority. The look also distinguished the director from his troupe. King, however, once explained the practical side of the "uniform":

> At that time, San Fernando Valley was where most of the pictures were made. It was all sagebrush and sand and if you . . . walked around for a location out there, why you'd be torn to shreds up to your waist so it was a matter of self-preservation. They were forced to dress that way: the puttees, the riding britches and the open-throated shirt. . . .

Between the megaphone, the garb and the aura of authority, when it came to silent movies, there was no mistaking the men who called the shots.

Chapter Eight

HOW DID THEY DO THAT?

As flickers became more complex both dramatically and creatively, new technology was needed to accommodate the developing art form. Soon it wasn't enough to just roll the film while people sneezed or kissed or gyrated. To keep spectators coming back for more, characters and stories had to be entertaining and rendered in an effective manner. Of course, some razzle-dazzle never hurt either. Early special effects using double exposures and miniatures, along with a little animation, was sure to leave the audience scratching their heads in amazement.

The controversial concepts of color and sound whispered their way around every studio. The color process was expensive and many believed that audience eyestrain would result. Who would want to leave the theater with tired, red eyes? Sound would be even more revolutionary. The studios would have to find a completely new way of working; movie theaters would have to be reconfigured; writers would be required to come up with snappy dialogue, which in turn actors would have to deliver, allowing story-lines to become even more complex and opening whole new frontiers as to the range of emotions films could convey. These were overwhelming ideas to an industry firmly entrenched in shades of gray and silence.

But determined men and women who believed that they were on to something had built the motion picture industry to its current state and were willing to push forward despite their critics. These revolutionaries weren't afraid to take a chance. Like it or not, they realized that a ground-breaking art form had no room for complacency. Progressive changes found their way in through the unique skills and imagination of many technicians behind the scenes and studio heads at the forefront who were willing to take a risk. Their names may not be legendary, but their specialized accomplishments that resulted in a film's awe-inspiring moments are hard to forget. These technicians and their mysterious knowledge base were well respected throughout the industry, giving them their own brand of Hollywood power.

In 1912, two Massachusetts Institute of Technology (MIT) graduates and professors, Drs. Herbert Kalmus and Daniel Comstock, teamed up with W. Burton Wescott to form Kalmus, Comstack and Wescott—a cutting-edge engineering firm. By 1915, they were ready to take on the challenge of color and set up their first film laboratory in Boston inside a railroad car. The boxcar was outfitted with a photochemical laboratory, darkrooms and the most modern equipment needed to develop film. It even had a sign on top that proudly announced the extension of their original company: "Technicolor Motion Picture Corporation." The "Techni" part was a reverential nod to Kalmus' and Comstock's alma mater.

The Technicolor team took their train to Jacksonville, Florida in 1917 where they filmed their first color movie, *The Gulf Between* starring Grace Darmond and Niles Welch. At that time, Technicolor consisted of only two color components—red and green. With Comstock acting as producer, the film was impressive, but definitely left room for improvement.

Showing the movie was another matter. It required a special projector and according to Kalmus "an operator who was a cross between a college professor and an acrobat."

As the team continued working toward improving their color process, influential members of the film community like Marcus Loew and the Schenck brothers noticed. By the time Technicolor released their next production, and the first color feature filmed in Hollywood, many enhancements were made. *The Toll of the Sea* (1922) starred Asian actress Anna May Wong, one of the few non-white actresses of the day, and did not require a special projector or an acrobat to run it. Chester Franklin directed the romantic drama while Technicolor engineer Joseph Arthur Ball manned the camera.

Ball was born in Cambridge, Massachusetts on August 16, 1894 to Elijah Ball who, at the time, was a baker, and his wife, Clara Peterson, who was originally from Sweden. Named after his paternal grandfather, Ball was a middle child with two brothers, Robert, the eldest, born in 1892 and Theodore, the youngest, who came along in 1898. Robert served in the Great War as a First Lieutenant in the U.S. Army. The twenty-six-year-old soldier never came home. He died on June 20, 1918 from battle wounds and was buried in the Aisne-Marne American Cemetery located in Belleau, France.

After graduating from high school, the middle Ball attended MIT where he earned his degree. He took an engineering job with Kalmus, Comstock and Wescott—the same team that eventually turned into Technicolor. The group got into the motion picture business when they were asked to stop the flickers from flickering. After extensive research, Kalmus and company concluded that flickers would always flicker, but maybe they could be colorized, so the men changed their focus. Technicolor incorporated in 1915 with Kalmus as president and Comstock vice president.

Encouraged by their accomplishments with *The Gulf Between* (1917), the group knew they could do better. It took another five years, however, before their next color production was released, the aforementioned *The*

Toll of the Sea, which was filmed under the watchful eye of producer Joseph M. Schenck. Hollywood was impressed, but there were still a couple of issues that needed fixing—the high cost of color film and its restricted hues. Color film ran about 27 cents per foot while standard nitrate film rang up at 8 cents—more than a 300 percent difference. Secondly, the color process itself remained limited to red and green—that elusive color blue was still at large.

By the time Ball took his turn behind the camera, he was a married man. He wed Isabel Osann on October 27, 1920 in Cambridge. Osann's father, Bernard, came from Hamburg, Germany and eventually settled in the Chicago area where he was a highly regarded traveling salesman for the United States Envelope Company. Isabel's older brother, Norman, graduated from the University of Wisconsin in 1912. He then furthered his education by enrolling in MIT's Electrical Engineering Program and also became an instructor at the school before joining Kalmus, Comstock and Wescott in their new venture.

Despite the drawbacks of cost and that still-missing shade of blue, *The Toll of the Sea* sparked interest from several of Hollywood's most influential citizens including Jesse L. Lasky, Douglas Fairbanks and D.W. Griffith. As a result, Kalmus sent several engineers including Ball, now a Technical Director, to the west coast. The group rented a building and set up their Technicolor shop—just a small extension of their Boston business.

In 1923, the Famous Players Lasky Corporation signed up to produce a colorized version of *The Wanderer of the Wasteland* (1924). The film was based on a Zane Grey novel and starred favorite cowboy hero Jack Holt. It was also the first western filmed in Technicolor—still a two-color process. Due to their limited facilities, however, much of the work had to be done in Boston. Shipping the film back and forth across the country was cumbersome and certainly not an efficient way to do business. Although Lasky didn't mind the long distance, other filmmakers did. Therefore, the group built a more sophisticated laboratory in Hollywood and, in 1924, they were ready to do business on a full scale—except for that hard-to-pin-down color, blue.

The following year, Kalmus and Comstock experienced a disagreement resulting in Kalmus' departure from the partnership. He took Technicolor, Ball and Norman Osann with him. It would take some time, and a whole lot of effort, but the face of film would one day transform. Ball commented on the future of colorized film:

> Any art which makes its appeal wholly through the eye must be severely limited if it has no color at its command, and especially if this art aims to affect our emotions. . . . The photoplay is such an art. . . . But there are some skeptical people who maintain that color is not wanted. This is to be expected for every innovation encounters opposition from skeptics. When motion pictures were in their infancy the same type of people said that pictures were and always would be a cheap and inferior imitation of the stage. Today, the photoplay is recognized as a new and separate art. . . . If it is assumed that the purpose of the photoplay is to hold a mirror up to nature, both for the mind and for the eye, then, obviously color is not only desirable but necessary by . . . excluding colors, we must exclude all other attempts at realism in pictures such as authentic sets, costumes and details generally in a scene . . .

Art director Cedric Gibbons had his own thoughts about color. Since the audience couldn't see it, the only reason he used color in his innovative sets was to benefit the actors. When it came to authenticity, however, he would have certainly nodded his head in ready agreement with Ball.

In the early days of film, interior scenes were thrown together in a clash of styles—a French chair may have sat next to a colonial table with a garish flower arrangement gloating on top. It wasn't unusual for a biblical picture to showcase a Victorian settee or a Roman lady sporting Twentieth Century jewelry. Clutter often ruled. Many scenes were filmed in front of a painted backdrop—much like a play. Realism and eye appeal didn't seem to count. In the beginning, it didn't have to. Spectators came to see pictures move. The details didn't matter. Now, however, the tide was turning.

The novelty of motion was wearing off and maintaining audience attention became ever more important. As author Austin C. Lescarboura explained in 1921:

> . . . the audience must be made to forget the mechanical end of picture production; and to this end every effort is made to have even the most insignificant details accurate and confidence-inspiring.

This new demand for realism made way for a new kind of filmmaking position—the technical or art director. It was his job to study the photoplay and determine the type of sets that needed building, how furniture and other props should be arranged on-screen, as well as overseeing the costumes worn by the players. As a result, this position required some impressive qualifications. According to Lescarboura:

> The technical director must be a veritable human encyclopedia. His must be a remarkably broad knowledge, acquired through travel, reading, and a wide range of acquaintances. And what he does not know he must be able to "dig up" at short notice.

Austin Cedric Gibbons not only fit the bill—he ultimately defined the role. An Irishman, he liked to say he was born in Dublin, but he really came from an Irish Catholic neighborhood in Brooklyn. His father, Austin Patrick Gibbons, was born in England to Irish parents and came to the United States in 1869 when he was five years old. As an adult, he owned an architectural firm in New York and married seventeen-year-old Veronica Fitzpatrick in 1889. The couple had their first son, Austin Cedric, on March 23, 1890, followed by Veronica in 1892 and Elliot in 1904.

Gibbons led a privileged life and, as a youth, was schooled at home. With an interest in paintings and sculptures, Patrick allowed his teenage son to visit several major European cities. Gibbons then entered the historic Art Students League of New York founded in 1875 where he studied art and architecture. He also collected books on these same subjects. His personal library eventually totaled over 4,000 volumes. With degree in hand, he took a job as a draftsman in his father's firm. After two years, he decided that his future was not in the family business, but in the movies.

His next stop was at the Edison Studios where he worked as an assistant to pioneer set designer Hugo Ballin—also an alumnus of the Art Student's League of New York. One of the earliest set designers who also worked in the theater mostly painting backdrops, Ballin was later known for his creative murals displayed in places like the Griffith Observatory and Burbank City Hall. Gibbons soon preferred the three-dimensional look, which meant replacing painted props with actual items—furniture, draperies, wall clocks, etc. Realism was slowly finding its way to the silver screen.

Ballin and Gibbons moved on to Goldwyn Pictures until The Great War interrupted. Gibbons joined the U.S. Navy and, after being discharged, returned to New York and Ballin who was still working for Goldwyn. By now, Goldwyn had established an official art department. Unlike other early studios that appointed a specific set designer to a movie, Goldwyn's art department was responsible for all productions. The head designers would read the photoplays and then sketch the sets, which would then be built by another team of artisans—all members of the unified art department. As a result, a Goldwyn set enhanced the story rather than distracted from it.

When the company moved to California in 1919, Gibbons went with them. One of his biggest successes was the small-scale set he designed to make the players look larger in *The Slim Princess* (1920), a fairy tale-like story where beauty was measured by girth—the larger the girl, the more desirable she was. Reviews for the Geraldine Ferrar vehicle even mentioned the unusual sets and praised them for establishing the movie's magical aura. The following year, Gibbons built a realistic version of the city of Verona for Will Rogers' *Doubling for Romeo* (1921). Shakespeare would have been proud. No doubt, Goldwyn was pleased.

Gibbons, an impeccable dresser, never settled for anything less than perfection—including the way he looked. Always classy with an air of sophistication, his tall, lanky form supported broad shoulders making him seem more like leading man material than one of Goldwyn's most successful and efficient department heads. In charge of the Art Department, his name surfaced in Hollywood social circles while his artistic influence crept into everyday life. He told the press in 1920:

> . . . art directors have a great opportunity to improve the general level of good taste in home decorations. There is no doubt of the influence of the screen in the lives of the American people . . . they observe closely the sets which they see in photoplays and that many of them copy our ideas in their own homes.

By 1923, Gibbons was considered a "radical" in his field and "the most original art director in the business." He viewed his sets as an extension of the story itself and because color was impossible for an audience to perceive, he effectively enhanced the film's aura through lighting. His simple philosophy served him well: "Never let a motion-picture set look like a motion-picture set."

Aside from pioneering Technicolor and experimenting with set designs, developing "camera lies" or "trick pictures" gave way to another specialized filmmaking position—the special effects technician. Movie magic was just beginning and spectators couldn't get enough of the amazing sights they witnessed on-screen.

Disappearing characters were one of the earliest tricks that left audiences wide-eyed. Stopping the camera at just the right moment, a smoking pot would be placed in the exact spot where a player was last seen. The camera would then resume rolling and, like magic, the spectators would see their favorite star vanish into a whirl of white mist. The same technique was used as characters or objects morphed into someone or something else.

Early filmmakers also brought inanimate objects to life through stop motion. By filming a toy soldier one frame at a time and slightly altering the little man's position before each shot, he appeared to march on-screen. Dancing forks, along with flying pigs, never failed to charm an audience and the possibilities were endless.

Double printing was another early method of screen magic. Done in the editing room, it was sure to amaze a spectator and often aid in the story telling. Lescarboura gives a clever example:

> . . . a fairy would appear in the bottle of a heavy drinker and dance about to his amazement. . . . the full-sized player was first filmed in a close-up with a dark bottle which . . . left a black or blank space on the negative. Then another full-sized player, dressed as a fairy, was photographed against a dead black drop at a sufficient distance away to bring down the size of the image to that required to fit the bottle. . . . Then the two films, with their subjects carefully registered, were printed on one positive with wonderful result.

This process also worked well when "identical twins" shared a scene or when it was necessary to "show" a character's deepest thoughts or daydreams.

Reverse motion resulted in another popular trick. To accomplish this outside of the editing room, the camera was simply turned upside down while filming. The result? Instead of a car racing down the street, the vehicle would appear to be traveling backwards. The camera could also film at a slower rate, which would then give the players a look of accelerated action once the film was shown at normal speeds.

As screen tricks became more complex, the role of the technical director grew more demanding. This part wizard, part scientist, part mechanical genius had to come equipped with a whole lot of imagination. Saying "that's impossible" was not allowed. Roy J. Pomeroy worked his movie magic so well that for a while, he stood alone with no equal.

A British subject, Pomeroy was born in Darjeeling, India on April 20, 1892. At that time, the Brits controlled India including Darjeeling, which is located in the state of West Bengal. Eventually, Darjeeling was home to a British sanitarium and health resort, as well as the historic Darjeeling Himalayan Railway. The English also found that the land was an ideal spot for growing the now internationally famous tea.

Pomeroy's father was an Englishman living and working in India and his mother was originally from Ohio. As a lad, Pomeroy was educated at Malvern Wells in Worcester, England. He then traveled to his mother's home state to attend Ohio Wesleyan University located about twenty miles north of Columbus. Before hitting Hollywood, he worked in New York as a self-employed artist. Jesse L. Lasky later recalled:

> We had discovered Pomeroy as a struggling artist with an inventive mind, who had some exceedingly original and useful ideas about the employment of miniature sets and background projection to affect enormous budget savings in picture-making. I hired him and he did some fine creative work on tricks and special effects. He was the first specialist in that field and there has never been a better one. . . . Perhaps it isn't strange under the circumstances that he came to feel he was God . . .

By the time he entered the movie business in 1922, Pomeroy had a receding hairline and a thin, waxed mustache, which made him look even older than his thirty years. He also had a deeply rooted passion for archery along with a new wife, Sylvia, who was originally from Kentucky. One of his first major tasks at Paramount was parting the Red Sea for Cecil B. DeMille 's biblical epic, *The Ten Commandments* (1923). Unlike Moses, who relied on his staff and a miracle, Pomeroy used a whole lot of gelatin, a few gas jets and some clever filming tricks. He also masterminded the blazing letters that spelled out each of the Ten Commandments. As a result, the movie-going crowd met the wow-factor and launched their long-term relationship.

Hollywood lore also says that it was Pomeroy's idea to bury the colossal sets of ancient Egypt in the sands of Guadalupe Dunes where the movie was filmed north of Los Angeles. He thought it made more sense than lugging the oversized statues, chariots and other props all the way back to the studio. DeMille supposedly loved the idea of some future archeologist digging up Egyptian ruins on a California beach. Sixty years later, the shifting sands revealed parts of a "sphinx" and other "Egyptian artifacts" that were left behind. Several archeological film buffs began uncovering what they called "The Lost City of DeMille." They even came across some Prohibition-era cough syrup—widely favored at the time for its alcohol content.

Wowing not only the spectators, but also his studio superiors and coworkers, Pomeroy enjoyed the awe he inspired. The special effects he continued designing only enhanced his reputation as something of a miracle worker, but the adulation encouraged some pompous behavior. Pomeroy held the trump card and he knew it. He never hesitated using this advantage to further his career or pump up his own self-worth. His success was so great that Pomeroy was given the position of head of Paramount's Special Effects Department, or as it was better known, The Pomeroy Department. This specialized group was responsible for resolving any technical issues that came up during filming and creating any magic that a photoplay required.

Next up was *Feet of Clay* (1924) where Pomeroy depicted life after death in a smoky haze of spirits and heavenly beings. Then for the groundbreaking production of J.M. Barrie's famous story *Peter Pan* (1924), he allowed the ageless boy and the Darling children to fly by attaching piano wires to corsets hidden under their costumes.

No one argued his brilliance, but his self-inflated ego and the fact that he often spit in the middle of a conversation didn't endear him to his associates. However, with the advent of sound in 1927 and his under-standing of how it worked, Pomeroy's power multiplied. Well-liked or not, he created a special effects empire that dominated the world of movies. His reign may not have lasted long, but for a few short years Roy Pomeroy, thanks to his technical know-how, was a major Hollywood force.

With experts like the scientific Ball improving the color process, the artistic Gibbons designing those stunning sets and the savvy Pomeroy in charge of miracles, spectators soon learned that anything can happen in the movies.

Chapter Nine

HEAD OF THE HOUSE

With directors directing, actors acting, writers writing and technicians keeping up with the latest innovations, the role of movie producer evolved from haphazard businessman into elite executive. While the director remained primarily responsible for the creative aspects of day-to-day movie making, the producer ran the business acting as a liaison between his production unit and the studio. It was the producer who approved the photoplay and cast, assigned the director, eyed the budget, viewed the daily rushes and acted as peacemaker when differences arose between employees under his regime. He also had to come up with resourceful solutions on the spot when unexpected crises surfaced.

Final decisions were his alone. To his filmmakers, he was the "go-to" guy who had the power to fix almost anything, but to his studio, the producer was all about the bottom line. He had to ensure their money was not squandered by seeing that his completed movies were properly marketed and distributed, and turned a profit once all the overhead was accounted for.

In the early studio days, the producer championed all aspects of his films from pre- to post-production. At the same time, he continued to solicit and approve new stories, supervise the writers, sign new talent, work through legalities, remain abreast of industry trends, take note of what was occurring at other studios and network with Hollywood officials to keep his momentum going. In addition, he often had to placate the censors. He lived inside a whirlwind of moving pictures that made Dorothy's Kansas twister look like a summer breeze.

Producer Harry Rapf had the energy and stamina the job required. He also had a nose for talent—human and otherwise—and he knew a good contortionist when he saw one. Short in stature with a sometime abrasive personality that hid a soft heart, his over-sized proboscis conjured dubious nicknames like "anteater" or "Mayer's sundial," but it didn't deter the way he did business. The eldest of four brothers, Rapf was born in New York City on October 16, 1880, to Eliza Brooks and her husband, Maurice Rapf. Maurice, originally from the Austro-Hungarian Empire, was a prosperous tailor who owned his own business.

Circumstances changed for the Rapfs when Maurice was diagnosed with tuberculosis before the turn of the century. At that time, doctors usually recommended TB sufferers get as much fresh air and sunlight as possible. Denver was considered an ideal place for these patients to live and seek treatment. As a result, the Rapf family, which now included Joseph, Matthew and Arthur, moved to the Mile High City where Maurice eventually lost his battle with the dreaded lung disease. Now the sole support of her boys, Eliza bought a grocery store while her eldest son took an interest in the stage. By the time he was eighteen, Rapf had organized and managed a small minstrel show out west.

Vaudeville performer and songwriter Gus Edwards, responsible for discovering such talent as George Jessel, the Marx Brothers and Ray Bolger, spotted the young man and thought he had potential. Edwards put Rapf in charge of a large revue and had him coordinate business matters through Edwards' New York secretary, Clementine Uhlfelder. For the next three years, Rapf and Uhlfelder corresponded sight unseen. The virtuous young woman often questioned what she deemed inappropriate business expenses causing some of their communications to be rather heated. When Rapf and Uhfelder finally met face-to-face, however, he fell hard for the good-looking girl known around the office as Tina. He asked her out and then married her in 1911 making it perfectly clear that his mother, Eliza, was part of the package.

By the time his oldest son, Maurice, was born on May 19, 1914, Rapf had left Edwards and struck out on his own. He produced top-notch vaudeville shows and gained a reputation for staging musical comedies featuring chorus lines of pretty girls or "girl acts" as the press dubbed them. *The Haberdashery* was one such show that opened in the fall of 1914. It showcased various musical numbers with plenty of girls, girls, girls—some in eye-popping lingerie. Also featured were British comedian Harrington Reynolds, singer Harry Bloom and contortionist Twisto the Great. True to his name, Twisto rearranged his append-ages in places they weren't meant to go. Audience members gasped in imaginary pain as he bent and curled his body to the titillating beat of *Queen of the Nile.*

Rapf's shows often shared the stage with early films made by many of the east coast studios such as Biograph and Essanay. Impressed by the flickers, Rapf took a professional leap from live theater and began producing movies starting with *The Argyle Case* (1917) directed by Ralph Ince, brother of Thomas. A proud father, he often took his young son to work with him and, without hesitation, put the boy in front of the camera. When his films were finished, the producer turned salesman. According to his son, Maurice:

> My father's early movies . . . were sold on a "state rights" basis. That is
> to say when a film was finished, my father put the cans under his arm

and traveled around to neighboring cities such as Philadelphia, Boston and Washington, D.C. to make deals for its distribution. . . .

Rapf's method of business changed in 1919 when he teamed up with Russian-born Lewis J. Selznick, father of famous sons, agent Myron and producer David. Formerly a jeweler, Selznick, was now running Select Pictures Corporation with partner William A. Brady. Their production studio was located in Fort Lee, New Jersey with offices in Manhattan. Rapf came on board as production manager where he supervised the making of such films as *The Invisible Divorce* (1920) and *The Greatest Love* (1920) while Select Pictures took care of distribution. Rapf's can-carrying days were over.

By 1921, the United States had a new president, Warren G. Harding, and Germany's Nazi Party had a new Fuehrer, Adolf Hitler. Harry Rapf had a new son, Matthew, and a new job—Head of Production at a struggling studio in southern California called Warner Bros. After a series of flops, the brothers Warner realized that they needed the expertise of a moviemaking professional if they wanted to save their business. They called on Harry Rapf. Their new producer got things rolling when he oversaw the making of Anna Q. Nilsson's *Why Girls Leave Home* (1921)—the only profit-maker released by Warners that year.

In 1922, Rapf put a freckle-faced teenager, Wesley Barry, under contract at the studio. Barry was already a popular player from the Los Angeles area who had worked in several films under the direction of Marshall Neilan. His first movie with Rapf producing was *Rags to Riches* (1922) in which he played the lead character, Marmaduke Clark—a rich kid who couldn't stay out of trouble. Barry's unruly hair and unaffected looks proved to be an audience favorite. The youngster became Warner Bros.' first box office draw and completed several more movies with Rapf at the helm. Harry Rapf was making himself known around Hollywood and the delighted Warners were finally making money.

Rapf's secret may have been his post-production poll. Before his movies were released to theaters, Rapf often consulted with a variety of people.

In the years before preview audiences were a routine part of the process, he'd run the film and solicit opinions from people he knew—his doctor, his barber, his chauffer, studio workers and anyone else he could think of. He'd also check in with their spouses and children just to be sure. If his motley test group didn't like something, he wouldn't hesitate to recall the cast and crew for a re-shoot.

Rapf rarely failed to deliver. He believed the average moviegoer liked nothing better than a pretty girl or "something to feast the eye on." He broke down his success in a very simple way:

> Almost everyone wants to get as much fun out of his spare time, his evening or afternoon at the theater, as possible. If we give them films with good clean fun therein, also something which is so human that they can catch a glimpse of themselves or their neighbors, they are satisfied and so are we. . . . Tragedy is not good business. I hold no brief for realism in making screen successes. Oh, once in a while, it is all right to make a picture, which is different and more realistic. But do people go to the motion-picture theater to cry? They do not; they go for amusement, fun and laughter, and that is what I, for one, want to give them.

At the same time Rapf and Twisto were creating a collective cringe among their patrons, the Schenck Brothers, without turning themselves into pretzels, were also entertaining. Joseph Michael Schenck was born on Christmas Day in 1876—three years before younger brother Nicholas. The boys and their numerous siblings grew up in Rybinsk, Russia near the Volga River. In November 1892, the Schenck family came to the United States and settled in New York. Joe and Nick worked together selling newspapers until they found employment at a drugstore. Two years later, they bought the place.

When they weren't working, they liked to ride the trolley to The Fort George Amusement Park—a favorite spot among New York City locals.

Realizing there was money to be made, Joe opened "The Old Barrel," a beer-selling concession that catered to park patrons as they waited for the trolley. The brothers later expanded the business by erecting a stage and hiring live acts to entertain the brew-buying crowd. Entrepreneur Marcus Loew was a frequent visitor at Fort George and he took a liking to the ambitious Schencks. Well-off, Loew had made his money investing in nickelodeons and penny arcades. He even owned theaters where flickers were shown. Loew agreed to back the young men on a new venture—their very own amusement park.

In 1910, Joe and Nick Schenck bought the Palisades Amusement Park located in Cliffside Park, New Jersey right across the Hudson River from New York City. They promptly re-christened the place "Schenck Bros. Palisades Park"—their name emblazoned over the main gate. Always thinking big and hoping to compete with popular beachside attractions like Coney Island, Joe and Nick installed the world's largest outdoor salt-water pool in the middle of their park. The concrete swimming hole was 400 by 600 feet and filled with more than a million gallons of water pumped in from the Hudson. The deepest end, complete with diving boards, measured 14 feet. An island in the center offered swimmers a place in the sun. In addition, several hundred tons of sand was carted from the Atlantic coastline and deposited around the pool. The Schencks even had a wave machine built to complete their beach illusion. When the pool officially opened on June 8, 1913, they claimed it could hold 10,000 people.

While the amusement park business thrived, Loew's movie house and theater chain expanded. The three men joined forces to become business partners in Consolidated Enterprises. With Loew holding the top spot, Nick was second in command. A callous businessman who enjoyed making people around him uncomfortable, Nick was quite different from his outgoing brother, Joe—now general manager of Loew's booking office. Unlike his frosty brother who preferred power to kinship, Joe's pleasant nature attracted people. He enjoyed flashy clothes, pretty girls, and risky bets despite his constant scowling. Their differences aside, the Schencks

Technicolor's Joseph Arthur Ball (Courtesy of Kevin Ball)

ABOVE: *Joseph Arthur Ball with his wife, Isabel, and their son, David* (Courtesy of Kevin Ball) BELOW: *Three generations of the Ball family in 1927: Joseph Arthur Ball holding his son, David, along with his father, Elijah* (Courtesy of Kevin Ball)

Hollywood's first super couple, Douglas Fairbanks and Mary Pickford, ca 1920
(Walter P. Reuther Library, Wayne State University)

Charles H. Christie around the age of 25 (Courtesy of the London Ontario Public Library)

ABOVE: *Charles H. Christie and his wife, Edna, in front of the fountain at Victoria Park, London, Ontario in wintertime ca 1915* (Courtesy of the London Ontario Public Library) BELOW: *Charles H. Christie with brother, Al, in the early 1920s; the words 'taken in kitchen set at the studio' were handwritten on the back of the photograph* (Courtesy of the London Ontario Public Library)

Western star Jack Holt (Jack Holt Photo File, The American Heritage Center, University of Wyoming)

Funnyman Harold Lloyd (L. Kenneth Wilson Collection, The American Heritage Center, University of Wyoming)

Director Raoul Walsh complete with eye patch (Raoul Walsh Photo File, The American Heritage Center, University of Wyoming)

did share one thing—a fondness for the horses. The upstanding Loew once told them: "I would never bet on anything that eats but can't talk."

While Nick immersed himself in the business, Joe's interest leaned toward making movies rather than exhibiting them—especially after he met actress Norma Talmadge, a top star at Vitagraph. Talmadge was the eldest of three sisters and the daughter of overbearing Peg who ran the roost. Deserted by her husband whom she always called "the skunk," Peg took charge of her chicks. She propelled Norma, Natalie and Constance into the moving picture world looking for financial security.

As early as 1910, fourteen-year-old Norma was working at Vitagraph in her first film *The Household Pest* (1910). She earned a steady living for the next few years playing everything from circus performer to guillotine victim. A reliable actress because Mama Peg, who ruled with an iron fist, "said so," the dark-haired, dark-eyed Norma was always appealing and spectators took a liking to her. By 1913, she was given lead roles, but continued living under Peg's powerful thumb.

It wasn't until the fall of 1916 that Norma made a move without consulting her mother. The twenty-two-year-old actress eloped to Connecticut with thirty-seven-year-old Joe Schenck. Their marital news didn't sit well with Peg who was shocked to learn that dutiful Norma went behind her back. All was soon forgiven, however, when Peg realized that this stocky man with thinning hair, whom Norma called "Daddy," could potentially help all of her daughters.

Now that he got the girl, Schenck left his brother and Consolidated Enterprises to be an independent producer. He founded Colony Studios in New York City with partner Lou Anger, a former vaudeville comedian and friend of performer Roscoe "Fatty" Arbuckle. The company's first floor was dedicated to Schenck's new wife and home to Norma Talmadge Productions; the second floor housed Constance Talmadge Productions specifically for Norma's sister, a popular funny girl; the third floor held The Comique Film Company that Schenck established for heavyweight comedian Arbuckle who only recently had left Mack Sennett's shop in California. Anger and Arbuckle were instrumental in recruiting another vaudevillian—Buster Keaton. He made his first film appearance in Arbuckle's initial movie for Comique, *The Butcher Boy* (1917). Keaton and Arbuckle teamed up to film more than a dozen productions in the house of Schenck.

Leaving the comedians to their own devices, Schenk lavished his attention on Norma. Her first movie under his supervision was the drama *Panthea* (1917). Set in Russia, Schenck who was still fluent in the language saw to every detail. Norma had only the best, beginning with the finest sets and costumes including the prestigious direction of Allan Dwan. Schenck also understood the value of good publicity. With much hype, he arranged for *Panthea* to open simultaneously at two different New York theaters—a first in film premieres. Thanks to "Daddy" and the popularity of *Panthea*, Norma's career soared establishing her as one of silent film's most important dramatic actresses. Mama Peg couldn't have been more pleased.

As for the funny men, both Arbuckle and Keaton put their careers on hold while they briefly served in World War I. Afterward they resumed making movies still under contract with Schenck, but now working in California. Schenck thought Arbuckle should be making features instead of shorts so he arranged for the big man to work at Paramount. In order to keep Keaton, Schenck picked up the Chaplin Studios, also in California, and renamed it the Keaton Studios. By 1921, Keaton was a star famous for his deadpan face and married to Natalie Talmadge—the one sister who didn't make movies. The jovial Arbuckle was finished. Falsely accused of murder, he was now an outcast. His movies that once pulled in millions of dollars were banned from theaters across the country as outraged spectators displayed their fickle side.

Schenck weathered the Arbuckle debacle in New York where he continued casting his wife in star vehicles. He also invested in United Studios, a California company, recently purchased by producer M.C. Levee.

By 1923, Schenck closed his New York business and moved to the West Coast where he took over the reins of United Studios from Levee. Schenck explained to the *L.A. Times*:

> Lou Anger, my friend and associate has finally prevailed upon me to become a resident of Los Angeles and to center the major portion of my activities in this city.
>
> As a result of this association and having received the earnest and competent cooperation of M.C. Levee, the president of United Studios, I have completed the deal . . .
>
> I intend to immediately move my offices, my staff and my stars, namely Norma Talmadge, Constance Talmadge, and Buster Keaton to our new home.

The "deal" Schenck referred to involved more than $1.5 million dollars and gave him control of the studio. A shrewd businessman, he kept Levee on as president, but make no mistake, one of Hollywood's original high rollers had arrived. And just in case things didn't work out, he always had Palisades Park to fall back on.

When Rapf left the boards for the silver screen and Schenk was setting up his New York studio, M.C Levee was working for Fox Films as a twenty-dollar-per-week prop man and before that he was a stenographer. Michael Charles Levee's parents were originally from Germany, but he was born in Baltimore, Maryland on January 18, 1891. Levee's family included brothers Louis, George and Sidney as well as one sister, Rose.

After one year of handling props, the ever-ambitious Levee was promoted to the general superintendent's assistant and by 1917, business manager. He eventually left Fox to accept a position as Vice President and General Manager at Robert Brunton Studios where he was also a major stockholder. Brunton, a Scotsman, built the fully equipped facility on Melrose Avenue in 1917 with the intent of renting it out to various independent producers.

Levee, however, had grander plans. By now, he was not only entrenched in making movies, but also a husband and father. His wife, Rose, a girl from Bay City, Michigan, presented him with a son, Michael C. Levee, Jr., on September 22, 1920. In January 1922, he struck a three-million-dollar deal, bought out Robert Brunton, reorganized the company and established United Studios, Inc. Among those who joined Levee on the new board of directors was moneyman F.L. Hutton of E. F. Hutton fame and New York producer Joseph M. Schenck.

Major stockholders included Lewis J. Selznick and his partner-son Myron, who soon merged their own company with United. As president of the new business, Levee put famous sisters Norma and Constance Talmadge, whose films were still controlled by Schenck, under contract. In addition to the Talmadge sisters, Levee picked up several other big names like Mary Pickford, Douglas Fairbanks and child star Jackie Coogan whose father also owned stock in the company.

Levee's new studio covered more than thirty acres on Melrose Avenue—room enough for twenty production units. According to the *L.A. Times*:

> ... The properties consisting of furniture, bric-a-brac, draperies, etc., are valued in excess of $300,000. The stock scenery equipment represents an investment of more than $150,000; the permanent exterior settings cost more than $250,000 and the electrical equipment represents an outlay of $150,000 ...

Levee also invested $800,000 on studio improvements. Under his guidance, roads were paved, sidewalks laid and the administration buildings moved for more convenient access. Older buildings were updated while new ones were built. Levee knew, however, that brick and mortar and movies would not be enough to keep a successful studio afloat. Community support was also key.

One of Levee's first civic duties under his new title was the symbolic $10 purchase of the first "patron certificate" presented by Los Angeles

Mayor George E. Cryer in 1922. This certificate entitled the bearer to an admission to the First Annual American Historical Revue and Motion Picture Industrial Exposition scheduled for the following year. The press photo depicting this momentous occasion showed the mayor signing the certificate and stage money representing the $10 bill. The censors condemned the use of real money in the photo op.

The local event, meant to promote the city as well as the motion picture industry, coincided with the centennial anniversary of the Monroe Doctrine and would be sponsored by the Motion Picture Producers Association. Levee described the purpose of the exhibition:

> The Motion-Picture Exposition will do more toward establishing in the eyes of people of Los Angeles, themselves, the importance of this vast industry in their midst than any other event since the beginning of the business.
>
> Just as charity begins at home so does the "selling" of a business begin among the people of the locality that houses it. Every person in the City of Los Angeles will have the opportunity to see for himself or herself just what this business "is all about."
>
> Thousands who live here will visit the exposition and will come away with a new regard for the "movie." If the exposition accomplishes nothing else, it will perform a mission that fully warrants its existence by reason of its "selling" the people of Los Angeles and vicinity on the motion-picture business—and what it means to every individual here.

In true Hollywood fashion, the event turned into a mini-World's Fair. A pueblo-style city complete with Aztec towers was constructed along with an outdoor arena used for staging live entertainment such as rodeos, circus acts and even a ballet. Twenty thousand people attended opening day festivities on July 2, 1923 when a bronze statue of U.S. President James Monroe was unveiled. During the next five weeks, several parades with more pageantry and color than any royal could hope for impressed thousands of onlookers. Each night, color cascaded across the darkness as fireworks zipped skyward. Lavish live shows and personal appearances by many of Hollywood's famous players added to the magic.

Foreign dignitaries were feted while the City of Angels publicly united with the motion picture industry declaring their mutual interests and claiming each other as business partners forevermore. Just days before the affair ended, however, the circus-like atmosphere turned somber. On the evening of August 2, 1923, Reverend Neal Dodd, a local clergyman, announced to the attending crowd that fifty-seven-year-old President Harding had unexpectedly died in San Francisco. A prayer was said, the orchestra played "Nearer My God to Thee" and the stunned audience went home. The fireworks canceled. Despite the emotional setback, the exposition ended on a high note after a three-day carnival called "Days of '49" brought the California Gold Rush to life.

But all wasn't perfect in the big city. A few months later, Levee and his sister, Rose, were returning home after attending the 1923 opening of the Millennium Biltmore Hotel when they, along with another couple, were robbed. The quick-thinking Rose slipped an expensive ring in her mouth when she saw the thugs approaching. Levee tossed another ring away from the melee. Despite their efforts, the thieves still got away with brooches, bracelets, watches and cash. Their booty was estimated at more than $17,000.

In addition to crime fighting, memories of the summer love affair between the City of Angels and the motion picture industry ran short. When the Western Motion Picture Advertisers' Association (WAMPAS) planned their annual splash—the WAMPAS Ball, Mayer Cryer refused their request to allow dancing after midnight. When group officials protested saying that they had been given permission to rumba after hours during past balls, Cryer stood firm. He claimed that anyone who allowed such a thing was acting beyond their authority. There would be no two-stepping in Los Angeles after midnight. WAMPAS moved their next ball to San Francisco.

By now, Joseph M. Schenck was firmly fixed as Chairman of the Board with Levee maintaining his position of president and studio manager at Universal Studios, Inc. In between the birth of his second son, John Harrison, and running the business, Levee continued touting Los Angeles. He tirelessly pursued east coast production companies enticing them to film at the new and improved California facility. Levee told the press:

> Many producers, who have never made their pictures here before are coming to Los Angeles . . . Never in the history of Los Angeles film production has the outlook been so encouraging. . . . Producers in the East have at last seen the light.

A big coup for Levee occurred in 1924. With Schenck's backing, he offered the use of United Studios to producer J.D. Williams, president of Ritz-Carlton Productions, persuading him to move west and bring his most famous player with him—Latin heartthrob Rudolph Valentino.

But Schenck wasn't the only producer who had amusement park roots. Milton Ely Hoffman once earned his living at a popular park located in Cleveland, Ohio—his birthplace. Hoffman was born on December 15, 1879, the first child of Simon and his wife, Rose Wolf. The couple had another son, Bert, in 1881 and daughter, Sylvia, in 1886.

Hoffman's career began in Cleveland where he was manager and publicity man for a local theater, The Coliseum Garden. He also had a brief stint as manager of Luna Park, which was established by Fred Ingersoll, a well-known maker of amusement park rides. The 35-acre playground opened in 1905 and soon became known as "Cleveland's fairyland of pleasure." Hoffman's first major venture into the world of film occurred in Michigan where he worked for Philip Gleichman at The National Film Company of Detroit headquartered in the downtown area. This outfit specialized in actologues—troupes made up of several "talkers" who stood behind the movie screens and spoke lines as the film rolled.

After Detroit, Hoffman served double duty as a manager and publicity agent for various theatrical stock companies with such well-known vaudeville names as Vaughn Glaser and Felix Isman. His work eventually brought him to New York. By 1910, he was living in Brooklyn with his sister, Sylvia, and her husband, Bernard Feigenbaur. Striking out on his own, Hoffman staged a well-received production of *The Blindness of Virtue* in Chicago, which was later turned into a movie by the Essanay Film Manufacturing Company. In 1913, the thirty-something Hoffman once again connected with former Detroiter Philip Gleichman who was now running the World Special Films Corporation in New York. The December 6, 1913 issue of *The Moving Picture World* had this to say about Gleichman's new hard-working publicity man:

> . . . With his personality there is no telling how much higher he will yet rise in his profession. He has an easy, imperturbable way and a capacity for getting through a lot of work without any fuss. He is a bear for system, and his chief delight is in bringing order out of chaos. As a press agent he has the right perspective, knowing full well that he is employed to advertise the production he is with and not himself. Perhaps the most surprised man on earth will be Milton Hoffman when he reads this sketch. He may even be a little angry because this space is used for him instead of his company . . . The picture [that accompanied the article] was stolen and the facts wheedled out of him with much subtlety. . . .

As busy as he was, Hoffman still found time for romance. He wooed bookkeeper Lydia Koch, a native New Yorker. Her parents, August and Flora, came to the United States from Germany in 1888. They settled in New York where August worked as a carpenter. Despite their thirteen-year age difference, Hoffman married the younger girl on October 14, 1914.

Two years later, when Jesse L. Lasky came calling, Hoffman was general manager at the Peerless Feature Producing Company in Fort Lee, New

Jersey. Lasky lured him away with a job offer on the west coast. Always willing to move, Hoffman packed up—this time with Lydia—and on April Fools Day, 1916, he began working in Hollywood as studio manager of the Jesse L. Lasky Feature Play Company. A baseball fan, Hoffman quickly organized a studio team and arranged for uniforms. Unfortunately, they lost their first game 6-4 when they played against the Hollywood Business Men's Association.

Later on, when Lasky's company merged with Adolph Zukor's Famous Players, Hoffman took on the challenge of general manager for the entire enterprise. After the Great War, Lasky established a studio in England. Located in London and housed at a large facility that was once a power station for the railroad, the building was extensively remodeled and the latest filmmaking equipment installed. In 1919, Lasky chose Hoffman to oversee his Famous Players-Lasky British Productions Limited, but this was small potatoes. Upon Hoffman's return to the States, he would be in the driver's seat when Hollywood officials decided to build a city.

Irving Grant Thalberg was in charge of another Hollywood city—Universal. A driven trailblazer, the twenty-year-old Thalberg whirled into movies before he could vote—despite his precarious health. Thalberg's story began on May 30, 1899 in Brooklyn. William, his father, was a passive man from Germany who imported lace. His mother, Henrietta Heymann, had all the family ambition. When doctors diagnosed the baby with a heart defect, they warned that he probably wouldn't live much past his thirtieth birthday. William resigned himself to his son's poor health. Henrietta had other ideas.

Thalberg spent his first seven years in bed while his mother took charge. She bathed, massaged, and encouraged him, determined that he'd eventually attend school. Doctors cautioned against it, but Henrietta firmly believed that her son needed an education. She refused to think otherwise and eventually got her way.

Young Thalberg may have faced more than his share of physical problems, but once enrolled in school, he excelled. Impressed with his smarts, many of his teachers tutored him at home when he was not well enough to attend class. He devoured books and through his reading he came to understand the makings of a good story. After a bout of rheumatic fever, which further damaged his heart, Thalberg graduated from high school. Believing college was a waste of his potentially limited time, he enrolled in secretarial classes. This, he thought, would be the quickest means to find a job—and he was right. His knack for typing and shorthand bought him a one-way ticket to the movies.

Thalberg became secretary to the general manager at New York's Universal Film Manufacturing Company founded by Carl Laemmle. Earning $25 a week, he quickly proved himself and before long became Laemmle's secretary. In between making appointments and handling correspondence, Thalberg previewed movies with the boss who came to value his young assistant's opinions. Universal actress Dagmar Godowsky recalled those very early days:

> When I was with Universal, I go in to see my general manager, and there was a very young man with a desk who took messages, and I would sit on the desk and talk to him. I thought he'd get places. He was intelligent and nice. We became great friends. He got ill, and I used to send my chauffeur over with chicken broth . . .

When Laemmle traveled to California's Universal City, he took his trusted secretary with him. During his first trip out west, Thalberg absorbed everything he could about moviemaking. He explored the studio and studied the dynamics that made it run—or not run. The three men in charge of the west coast facility couldn't agree on anything and as a result, the place was in an uproar. As headline talent fled to other studios, Universal's bottom line suffered. Instead of firing the middle-aged executives, however, Laemmle added a fourth—twenty-year-old Thalberg.

The three chiefs were outraged. They resented the youngster's intrusion. The head honchos tried to oust him, but Thalberg had something they didn't—the backing of Carl Laemmle. Within six months, Thalberg offered his documented assessment to the boss: the studio was failing because of bad management and bad movies. He suggested that one person oversee all production. Laemmle gave him the job. Thalberg, as the new General Manager, took charge with an energy that belied his delicate heart.

Now earning $450 each week, Thalberg dealt with talent agents, held writer's conferences, met with casting, viewed newly filmed scenes and edited final cuts. With his uncanny flair for storytelling and unwavering self-assurance, he touched every film around him. In between his many daily duties, he also managed sudden emergencies as well as difficult directors. When he took on the formidable Erich von Stroheim, Hollywood was stunned.

Von Stroheim went over budget while filming *Foolish Wives* (1922) at Universal. He resented young Thalberg for questioning his lavish spending. Thalberg realized that stopping production wasn't financially smart, but he kept close watch on both the filming and the cost. Once he felt enough footage was shot, he simply took the cameras away. The unhappy von Stroheim's final cut ran more than five hours. Thalberg pared it down to three.

The Thalberg-von Stroheim feud continued into their next production, *Merry-Go-Round* (1923). The director went on overspending as the general manager kept tabs. After six weeks and with only a quarter of the filming completed, Thalberg had enough. He fired von Stroheim who went straight to Laemmle who stood firm behind his general manager. Von Stroheim was out and Hollywood reeled with the news of the boyish producer who dared stand up to the overbearing director.

In just three and a half years, Thalberg restructured Universal, improved its efficiency, oversaw the making of more than 100 movies, retained talent through better contracts and most importantly, increased profits. The Hollywood heavyweights took note. So did writer Malcolm Stuart Boylan who penned an article for the *L.A. Times* entitled *Great Executive*

Job Held By a Boy of 22—How Irving Thalberg Became the "Big Boss" of One of the Biggest Institutions in the World. Boylan listed Thalberg's "rules of success":

- Never hold an unassailable opinion
- The clearness with which I see my goal determines my speed in reaching it
- Expect help from no one
- Pride goeth before a fall. The height of the pride determines the severity of the bump
- Never take any man's opinion as final

Laemmle's daughter, Rosabelle, also took note of the powerful yet frail-looking fellow. She liked Thalberg, who was quickly becoming one of Hollywood's most eligible bachelors. The pair dated for a while with Laemmle's approval. Henrietta, however, wasn't buying into any marriage business. Now living with her son, she felt that, physically, married life would be too taxing on his delicate health. Thalberg himself didn't seem overly eager to commit to the boss' daughter either. This caused Laemmle to revise his opinion of the boy genius. Now worried about someone with a heart condition controlling his empire and feeling threatened by Thalberg's authority, Laemmle refused him a raise. Their relationship soured and Thalberg went looking for another job.

Producing a movie was not for the faint-hearted. The job demanded stamina and an endless supply of energy—or in Thalberg's case, willpower. Between bossy mothers, dictatorial directors and over-the-top exhibitions, the head of the house took charge of the mayhem and managed to make a buck.

Chapter Ten

THE GUARDIANS

Once Harris Newmark came to Los Angeles in 1853, the City of Angels was never the same. That April, the Prussian-born lad followed his older brother, Joseph, and sailed from Europe to New York. He then bought passage on a second ship, which traveled through the Isthmus of Panama before reaching San Francisco. From the City by the Bay, he boarded a steamer that finally docked in San Pedro, California in October 1853 to complete his six-month journey.

Upon his arrival, Newmark spoke several languages, but English wasn't one of them. It wasn't until his aunt and uncle immigrated the following year that he learned to read and write the language of his new country. Newmark started out selling groceries and dry goods. He even tried his hand at sheep farming, but it was real estate where he finally prospered.

A benevolent man who believed in community spirit, once he made his fortune, Newmark founded the Los Angeles Public Library in 1872 as well

as the Jewish Orphans Home in 1911. He was also a member of the Los
Angeles Chamber of Commerce and influential in bringing the railroad
to the west coast. He penned his memoirs in 1916, *Sixty Years in Southern
California 1853-1913*, which is still considered one of the finest personal
accounts ever written about Southern California history.

In between his business activities, Newmark married his first cousin,
Sarah. The couple had eleven children—five died young while six survived
including daughter Estelle, who married Leopold Loeb in 1879.

Originally from Strasburg in Alsace-Lorraine, Loeb's parents, Jacob
and Rosalie Levi Loeb, were part of a prominent Jewish family that
boasted a long line of leaders both spiritual and civic. Loeb's cousin,
Eugene Meyer, was already living in Los Angeles and the established
owner of Salmon Lazard, a dry goods store that carried clothes and
furniture. Starting out as a clerk in Meyer's store, Loeb worked his way
up over the next several years.

The Loebs gave Newmark three grandchildren: Rose born in 1881 followed by Joseph in 1883 with Edwin bringing up the rear in 1886. By the
time their last child was born, Cousin Meyer had moved to San Francisco
and sold Salmon Lazard to Loeb who renamed the store The City of Paris.
Meyer also acted as the French Consular Agent and suggested that Loeb
fill the vacancy he left behind. Meyer wasn't just trying to keep things in
the family. His recommendation was sound. Loeb provided outstanding
service as Consular Agent for over fifteen years. The French government
even awarded him the decoration of an Officer of the Academy—one of
their highest honors.

Some of Loeb's civic-mindedness must have rubbed off on his youngest
son. While still a student at the Cambria Street School in 1898, eleven-year-
old Edwin composed a patriotic essay about the Spanish-American War:

> Spain when she blew up the Maine little realized that her treacherous
> crime would be discovered. But she realizes it now, and though she
> may call us pigs, she little knows what a bull she is making.

From Cambria Street School, Loeb went on to Los Angeles High. After his 1904 graduation, he enrolled in the University of California, Berkeley. While he took his studies seriously, Loeb also found time for extracurricular activities. He co-wrote his sophomore class' annual burlesque show and called it *A Comedy of Terrors*. He also entered into an agreement with a fellow student that required both young men to travel around the world in opposite directions and eventually meet in England. The youths planned to cash in by writing magazine articles depicting their journey. Until then, Loeb worked as a cabin boy on the steamship that carried him to Australia.

After Loeb completed his travels, he received his law degree and passed the bar. He then partnered up with older brother Joseph, already an attorney, and the two founded their law firm in 1909. As lawyers, they made their mark when they represented their enterprising cousin Kaspare Cohn of the Kaspare Cohn Hospital, as well as the Kaspare Cohn Bank—known today as Cedars-Sinai Medical Center and Union Bank, respectively.

Joseph, the more serious brother, took on the regular business accounts, while the outgoing and animated Edwin was a much better fit for the movie colony. It was producer David Horsely of Nestor Studios who first approached Edwin Loeb for legal representation. Horsely had a problem with a couple of filmmaking brothers and he needed a lawyer. He wrote to his New York attorney asking him to recommend a well-versed litigator on the west coast. The east coast lawyer contacted San Francisco attorney Jesse Steinhart who knew the Loeb Brothers quite well. He didn't hesitate to recommend them for the job. According to Joseph:

> . . . My brother, Edwin, handled the row. Edwin made such a good arrangement for David Horsely that he was tickled to death. One of these brothers said to Edwin, "Why you dirty little so-and-so, the way you treated us is terrible, and if we ever need a lawyer, we are coming to you." Believe it or not, he did.

Then the two of them kept saying to Edwin, "We want you to meet our brother-in-law." And Edwin would come to me and say, "What shall I do? These boys want me to meet their brother-in-law. I've had trouble enough with them." Finally, one day Edwin said to them, "Who is your brother-in-law?" They said, "He's Carl Laemmle, the president of Universal Pictures" and so Edwin decided that he would meet the brother-in-law. . . . and because we handled the case for David Horsely against the brothers-in-law of Carl Laemmle, we got into the motion picture business. . . .

A small man with a large personality, the younger Loeb attracted many more movie clients to the firm such as Mary Pickford, Douglas Fairbanks and Charlie Chaplin. He often represented legal matters for the major studios as well. While Joseph was serious and refined, his gregarious kid brother liked to laugh and tell a rowdy tale. He also delighted in a good hand of poker. It wasn't unusual for the likes of Carl Laemmle, Irving Thalberg or Louis B. Mayer to deal in on a regular basis.

In the early days, the Loebs had no legal assistants or office managers. Edwin and his secretary ran the place. At home, the younger Loeb partnered up with Bessie Brenner, the daughter of San Francisco business leader and Chairman of the Republican State Central Committee Gustave Brenner, and his wife, Julia. While Loeb took care of the legal business, his wife took care of the homefront. Subsequently, they had two daughters, Marjorie and Virginia.

As their law practice flourished with Hollywood-related business and otherwise, another bright young attorney signed up for duty at Loeb and Loeb—George Washington Cohen. Like Leopold Loeb and Harris Newmark, Cohen's father, Isaac, was a long-time and well-respected Jewish resident of the Los Angeles area. Cohen was originally born in Germany and settled in San Francisco in 1868 after a brief stop in Kentucky. On May 2, 1887, he married the German-born Emma Stencel. The couple moved to Los Angeles and Isaac worked for the Internal Revenue Office for the next five years. He eventually moved to Redondo Beach and then to Anaheim where he served as mayor for two years in each city. The Cohens then returned to Los Angeles and Isaac entered the clothing business.

Their eldest child and only daughter, red-haired Gertrude, was an accomplished pianist by the time she was ten. When the brilliant musician Ignace jan Paderewski heard her play, he was so impressed that he suggested she study music in Europe. He even arranged a meeting with renowned composer and teacher Theodor Leschetizky in Vienna. After studying with Leschetizky for three years, Gertrude went on to enjoy a successful professional career. The Cohens also had a son, Herbert, who joined the family business until 1914 when he opened his own store selling furniture. When the United States entered The Great War, Herbert sold his company and enlisted. He was assigned to the aeroplane division and served out his time in Oregon.

George was the youngest Cohen and a great debater. While attending Los Angeles High, he represented the school in six interscholastic debates winning them all. He even took the first place gold medal in a championship debate against Anaheim. In 1916, while attending the University of California, Berkeley, one of his professors urged he be given a spot on the senior debate team even though he was just a junior. As a result, he won the Carnot Medal—the highest debating honor in the West. After winning the prestigious award, he wired his parents one brief word: "Yes!" He must have been all talked out.

Baron Pierre de Coubertin established the Carnot Medal in 1894 specifically for debating contests between students of the University of California and Stanford. His one stipulation was that the debate itself had to center on contemporary French politics. The medal was named after the recently assassinated President of France, Marie Francois Sadi Carnot. In addition to the debate award, de Coubertin is also considered the founder of the modern-day Olympics.

After his win, Cohen was elected president of his senior class. Like his older brother, he also enlisted during World War I. He was stationed at

Fort Sam Houston in Texas and earned a lieutenant's commission. During wartime, Cohen was sent to various training camps including The Presidio. By the time he was twenty-two, he was a captain and on his way to the French battlefields when the fighting ended. Cohen returned home in January 1919 and that fall attended Harvard University's law school.

Cohen passed the bar in 1921. He then married Carolyn Furth. Her brother, Albert, eventually rose to the position of assistant editorial director to Henry R. Luce, editor-in-chief of Time-Life fame. The Cohens had their first son, Donald, in 1924—the same year Cohen joined the law firm of Loeb & Loeb. The circle of Hollywood's legal protectors was expanding.

Unlike Loeb and Cohen, Frederick William Beetson was not a native Californian. He hailed from New York where he was born on February 26, 1880 to his father, Frederick who worked in the silk industry and his wife, Margaret. The couple also had a daughter, Fredericka, born two years earlier. Brother Frank came along in 1882. As a young man, Beetson worked in sales traveling throughout the east coast and Midwest. He also met a girl named Mabel.

Mabel Duryea Mitchell was the daughter of Herbert James Frost and Alice Duryea. In 1896, her father founded Frost and Company, which specialized in the selling of fishing equipment. Her mother was a member of the prominent Duryea family who established the Duryea Starch Manufacturing Company in New York City. Beetson wed Mabel on May 17, 1905 and following their nuptials, the newlyweds sailed to Europe for a two-month honeymoon. Seven years later, they had a son, Frederick William Beetson, III.

When the United States entered World War I after the sinking of the *Lusitania*, which killed theatrical producer Charles Frohman, Beetson was thirty-eight years old, living in Washington D.C. and working as the Assistant Secretary to the Republican National Committee. The Republican National Committee Chairman, William Harrison Hays, Sr., was also a lawyer and savvy campaign manager for presidential candidate Warren G. Harding. In 1921, the newly elected president appointed Hays to the office of Postmaster General. Within one year, Hays resigned from his official position to take on the presidency of the newly formed Motion Picture Producers and Distributors of America (MPPDA).

Prior to the MPPDA, the National Board of Review of Motion Pictures was founded in 1909 after New York City Mayor George B. McClellan, Jr. revoked motion-picture exhibition licenses on Christmas Eve, 1908. The board was meant to establish some form of early censorship and give the thumbs-up or sometimes thumbs-down to newly released films. For decades starting in 1916, many movies carried the words "Passed by the National Board of Review" for the public to see.

By the time Hollywood entered the Roaring Twenties under the auspices of Prohibition and scandal after scandal hit, from drugs to murder, like that of director William Desmond Taylor, a stamp of approval from the National Board of Review of Motion Pictures wasn't enough. Tales of sensational murders, violent rapes, illegal drugs, illicit love affairs, underground abortions and heavy drinking despite the liquor ban, resulted in a major public outcry directed at what they now called "Sin City." The press ran with each titillating tidbit, selling out their print run with each sordid headline. Well-respected church groups condemned the industry urging their faithful members to boycott movies. The box office was threatened. Something had to be done to restore Hollywood's good name and assure stable profits.

Making matters worse, the United States Supreme Court had declared, in the landmark case of Mutual Film Corporation v. Industrial Commission of Ohio, that movies were not an art form, but a business and therefore not covered under the Constitution's First Amendment and freedom of speech. The Ohio State Government had established a censorship board that was responsible for reviewing all films to be shown in the Buckeye State. Anyone running an unapproved film was subject to arrest. The Mutual Film Corporation, a movie distributor, challenged the censorship board's authority. When the Supreme Court unanimously ruled in Ohio's favor, Hollywood officials worried that Federal censorship of their films was just around the corner. Hays disagreed with the Supreme Court decision when he later stated:

> Had motion pictures been in vogue when the Constitution was written, they would have been protected against legislative inroads as were the press and our freedom of speech. For pictures are only another medium of expression.

In the meantime, censorship bills pended in many state legislatures. Local censorship boards popped up from coast to coast banning what they considered immoral movies in an attempt to protect their citizenry, especially their innocent children, from such corruption. Standards varied between cities and states allowing films to be run in one town but forbidden in another. In order to regain some control, Hollywood officials decided to police themselves. They created the MPPDA and called upon Will Hays to commandeer it. After all, he was a well-respected Republican hailing from Indiana and an elder in the Presbyterian Church. What better representative to counter Hollywood's woes than a Midwestern churchgoer firmly fixed in his conservative beliefs?

Hays wasted no time. One of his first agenda items barred Roscoe "Fatty" Arbuckle from making movies. Up until Labor Day weekend in 1921, the rotund Arbuckle was by far the most popular film comedian of his time. Spectators couldn't get enough of his onscreen antics. Literally, overnight something went wrong, however, and Arbuckle fell from grace to become the man everyone hated. That holiday weekend, Arbuckle and his groupies traveled to San Francisco where they partied together at the posh St. Francis Hotel.

One partygoer, actress Virginia Rappé, was not feeling well. It is believed that Rappé may have had several abortions and suffered from gonorrhea at the time. She ultimately died in a San Francisco hospital less than one week after the holiday. There were no signs of rape or violence, but sadistic rumors about Arbuckle persisted and the press vilified him.

The actor was soon summoned back to San Francisco where he was arrested and charged with rape and murder. Three trials later (the first two ended in hung juries), the big man was ultimately cleared from all charges and no one ever proved that a crime actually occurred. Despite his exoneration, Arbuckle remained a pariah for the rest of his days thanks to vicious gossip, the public's desire to believe he was guilty and Hays' choice to make him an example of Hollywood excess.

But Hays didn't stop there. He also developed the infamous "morality clause" that all filmmakers were expected to adhere to in their personal lives or else. Inserted into their contracts, adultery was forbidden, pregnancy outside of marriage was a major offense and any other disgraceful or illegal behavior could result in permanent excommunication from the industry. Of course, one had to first get caught in the dastardly deed before punishment was doled out. Hays' quick moves publicly demonstrated that Hollywood was serious about cleaning up its act. As a result, moviemakers dodged federal government censorship, which could have set a disastrous precedent in an era of renewed social conservatism.

Once he got things up and running, Hays summoned fellow Republican Fred Beetson to Hollywood to oversee the MPPDA. Beetson, the association's first secretary and treasurer, also brought along his second wife Minnie, a girl from Maine. Once Hays, now known, as the Movie or Cinema Czar, was satisfied with what he had put in place, he announced in January 1924:

> I believe we are on the right track at least. Waste in the production of motion pictures has been the most eminent fault of the industry. It is our purpose to do everything possible to eliminate it.

As second in command at what was dubbed the Hays Office, Beetson's job was to protect the public from the potential evils of film and he took his work quite seriously. He often mediated volatile issues between filmmakers, his own office and the many censorship boards that cried foul across the country. Beetson even intervened with international censors when the need arose. The Hays Office advised the studios just what these boards would and wouldn't approve, but it was really anybody's guess since the boards themselves had no standardization or common denominator between them. A film that might be run in Manhattan or Detroit could be banned in Pittsburgh or Paris.

Censorship, however, wasn't the only issue that concerned Beetson. He also looked out for the animals that were used on-screen. At the end of 1924, he made an arrangement with the Society for the Prevention of Cruelty to Animals to protect the non-human players. Actor William S. Hart topped off the deal by presenting an ambulance to the Society.

Shortly after he took care of the creatures, Beetson's attention turned to the screen actors. He met with producers Joseph M. Schenck, John McCormick, Irving Thalberg and Jack Warner to come up with a process for all actors—stars and extras—to present grievances in front of a fair-minded committee in an unbiased arena without consequences. The goal was to seek solutions agreeable to all parties involved, minus any backlash.

Despite the negative hoopla, star-struck hopefuls trying to break into the movies as extras inundated Hollywood. Hays commissioned the Russell Sage Foundation, which specialized in social studies, to investigate and report on conditions related to the extras. Their investigation revealed some disturbing facts. With more people than work available, unscrupulous agents commanded exorbitant fees to find extra roles for their unsuspecting clients, and scam agents sometimes walked away with a significant amount of a desperate actor's earnings before they wised up. The hopefuls were often mistreated, taken advantage of and lied to. In response, Hays, with Beetson's help and the approval of the MPPDA, established the Central Casting Corporation in 1926.

This new organization, financed by the producers' group, provided a registration process and, with one simple phone call, a job hopeful could at no cost find out whether work was available. According to the biennial report of the Bureau of Labor Statistics of California, Central Casting also committed to the following:

1. To do away with the high fees charged by private employment agencies to extras in the motion picture industry.

2. To eliminate the violations of the law arising out of methods of paying off the extras.

3. To discourage the constantly increasing influx of persons as extras in the industry, and

4. To develop a residue of efficient extras who would be called upon frequently and who would be able to derive a decent living from the employment as extras.

With Beetson as president, the Central Casting Corporation made the job search much easier for extras and aspiring actors. They no longer had to hustle from studio to studio looking for work. It also helped them avoid schemers. It did not, however, deter men and women from coming to Hollywood hoping to be the next Mary Pickford or Douglas Fairbanks, both of whom by now were huge stars: she "America's Sweetheart" and he a beloved matinée idol. While hundreds found steady work, thousands registered but remained on the outside looking in.

In a short twenty years, with one World War behind them and Prohibition cramping their style, the movie industry went from John Q. Public's favorite pastime to national nemesis. With the Temperance Movement already culminating in the banning of alcohol, many so-called civic-minded groups turned their attention to Hollywood where they believed depraved lives of excess and immorality were just waiting to be saved. Where else were divorces so common? Illicit affairs ongoing? Illegal drugs and liquor so brazenly consumed? Crimes covered up? And if the high-paid celebrities were leading exemplary lives then they still had to be guilty of something—like over-the-top indulgences, no matter how harmless they seemed.

Even matinée idol Wallace Reid, who represented the all-American hero with his good looks and strong build, succumbed to a morphine addiction. His untimely death in 1923 at the age of 31 shocked spectators and came on the heels of the Arbuckle scandal and the William Desmond Taylor murder. Instead of playing down her husband's death, Reid's widow, former actress Dorothy Davenport, spoke out touring the country denouncing drugs and warning anyone who would listen of their deadly ramifications.

Of course, scandal also sold newspapers and magazines so the press gladly reported each and every one whether they actually happened or not. A bloodthirsty public soaked up one salacious story after the other reading with enthusiasm, but condemning the evildoers all the same.

The hardworking men and women in the industry found that along with making movies, defending Hollywood became a full-time job as well. In order to keep business going, filmmakers had to protect their investments and clean up their acts—literally. While lawyers like Loeb and Cohen assisted with legalities ensuring that business matters stayed above the law, Hays and Beetson struggled to protect the citizenry from those wicked Hollywood hooligans and their potentially corrupting influence, along with some genuine scam artists and predators.

Would all of their efforts make things right? Would the public once again embrace the movies? Could a crisis be reined in or did Hollywood higher-ups need to take control and write their own happy ending?

In 1927, thirty-six top movie officials opted for the latter.

Part Two

YOU AIN'T HEARD
NOTHIN' YET!

Chapter Eleven

ON TOP OF THE MOUNTAIN

After director Cecil B. DeMille decided Flagstaff, Arizona wasn't the right place to film his feature *The Squaw Man* way back in 1914, he and his troop from the Jesse L. Lasky Feature Play Company continued heading west. The group ultimately set up shop inside of a horse barn about ten miles north of Los Angeles in a dusty little town that locals called Hollywood. The film company shared the space on Selma Avenue and Vine Street with barn owner Jacob Stern who reserved just enough room for his horses and carriage. DeMille recalled keeping a waste can handy, describing it as "a very convenient refuge for my feet whenever Mr. Stern washed his carriage and the water ran under my desk."

By the time Lasky himself paid a visit to the barn, filming was well underway. The story centered on an innocent Englishman, played by actor Dustin Farnum, who took the fall for embezzlement charges on behalf of his cousin, the earl. The gentleman leaves his homeland in shame for America's Wild West where he tries his hand at cattle ranching. He also meets and falls in love with an Indian girl, Nat-U-Ritch, portrayed by the Native American actress Red Wing. Meanwhile, the real crook is killed in a mountain climbing accident, but just before he goes on to his greater reward—or not—he pens a note admitting to his dastardly deed paving the way for our hero's triumphant return to England. Of course in between, there is plenty of gunslinging, brawling and even a daring rescue at sea.

DeMille, who co-directed the six-reel film with the more experienced filmmaker/mentor Oscar Apfel, went over budget causing Lasky and his brother-in-law-partner, Samuel Goldfish, no end of headaches. *The Squaw Man* had already been touted, and exhibition rights sold to various distributors throughout multiple states, by Goldfish long before it was finished. Without a back-up plan, Lasky had no choice but to let DeMille carry on in his brazen fashion and complete the film. When it finally came time to exhibit the movie, Lasky and company were forced to stop the very first show. The film jerked inside the projector making the off-kilter picture shake and shiver on-screen. Confusion reigned as a jumble of heads, hands and feet appeared in all sorts of odd places.

Fearing that their final product was nothing but junk, their large investment lost and their movie-making days over forever, Lasky and DeMille sought technical assistance. They took their film to Sigmund Lubin, a well-known exhibitor from Philadelphia. He quickly found the problem—DeMille had inadvertently punched too many sprocket holes along both sides of the film with sixty-five per foot instead of the customary sixty-four. These sprocket holes were used to pull the film through the projector at a standard pace, which kept the moving picture in sync. Once the film and the sprocket holes were repaired, the movie played without a hitch or a spasm. The crowd-pleasing feature was hardly junk at the end of the day, pulling in more than a quarter million dollars and officially admitting the Jesse L. Lasky Feature Play Company into the movie business as major players.

A more confident DeMille followed up that first picture with two more hits, *The Call of the North* (1914) and *The Virginian* (1914). Now recognized as one of film's top directors, DeMille along with partners Lasky and Goldfish were part of an elite group of leading moviemakers. The company then bought Stern's entire barn, as well as the adjoining property. DeMille sent for his wife and daughter and moved the family into a home in Cahuenga Pass. The couple soon adopted a son, John, making them a foursome. DeMille's older brother, William, was somewhat skeptical about the flicker business, but he conceded and also moved west as head of the Scenario Department.

Later that same year, DeMille directed another western, *Rose of the Rancho* (1914). He cast former Universal actress Jeanie Macpherson in the role of Isabelita, the daughter of a ranch owner whose property is seized. While working at Universal, the very feminine Macpherson occasionally directed and wrote photoplays of her own, which intrigued DeMille. He soon noticed her knack for storytelling and took more than a casual liking to the attractive young woman with red hair and dark eyes. The demanding DeMille admired her pluck. Much like the imperious director, the tough-talking Macpherson always gave as good as she got.

After casting her in two more films, DeMille asked Macpherson to pick up a pen. She developed the photoplay for *The Captive* (1915), based on DeMille's stage play by the same name. The story took place in Montenegro during the Balkan Wars and marked the beginning of a life-long professional partnership between the domineering DeMille and the innovative Macpherson who was one of the few people in the business that stood up to him, both personally and professionally. While the ever-tolerant Mrs. DeMille looked the other way, her husband and his new associate also became on-again, off-again lovers, but it was their professional collaboration that far outlasted their clandestine trysts.

While DeMille and Macpherson were getting better acquainted, Jesse L. Lasky also moved his family to California. Originally from the San Francisco Bay area, he welcomed the chance to return to the warmth of the west coast. By now, Jesse and his wife, Bessie, were parents to a four-year-old son, Jesse Louis, Jr. On the business side, Lasky's premise was basic—he generally bought the rights to various stage plays intending to turn them into movies. If a theatrical feature could resonate with an audience and sell tickets, the movie version should do the same.

By 1915, Lasky was in charge of what was now considered one of Hollywood's most successful motion picture production companies. In order to stay in business and keep making movies, he needed a distributor that would ensure his films reached the widest possible audiences and thus sell the maximum number of tickets. Lasky struck a deal with a new film exchange founded by salesman W.W. Hodkinson who grew up near Utah's Wasatch Range. Paramount Pictures was the brainchild of Hodkinson and his business partners. It is commonly believed that their snowcapped mountain logo was originally based on one of the larger mountains located in the Wasatch Range—possibly Mount Ben Lomond measuring in at 9,712 feet. Other stories claim that Colorado's white-topped Pike's Peak was behind the logo. Whatever inspired him, Hodkinson's vision of a snow-capped mountain remains firmly linked with Paramount Studios.

Paramount also distributed films for furrier-turned-film-producer Adolph Zukor, head of the Famous Players Corporation in New York. Zukor, originally from Hungary, was orphaned at an early age and sent to live with his uncle. At sixteen, he realized that Hungary held no future for him and immigrated to New York. He eventually found employment with a furrier and, in what would become his standard operating procedure, he studied every aspect of the fur trade, absorbing even the smallest of details. Within three years of his arrival in the United States, Zukor earned a comfortable living designing furs.

From New York, he moved to Chicago after a visit to the World's Fair in the early 1890s. Once in the Windy City, he met fellow furrier Morris Kohn, another Hungarian immigrant. The two men partnered up to form Kohn and Company. While Kohn covered the finances and sales, Zukor designed and created the fashionable furs. Business boomed and when he wasn't fingering fur, Zukor was courting Kohn's niece, Lottie Kaufman.

Out on a date, the couple visited a local theater where they watched an amazing sight—a brief flicker, called *May Irwin Kiss* (1896). The short film depicted theatrical players May Irwin and John C. Rice engaged in a lingering kiss—a shocking demonstration of intimacy for the day along with a display of movement that left patrons wanting more. Despite the great success of Kohn and Company, the image of that kiss remained in Zukor's head—even after he married Lottie and returned to New York to expand the fur business.

Once in New York, Zukor's cousin approached him about investing in a penny arcade. Zukor and Kohn not only came up with the money, but were so impressed with the peep shows and moving pictures, they opened a nickelodeon of their own called Automatic Vaudeville. Intrigued by their new business and the hundreds of dollars taken in each day, the two partners established Automatic Vaudeville arcades in New Jersey, Massachusetts and Pennsylvania. With ticket money pouring in, the partners lost interest in minks and sables. Kohn and Company was dissolved allowing the men more time for their entertainment business. By 1910, Kohn and Zukor joined another former furrier, Marcus Loew, who already owned and operated his own chain of theaters. The group formed Loew's Consolidated Enterprises with Zukor as treasurer.

Still infatuated with moving pictures, but not happy with the partnership, Zukor eventually dropped out of the business to strike out on his own. He realized early on that motion pictures were more than just a passing fad. Creating flickers, not just exhibiting them, could easily morph into big business and he wanted in. For the next several years, Zukor methodically studied and learned everything he could about the movies. In the end, he came up with a similar conclusion to Lasky's—movies were just another version of theatrical plays. He penned the words "Famous Players in Famous Plays," which later translated to "The Famous Players Film Company" and set up his shop near New York's theater district.

Zukor knew he could not succeed alone so he recruited more experienced filmmakers such as Edwin Porter, who wrote and directed *The Great Train Robbery* (1903), a flicker that was by and large a household name. By 1913, Zukor had expanded his enterprise and filmed several successful features including classic tales like *The Count of Monte Cristo* and *The Prisoner of Zenda*, both directed by Porter. Zukor also had a certain curly-haired girl named Mary Pickford under contract. Pickford had left Biograph and returned to Broadway only to realize that she missed making films. With Zukor, Pickford perfected her innocent-young-girl-who-conquers-all persona in movies like *Heart's Adrift* (1914), another Porter film—this one penned by the star herself. Spectators always favored Pickford, but now they fell in love with the impish girl they adoringly called their "sweetheart" and her film legacy as "America's Sweetheart" was cemented.

At home, the grown-up Pickford had not yet met the dashing Douglas Fairbanks, but lived within the constraints of a messy marriage with actor husband Owen Moore. He was hardly the Prince Charming he portrayed opposite his wife's starring turn in the fairytale movie *Cinderella* (1914). Off-screen, a drunken Moore often belittled her—jealous of her success, as well as the unshakeable bond she shared with her mother. Charlotte was always displeased that Mary had tied herself to a drunk, despite her own unsavory experience with a bottle-toting husband decades before. Pickford left Moore again and again only to return once he sobered up and begged her forgiveness.

While her relationship with Moore remained anything but amorous, Pickford took a liking to her cigar-smoking boss. He was hardly anyone's favorite. Most of Zukor's subordinates referred to him as "Creepy" when he wasn't around. Not Pickford. Perhaps because she always lacked a strong man in her personal life from her father to her husband, she looked up to Zukor and called him "Papa." In turn, Papa Zukor, with an unusual display of warmth, referred to Pickford as his "sweetheart honey." Their chaste father-daughter relationship would continue as long as they worked together.

By now, Zukor, much like Lasky, was a major industry force and known throughout the motion picture business in America as well as Europe. Both the Famous Players and the Jesse L. Lasky Feature Play Companies distributed their features through Hodkinson's exchange. Their movies represented the vast majority of Paramount's films. Unlike Lasky, however, Zukor wasn't satisfied. He took note of *The Squaw Man* (1914) and its box office success, and then wired his congratulations to Lasky. The movie shark was circling.

If filmmaking creates strange bedfellows, Lasky and Zukor were among the oddest of couples. While both men built their success on turning screenplays into films, the easygoing Lasky who loved his work and his company was the complete opposite of the ruthless Zukor whose drive to succeed dominated every calculating decision he made. The well-liked Lasky was often called "the nicest man in show business" while "Creepy" Zukor was known best for his coldness and cunning. Zukor slowly gained Lasky's trust and when the two finally joined forces on June 28, 1916, they created the world's largest motion picture company to date, known as the Famous Players-Lasky Corporation.

With Zukor as President and Lasky as Vice-President in Charge of Production, DeMille retained his title of Director General and Goldfish became Chairman of the Board. The outspoken Goldfish, however, soon fell out of favor with Zukor who simply could not handle someone questioning his authority. Now divorced from Lasky's sister, Blanche, Goldfish no longer fit in with the business or the family. In the end, the overpowering Zukor won out. Goldfish was given almost one million dollars to resign, but his career in the movies was far from over. He would soon team up with another partner, Edgar Selwyn, to form Goldwyn Pictures Corporation—the company that would one day become part of the great triumvirate, Metro-Goldwyn-Mayer. This new partnership also prompted Goldfish to change his name to Goldwyn.

With the Famous Players-Lasky Corporation now established, minus the troublesome Goldfish, Zukor and Lasky turned their attention to

Paramount Pictures, which had been distributing for them since 1914. The two men pooled their Paramount stock together and seized control of the film exchange effectively ousting the current executives. With all three companies now under his dominion, Zukor's painstaking methods had finally paid off. He had reached the top of the mountain, from apprentice furrier to media mogul.

After the merger, Milton E. Hoffman, who was Lasky's studio manager, stayed on as general manager of the larger company until 1919 when he was sent to England to open their London studio, Famous Players-Lasky British Productions, Limited. Hoffman, accompanied by his wife, Lydia, was optimistic about his mission:

> This will be my first trip to London and I anticipate a busy and enjoyable time under the new auspices. While it is true that since the beginning of the war production activities in England have been more or less at a standstill, the pictures that had been made up to that time had shown an unusual amount of real quality and I am satisfied that, with a foundation of this kind to build upon, there should be no difficulty in again reaching that standard and maintaining it.

Hoffman was right. Talent awaited him in Britain. After outfitting the old power station on Poole Street with two stages, several workshops, and the newest filmmaking equipment available, the production company got down to business. Under Hoffman's guidance, the new studio began manufacturing quality movies. Many of the London facility's first films, including *The Call of Youth* (1921) and *The Great Day* (1921), employed the services of a young but gifted title writer by the name of Alfred Hitchcock.

In addition to Hoffman, Lasky also hired one of filmdom's original scenarists, Frank E. Woods, as Supervising Director. The forward-thinking Woods is credited with developing new production methods such as regular writers' meetings, story conferences and individual production units headed by a single supervisor. During his off time, he also helped create the Actors Fund Motion Picture Committee and served as the group's first chairman. Through this group, any person who worked in the motion picture industry for at least one year could submit an application requesting personal financial assistance. The committee reviewed each one and granted aid to "the sick and those in destitute circumstances." It seems that even the bigwigs did not forget when they too once struggled to make ends meet.

By 1921 Woods had climbed to Supervisor and Chief of all studio activities under Zukor and Lasky. That same year, when one of their own, Roscoe "Fatty" Arbuckle, encountered unfounded manslaughter charges, Woods commented on the unfortunate situation to the press:

> . . . I should like to say a good word for Arbuckle now that everyone is kicking him when he is down. He was simply guilty of trying to be a good fellow, and I, for one cannot believe that he is guilty of all of the crime charges against him. The public knows, however, that he did not live a sane, regular life, and that he thought only of pleasures of eating and drinking, and the public has put its stamp of disapproval on his conduct. He gave parties in his Los Angeles home that, in those days now past, many prominent people of this city were glad to attend, but now that he is down, these people are kicking him.

Amidst all the corporate switching and twitching, DeMille and Jeanie Macpherson were still making movies together. In 1916, they took on their first historical epic based on the life of the French-warrior-saint, Joan of Arc. Driven by authenticity, DeMille recreated replicas of medieval buildings still standing in France and used real period weapons purchased from various museums. He cast famed opera singer and silent screen star, Geraldine Farrar in the title role. While DeMille focused on the pomp and circumstance, Macpherson emphasized Joan's human side. She wrote the part depicting a young, bewildered woman who wanted to do the right thing during extraordinary times. It was Macpherson's idea to call the movie *Joan the Woman*, which captured the person instead of the saint. Macpherson once explained her philosophy:

> . . . The pictorial qualities of a photoplay will always be important, but what people want to see is what happens to the hero, the heroine and the other integral characters. It's the reaction between humans not beautiful backgrounds although of course beauty of a background helps to distinguish a poorly from a well-built picture . . .

In that sense, DeMille's desire for grandeur and Macpherson's need for personalization complemented each other and made for some spectacular motion pictures. Despite DeMille's best efforts and the critics' approval, *Joan the Woman* (1916) wasn't one of them. Perhaps part of the problem was the forty-four-year-old actress trying to play a teenager. Whatever the reason, the poor ticket sales sent the director's career into a temporary downswing and only added to his already tense relationship with Zukor whom he found domineering and unreasonable, traits that grated on DeMille.

Despite the disappointing box office for *Joan the Woman*, DeMille and Macpherson continued their on-and-off-screen pairings. By 1919, they had adjacent offices at the studio, as well as his and hers pilot licenses. DeMille not only owned a plane, he formed the Mercury Aviation Company, considered California's first commercial airline. Located at Fairfax Avenue and Melrose, the "DeMille Field" offered charter flights, flying lessons and sightseeing tours—from the air, of course. They also flew regularly scheduled roundtrip passenger flights to surrounding areas like Catalina Island and Pasadena. In addition, the airfield was home to filmmakers who soon realized that aeronautical thrills equated to box office dollars. Many early aviators were often willing to loop de loop, wing walk or parachute out of a burning plane for a good price and a little publicity.

In between directing and flying, DeMille and Constance expanded their family, his affair with Macpherson notwithstanding. The couple adopted a daughter, Katherine Lester, in 1920. The nine-year-old was left without parents after her father died in The Great War followed by her mother who succumbed to tuberculosis. Two years later, they adopted their final child, Richard. The family claimed he was a foundling, but the boy displayed a remarkable resemblance to the DeMille side of the house.

As another frequent flyer, Macpherson was recognized as one of the most able aviatrixes in the country. An expert stunt flyer, she often took part in air shows, or circuses as they were sometimes called, and displayed her flying mettle in her Curtiss aeroplane. She learned from the best like stunt pilot Ormer "Ormi" Locklear, world-famous for his above-ground tricks and steely nerves. The two flew together often and Macpherson carried a deep respect for Locklear's airborne skills. When he died in a fiery crash while filming his second movie, *The Skywayman* (1920), the normally unruffled Macpherson was shaken. The crash itself was caught on film and used in the movie's final cut.

Locklear's tragic death did not keep Macpherson grounded for long. In addition to her love of flying, Macpherson also liked speed. In March 1922, she took a spin with Italian racecar driver Pietro "The Red Devil" Bordino. Born in Turin, the dashing Bordino started out as a racecar mechanic for Fiat. By 1921, he was not just driving for the burgeoning car company, but he was one of the racing circuit's major contenders. When Bordino visited the Beverly Hills Speedway, the daring Macpherson rode the track with him. Cranking his Fiat up to 110 miles per hour, she declared the exhilarating pace felt like "two streams of hot chocolate rushing into your eyes."

Macpherson met her match, however, when she entered a Detroit women's penitentiary—all in the name of research. While working on her photoplay for *Manslaughter* (1922), Macpherson decided to serve time. She went to Detroit and, as "Angel Brown from San Francisco," got herself convicted on a bogus charge of thievery. After pleading guilty, the judge gave her a choice—either pay a $10 fine or spend ten days in jail. She happily chose the latter. After getting her coveralls and cell assignment, Macpherson dined on her first prison meal of what she later described as sour soup and bread. That night, while confined to her cell, she met the local vermin. Sleep was out of the question. After 72 hours of penitentiary living, even the fearless Macpherson had enough. She managed to contact her mother who came through with the $10 fine. Macpherson claimed to have lost ten pounds during her lock-up. She described her ordeal in an article for *Movie Weekly* entitled "I Have Been in Hell."

Back in California, Macpherson and DeMille teamed up once again to produce another historical epic. This time they picked the biblical story of Moses. After the dismal failure of *Joan the Woman*, no one seemed interested in DeMille's vision of the desert wanderers. Zukor refused to let him travel to Egypt for location shooting so DeMille settled for Guadalupe Dunes in central California. Taking thousands of workers and animals with him, DeMille replicated Egypt on a California beach. The oversized sets and special effects caused the shoot to go over budget once again, increasing the tension with Zukor. In the end, *The Ten Commandments* (1923) brought DeMille international acclaim and Zukor financial success. The spectacle-making director had found his strong suit and thanks to the magic of Roy Pomeroy, the parting of the Red Sea made movie history.

As head of his own special effects department, Pomeroy continued delivering spectacular film footage. Often described as a "technical wizard," his attributes were once listed as:

1. He is a picture technical expert.
2. A camera expert.
3. A sound engineer.
4. A director.
5. An oil painter.
6. An electrical engineer.
7. A mechanical expert.
8. A mathematician.

He is also widely read on history, literature, drama, music and kindred arts.

They forgot the part about "miracle man." With his technical know-how, the coming of sound would ensure his position but also cause his downfall. Even miracle workers can get tiresome.

While moviegoers liked spectacle, they also liked adventure, cowboy-style. Lasky's most popular Western star, Jack Holt, oozed brawn and muscle as he battled the bad guys with guns and horses. Unlike his contemporaries, Tom Mix and Buck Jones, Holt's cowboy was a no-nonsense tough guy who wore a mustache—a rare sight for a hero in early Hollywood. The good guys were almost always clean-shaven with facial hair reserved for the wicked and villainous.

Most of Holt's movies took him away from the studio. Filming often occurred in places like Arizona's Fish Creek Canyon near the Apache Trail. The travel and the authentic locations suited Holt just fine. He much preferred the road to the back lot and spent several months of the year away from home. While he still fit in a modern drama here and there, Holt was at his best in the saddle—both on-screen and off.

When he wasn't working, the actor spent much of his time playing polo and caring for the horses he kept at the Midwick Country Club Stables. The prestigious association, located near Monterey Park, opened in 1913 with over 200 acres devoted to polo, golf and tennis. Many top Hollywood figures joined in order to participate in one or more of the sports offered. Holt, an expert horseman, was a valued member of their polo team.

As for Zukor and Lasky, they continued their partnership, but it would be a while before The Famous Players-Lasky Corporation formally adopted the Paramount name, even after they bought it out. In the meantime, Lasky, still "the nicest man in show business," oversaw film production while the cigar-smoking "Creepy" Zukor looked down from his mountain top.

Chapter Twelve

LIONS AND TIGERS AND BROTHERS, OH MY!

The Warner Brothers had come a long way from the Ohio bicycle shop they opened in 1899. In less than ten years, they established a successful movie theater and an even more financially prosperous movie exchange that they called The Duquesne Amusement Supply Company. Pulling in $2,500 per week from the exchange, the brothers sold their movie theater in 1909 and opened a second exchange in Norfolk, Virginia.

By now, Harry and Rea were parents to infant son Lewis, born on October 10, 1908. They also owned a home just outside of Pittsburgh. Recently married Abe worked closely with Harry to run the Duquesne exchange. He and his new bride, Bessie Krieger, lived with her family on Fifth Avenue in Pittsburgh. Bessie, the eldest of seven children, was the daughter of shoe salesman Leon Krieger and his wife, Jennie, who immigrated to the United States from Russia. Single brothers Sam and Jack were rooming in a Norfolk boardinghouse while manning the exchange in Virginia. Warner life was good until Edison and the Trust choked their evolving business.

In 1910, members of the Trust formed the General Film Company in an attempt to take over all of the independent exchanges and establish themselves as the sole monopolizer in the business. If owners refused to sell out, the new company just cut off their film supply forcing them to shut down. In some cases, the Trust employed tough guys who got their underhanded point across with a well-aimed punch or two. A representative from the General Film Company visited the Warners with such an offer. The brothers protested. They didn't want to unload their lucrative business. Threatened with the termination of their film resources, however, the Warners realized that they had no choice but to close their doors. Brother Sam described the moment:

> [The representative] said he was going to give us a fair break and allow us $52,000 for our exchange. He handed us $10,000 in cash, $12,000 in preferred stock and the rest in four payments to stretch over a period of three years.
>
> Here we were—$10,000 among the four of us, not enough for a first-class peanut stand. . . .

Despite their troubles, something about those silent flickers kept nagging at all of the brothers. Harry admitted temporary defeat and purchased a grocery store in Youngstown. He had a wife and a son to support, after all. Abe took to the road as a traveling salesman while Sam and Jack went to New York to somehow keep their hands in the motion picture business. Jack found work as a film splicer while Sam discovered a five-reeler that the Trust didn't own. Sam's foreign film, *Dante's Inferno* (1911), provided the necessary jolt that the brothers needed to get back into the movie business.

The Italian-made movie was hand-tinted and based on Dante's famous poem. The film's frightening depiction of a fiery Hell and depraved Lucifer fascinated Sam. He was sure the graphic action would have the same effect on paying spectators. He summoned Jack, and together they found an unemployed thespian with a fondness for liquor, a working wind machine and an ordinary sheet of metal. Then, with everything in place, they staged a showing. While the film rolled in front of an eager audience, the actor bellowed out the poem. At the same time, Jack created mechanical wind gusts and shook the sheet metal to emulate rumbling of thunder. Pulling in a profit, they took their show on the road. The Warners were making a comeback despite the unlucky craps game that took Sam and Jack for the $1500 they had just earned during a celebratory night out.

The four brothers pooled their money allowing Sam and Jack to rent an empty foundry in St. Louis. In their makeshift studio, they directed and produced a western film starring Chicago-born actress Dot Farley who knew how to hang on to a horse. They even put members of the National Guard to work as pioneers heading west. *The Peril of the Plains* (1912) was the first film made under the new production company, Warner Features. Harry, still the brains behind the business, wasn't impressed. Abe, the would-be film salesman, knew they were in trouble: "Soap I can sell. Pots and pans I can sell. Junk I can't sell."

Ever the realist, Harry knew that with their limited budget, they couldn't make a better movie. They were stuck with the footage they had. If there was any hope for Warner Features Company, the brothers had to escape the Trust and distribute the film themselves—no matter how bad it might be. With some financial help from their folks, the Warners split up. Sam established an exchange office in Los Angeles; Jack did the same in San Francisco; Harry and Abe opened a business office in New York.

At home, Abe and his wife, Bessie, remained childless while Rea presented Harry with daughter Doris on September 13, 1913. Sam was content with the single life, but Jack met a girl in San Francisco through theater owner Sid Grauman. Irma Claire Salomon came from an affluent family of Jewish-German descent. Jack fell hard for the pretty young girl and persuaded her to marry him on October 14, 1914. Jacob and Alice

Salomon didn't approve of their daughter's mate, but Jack laid on the charm and soon won them over. The couple had a son, Jack L. Warner, Jr., on March 27, 1916.

The following year, Jack joined Sam in Los Angeles where the two hobnobbed with experienced filmmakers. There, the brothers hoped to find a worthy project that they could turn into a moneymaking movie. Sam discovered exactly what he was looking for in a bookstore window—*My Four Years in Germany*. James Watson Gerard, the former American Ambassador to the German Imperial Court, penned the nonfiction book. He detailed the years he spent in Germany from 1913 to 1917 at which time the German government ordered him to leave. With The Great War in full swing, the timely memoir generated public interest. Sam bought the book and after reading it, pitched his movie idea to Harry.

With actor Halbert Brown playing the part of Gerard, *My Four Years in Germany* (1918) depicted the stark atrocities of a country at war—mistreated prisoners, ruthless executions and merciless leaders whose twisted minds plotted unthinkable horrors. Billed as "fact, not fiction," the explicit film made an unforgettable impression on American moviegoers, stirring up a fervent patriotism in the midst of World War I. The box-office success of this documentary-style motion picture turned Harry, Abe, Sam and Jack into serious Hollywood contenders.

The brothers then rented a shabby studio near the Selig Zoo in Edendale. Early filmmaker William Selig bought what was now the zoo property in 1913 and turned it into a home for the animals used in his movies. The still-struggling Warners started filming serials, but they-couldn't afford highly paid actors. Instead they featured beasts borrowed from the neighboring zoo. These non-human players were cheaper to hire, but not always pleasant to work with. Both cast and crew faced tigers with big tempers, monkeys with sharp teeth and elephants with bad attitudes. Despite the hazards, however, one pretty girl being menaced by lions, tigers and bears on a weekly basis caused audiences to come back for more.

Within a year, the Warners moved on up to a new location in an area known as Poverty Row. Located on Sunset Boulevard between Gower and Beachwood, this new studio was so bad the brothers didn't even hang a shingle to identify themselves. Convinced that Poverty Row was just another temporary place, Sam found ten acres on Sunset Boulevard and Bronson. The site already had an office building where they could conduct business and a barn to film in. With zero dollars down, the Warners bought the property for $25,000. Shortly after, Harry and Rea completed their family with daughter Betty May born on May 4, 1920.

Warner Bros. was the only family-run studio in town. As always, Harry, the eldest, was the headman in charge. Generally a quiet, conservative man who maintained his sense of honesty, Harry installed himself as President. Abe, an oversized guy with an intimidating physical presence, was really on the shy side. He acted as Treasurer and overseer of exhibitor relations. Sam's gregarious personality made up for Abe's timidity. Sam, always fascinated by mechanical gadgets, was a fun-loving forward-thinker who couldn't wait to try something new. As Vice President and Sales Manager, he acquired stories and kept up with the latest technology. Unofficially, Sam also acted as peacekeeper/referee between Harry and Jack during their many rowdy confrontations.

Jack, Vice President in Charge of Production, liked his film executive job as much as he liked making movies. His biggest problem was Harry. Jack still resented his older brother's authority. Complete opposites, the two Warners were a constant source of irritation to each other—on the job and off. At home, Harry was a devoted family man who didn't approve of Jack's philandering. At the studio, Harry believed in an honest day's work. Jack did, too, but he also liked to have fun—a little too much fun for Harry's tastes. The two often clashed at work where studio employees claimed to have once seen the usually subtle Harry chasing Jack with a lead pipe.

Jack once again paired up with his favorite brother Sam to direct another serial, *A Dangerous Adventure* (1922). In this fifteen-part series, the animals were back under the guise of a traveling circus. This time, the public wasn't interested in mad monkeys and even madder elephants, so the brothers trimmed multiple episodes down to one feature-length film and then released it. Their new strategy worked and earned some sorely needed cash.

The Warners realized, however, if they wanted to stay out of the red, they needed someone on their staff with more filmmaking savvy. Successful New York producer Harry Rapf seemed like a good choice so Warner Bros. made him an offer. Rapf accepted and moved his mother, Eliza, along with his family to California, where Mama Rapf continued her reign over their household. It was Eliza who approved the move, did the grocery shopping and supervised meals, making sure the cook knew how to fix her son's favorite foods, while wife Tina mostly stayed out of her way.

With Rapf as Head of Production, Warner Bros. released only three pictures that year including Rapf's film *Why Girls Leave Home* (1921). It was his first success under the Warner banner and the studio's only profit-making film for 1921. Secure in his new job, Rapf then signed on the Warners' first contract player, the young actor Wesley Barry.

With their company finally making money thanks to the good movie sense of Harry Rapf, the Warners' finances improved. Eventually, they remodeled their studio and moved out of the barn. With the financial backing of one of their greatest supporters, banker Motley Flint, the four men officially incorporated to form Warner Bros. Pictures, Inc. on April 4, 1923. Not long after, Abe Warner lost his wife Bessie to a bout of influenza.

Just because they were official, however, didn't mean they would stay afloat. It was more important than ever to make profitable films, as competition from other studios like Universal and Paramount was growing. Harry Rapf came to the rescue with a canine hero, but first he had to persuade a skeptical Jack Warner to get back into the animal business. Jack had had his share of being bitten, charged and growled at. The last thing he wanted was another unpredictable creature running amok in his studio. Rapf disregarded his boss's lack of enthusiasm when he brought a German Shepherd and its owner, Lee Duncan, to Jack's office. Duncan put his pet through the paces and, despite his misgivings, an impressed Jack Warner agreed to give the dog a chance.

Rin Tin Tin was found by U.S. Corporal Lee Duncan in Lorraine, France during World War I when he and his troop came across a bombed out dog kennel. Huddled inside the ruins, Duncan and company discovered a female German Shepherd with several newborn pups. Duncan personally kept one male and female, while battalion members cared for the rest. Duncan named his dogs "Rin Tin Tin" and "Nanette" after tiny French dolls that soldiers sometimes carried for good luck.

After the war, Duncan returned home to Los Angeles and made arrangements to bring his pets with him. Sadly, the long trip across the Atlantic was too much for Nanette and she died, but the highly clever and energetic "Rinty," as he was nicknamed, flourished on American soil. So impressed with his dog's abilities and intelligence, Duncan taught him to perform. Duncan then set his sights on making Rinty a movie star. He wrote a story called *Where the North Begins* and shopped it around to several studios—none of which were interested until he finally stumbled across Harry Rapf at Warner Bros.

Where the North Begins (1923) was Rin Tin Tin's first smash hit, running in sold-out theaters nationwide. The likeable canine played an orphaned dog raised by wolves. When he heroically rescued a fur trapper from certain death, Rinty became a superhero. He could swim rapids with ease, operate machinery, open locked doors and woo his favorite female—all in the name of justice and love. Within a few short years, Rin Tin Tin was one of the top box-office names in Hollywood earning thousands of dollars each month. His personal appearances drew enthusiastic crowds wherever he went. Fan letters poured in to the studio by the truckload. Rinty's famous face even appeared on boxes of dog biscuits. Living up to his superstar image, he donned a diamond-studded collar, dined on steaks and even had his own orchestra for mood music—not to mention his very own radio show.

Rinty was the first animal to reach international stardom. He went on to make dozens of movies for Warner Bros. and brought the financially stressed studio to solvency. The once-skeptical Jack took to calling Rinty the "Mortgage Lifter." The studio wisely kept eighteen other Rin Tin Tins trained and standing by just in case of an emergency. When the real Rinty died in 1932, he went the way many red-blooded American fellas only dreamed of going—in the arms of a sobbing Jean Harlow who happened to live across the street from Lee Duncan's Beverly Hills home.

Now that Warner Bros. had established itself, they needed some key players, as well as theaters to show their films. Harry brought in popular German director Ernst Lubitsch who then filmed *The Marriage Circle* (1924), one of the year's most popular movies. Harry also signed on the flamboyant stage actor John Barrymore giving him the star treatment with more than $76,000 per movie, approval of his leading ladies, as well as a chauffeur-driven limousine and a suite at the Ambassador Hotel. Harry also authorized the building of Warner Bros. movie theaters in several major cities.

Still single, brother Sam took a shine to the radio. Always intrigued by sound transmission, he convinced Harry that Warner Bros. needed their very own radio station. That way, they could advertise their own movies however and whenever they wanted. Sam purchased an existing station and moved all of the equipment to the movie studio. Their first broadcast on KFWB introduced new singer Leon Zuardo—a.k.a Jack L. Warner. The innovative brothers also placed microphones on live film sets so curious listeners could hear the actual sounds of movies in progress.

With several moneymaking motion pictures and a theater chain behind him, Harry's attention turned to the financially troubled Vitagraph Studio, which was failing and deeply in debt—they owed creditors almost one million dollars. When Harry approached Vitagraph officials about a buyout, they offered their company up for $800,000 plus the money they owed. Harry agreed to their terms. With his well-respected business sense, he had no trouble obtaining a loan for the take-over. Now armed with Vitagraph's multiple film distribution networks or "exchanges" throughout North America, Warner Bros. became one of the biggest independent movie companies in the world.

The same day that Harry closed the Vitagraph deal, widowed Abe took a second wife—another Bessie. She, too, was a widow who had been married to one of Abe's best friends, Jonas Siegel. Bessie's husband, who changed his family name to Steel, died around the same time as the first Mrs. Warner. After losing their respective spouses, the already familiar Abe and Bessie grew closer. They married on April 23, 1925. Opposites in many ways, the two complemented each other. Always self-conscious about his lack of education, Abe especially liked the class that Bessie brought into his life. He enjoyed nothing better than a good cigar or a horse race that finished by a nose. She preferred fine art and priceless antiques. He'd never had children. She had one son, Arthur, whom Abe loved and treated as his own.

While the newlyweds honeymooned in Atlantic City, Sam had a serious romance of his own. On one of his many visits to New York, Sam met Ziegfeld Follies girl Lina Basquette. Lena Copeland Baskette was born in San Mateo, California to Frank and his wife Gladys on April 19, 1907. After Frank's death, the overbearing Gladys married dance instructor Ernest Belcher and had a second daughter, Marjorie, nicknamed Marge, and the future Mrs. Gower Champion.

By the time Lena was nine, her mother had the child under contract with Universal Studios. After several movies, Gladys pushed her eldest daughter into the Ziegfeld Follies of 1923. The sixteen-year-old was presented as "America's Prima Ballerina" and her name changed to the more intriguing Lina Basquette. Two years later and still working for Ziegfeld, Basquette met the one Warner brother who had so far remained single— thirty-seven-year-old Sam.

Smitten with the young dancer, Sam asked her out—along with her mother. Sam knew that without Gladys' approval, his chances with Lina were slim. He needn't have worried. Mama Gladys was overjoyed with her daughter's new suitor—a big-time producer who didn't drink. She even overlooked his occasional cigar. More importantly, she knew that Sam could fast-track Lina's career. With Gladys' blessing, the couple married on July 4, 1925 in New York. Their only child, a girl also named Lina, was born the following year.

In the meantime, Harry made business plans for 1926. Among the dozens of movies Warner Bros. would release that year, one of their biggest would be *Sea Beast* (1926). Former MGM scenarist Bess Meredyth penned the photoplay based on Herman Melville's novel *Moby Dick*. The classic film starred Barrymore who so thoroughly approved of his leading lady, newcomer Delores Costello, that he made her the third Mrs. Barrymore.

Meredyth had completely given up acting for the pen after her 1917 marriage to actor Wilfred Lucas. In between dozens of photoplays, she gave birth to a son in 1919 and officially named him Wilfred Meredyth Lucas, but everyone called him Jack. Eventually, he legally changed his name to John.

By the time she signed on with Warner Bros., however, she and her husband were divorced. Now a single mother, the outgoing blonde had also caught the eye of Michael Curtiz, a talented Hungarian director recently put under contract by Warner Bros. Aside from her personal problems, Meredyth was one of the highest-paid female scenarists in Hollywood ranking with the likes of Jeanie Macpherson, Frances Marion and June Mathis. Meredyth believed in simple stories with just a few characters planted in the midst of intriguing circumstances. Like too many cooks who spoiled the broth, she believed that too many characters could turn a good movie bad. The *L.A. Times* described the energetic writer known for her quick wit:

If effervescence of spirits has anything to do with the intelligence of a person, and this intelligence heightened by the ability to converse, at length, understandingly and interestingly on any subject broached, then Bess Meredyth is a very superior sort of person. For she is literally bubbling over with good humor, and anyone who leaves her feeling the least bit low is ready either to drape the interior of a coffin or take up quarters in a select asylum. . . .

While the Warners tapped Meredyth to write the photoplay for Barrymore's next movie, *Don Juan* (1926), Sam picked this period film to experiment with sound. At Sam's urgings, the brothers partnered up with Western Electric forming the Vitaphone Corporation. Sam championed the simple disc system whereby a large record captured the sound and then played it back as the corresponding film rolled through the projector. These early attempts at pre-recorded sound were primarily for music used to accompany shorts—an effective replacement for live musicians. Sam, however, wanted to take things further. The Warners reconfigged Vitagraph's Brooklyn studios for the purpose of recording sound. They even bought the Piccadilly Theater in New York and wired it for sound in order to have a place to run their cutting edge films. The *New York Times* reported on April 26, 1926:

Perfection of a new apparatus which makes possible the release of music and reproduction of the human voice in their natural tones, to be used in connection with motion pictures, has been attained . . . and rights for the exclusive use of it have been purchased by the Warner Brothers . . .

Don Juan let Barrymore show off his dashing side as he brandished a sword with bravado and leapt into the arms of his ladylove played by fan favorite Mary Astor. The adventure film also let Sam try out the Vitaphone process on a full-length feature. Although the experiment with its musical score and clanging swords was a success, dialogue was not spoken. In addition, the vast majority of movie theaters were not equipped for sound, forcing most patrons to view the typical silent treatment anyway.

Sound, however, was not about to go away, and it would be Sam Warner who finally got the ball rolling after nearly three decades of silence, despite brother Harry's vociferous qualms: "Who the hell wants to hear actors talk?"

Chapter Thirteen

THE LUNATICS

The year 1919 was a time of worldwide change. The Treaty of Versailles officially ended World War I after more than 15 million lives were lost: in some countries, a whole generation of young men. The League of Nations was formed in Paris and Benito Mussolini founded the Fascist Party in Italy. Health officials announced that the deadly, globetrotting pandemic known as the Spanish Flu was over, which had been claiming lives by the millions alongside the machine gun fire. Walter Owen Bentley established Bentley Motors Limited in England.

Events in the United States were also unfolding. Congress made the Grand Canyon the country's seventeenth national park, preserving its beauty forever. A few months later, these same seemingly wise men also passed the Volstead Act triggering Prohibition, which paved the way for underground speakeasies, bathtub gin and bootlegged hooch. The Purity Distilling Company of Boston experienced an explosion that let loose a giant wave of molasses covering city streets and killing 21 people in its path. The Black Sox Scandal gave Cincinnati the World Series Championship and baseball a lingering black eye. A deadly hurricane devastated the Florida Keys, as well as Corpus Christi, Texas causing more than 700 deaths.

On the west coast, the University of California established its second campus in Los Angeles and four major Hollywood players banded together to form their own film company, United Artists Corporation (UA). In response to this radical move, disgruntled Metro Pictures president Richard Rowland is often credited with saying: "The lunatics have taken charge of the asylum!" The aforementioned crazies were Hollywood icons Douglas Fairbanks, Mary Pickford, D.W. Griffith and Charlie Chaplin.

Douglas Fairbanks was a successful theater actor before he headed west to work for D.W. Griffith at Triangle Films. He was also a married man who had fallen in love with Pickford who was still the unfortunate Mrs. Owen Moore. As their affair became physical, the situation got touchy. Silent film stars were presented to the public as wholesome, morally upstanding citizens—their private lives flawless. To movie fans, Fairbanks was an incomparable hero with noble values and Pickford was America's Sweetheart with uncompromising virtue. An adulterous scandal could destroy both of their careers and rattle the movie industry's fragile foundation. As rumors enveloped them, the couple repeatedly denied each one.

Fairbanks' best friend and confidant was the equally famous Charlie Chaplin. According to Chaplin's autobiography, he and Fairbanks met through their mutual friend, actress Constance Collier. The two male stars were also a little wary of each other, as Chaplin described it:

> From Constance I had heard much about Douglas Fairbanks' charm and ability, not only as a personality but as a brilliant after-dinner speaker. In those days I disliked brilliant young men—especially after-dinner speakers. However a dinner was arranged at his house.

. . . Before going I had made excuses to Constance that I was ill, but she would have none of it. So I made up my mind to feign a headache and leave early. Fairbanks said that he was also nervous, and that when the doorbell rang he quickly descended into the basement where there was a billiard table, and began playing pool. That night was the beginning of a lifelong friendship.

There are other versions of the story—some even told by Chaplin and Fairbanks themselves, but whatever the circumstances, the two actors were each other's greatest fan. In many ways, they were opposites—Chaplin was quiet and disliked attention off the stage/screen while the gregarious Fairbanks thrived on it. Chaplin was moody; Fairbanks upbeat. Their on-screen personas also differed—Chaplin the master of physical comedy as the Little Tramp and Fairbanks a dazzling heartthrob known for his acrobatics. Yet they also shared similarities. Both had errant fathers who imbibed more than they should have, leaving mothers to raise their children alone. Unlike Ella Fairbanks who had been a strong parental figure in her son's life, Hannah Chaplin suffered from mental illness most likely due to syphilis and was institutionalized while her son was just a boy, leaving Chaplin essentially orphaned.

Hollywood beckoned both men from the stage, and the films they made catapulted them into box office deities. The clever Chaplin, with his baggy pants and cane, created a resourceful, endearing character that movie fans found irresistible; the agile Fairbanks with his good looks and romantic action films left women swooning and men wishing they had just some of his bravado. Then there was Little Mary who retained her curls, as well as her title, "America's Sweetheart," despite being a mature, poised, even shrewd, business-minded woman off-screen. The child-like Pickford, who symbolized purity and innocence, remained the public's all-time favorite female star during those years. For movie fans, Chaplin, Fairbanks and Pickford were no less than Hollywood royalty.

It was no wonder that the White House requested their help selling Liberty Bonds as Americans joined in The Great War. Fairbanks welcomed the nationwide bond drives. Not only could he partake in shenanigans with Chaplin, the tours also allowed him some cozy time with Pickford—all in the name of patriotism, of course. As for Chaplin and Pickford, each respected the other's talent and good business sense, but the Little Tramp and America's Sweetheart merely tolerated each other. Their common ground was always Fairbanks. If he wanted them to get along, by golly, they would.

As the lovers' secret trysts continued, Fairbanks's respect for Pickford's uncanny sense of business grew. While most men talked down to her, Fairbanks never did. He valued her smarts and savvy insights into the motion picture industry. In turn, Pickford enjoyed something she, along with most women of this era, wasn't accustomed to—being treated as an equal. Before long, their romance was well known throughout the film colony, but the public remained blissfully unaware of the unholy alliance taking place right under their noses.

Oddly enough, it was their spouses who first mentioned the covert affair. In April 1918, Beth Fairbanks told the press that her husband had met a mystery woman whom he felt was the great love of his life. Neglecting to specifically name Pickford, she referred to her husband's mistress as one of his business associates. Moore, on the other hand, defended his wife to her fans, perhaps out of guilt for his continued addiction to the bottle, or maybe just to save face. He claimed that Fairbanks was taking advantage of his poor, little Mary who just didn't know any better. Privately, Moore threatened to hunt down his rival and kill him, which drew a loud laugh from the much nimbler, and more sober, Fairbanks.

The following October, Mrs. Fairbanks had enough. She filed for divorce in New York where the only legal grounds was infidelity. Her soon-to-be ex-husband publicly refuted the charges, but the divorce was granted giving her custody of their only child, Douglas, Jr., as well as a cool half million dollars. With Fairbanks a free man, Pickford wavered.

Unsure of what to do, she stayed with Moore. The thought of a scandal was more than she could handle, and any public condemnation of their affair would most likely have fallen harder on Mary, as a woman, due to an unfortunate social double standard.

Professionally, Fairbanks had left the Triangle Film Company and in early 1917 formed the Douglas Fairbanks Pictures Corporation, about two years before United Artists was established. He felt that Triangle was making millions off of him and not compensating him accordingly. For the first time, Fairbanks produced his own pictures beginning with the comedy *In Again, Out Again* (1917) penned by Anita Loos.

Pickford, too, had her own production company, but she was still under contract with producer Adolph Zukor who had recently merged his Famous Players Film Company with the Jesse L. Lasky Feature Play Company. Along with this merger came Zukor's concept of block booking. He sold the company-owned movie theaters a set number of films of his choosing. Theater owners had no say in which pictures they ran. They had to take the good with the not so good and could only hope that the better films outnumbered the duds.

In retaliation, a powerful group of nationwide theater owners banded together calling themselves the First National Exhibitors Circuit. They had the money to finance their own films for their own theaters. All they needed were box office names to make their idea work. They first recruited Chaplin and then, in late 1918, Pickford, by offering each of them an unheard sum of one million dollars. An emotional Pickford left "Papa Zukor" who gave "sweetheart-honey" his blessing. Before Pickford even settled in, however, rumors ran wild that her new employer was about to merge with Zukor and his Famous Players-Lasky Corporation.

According to Chaplin, he, along with Fairbanks and Pickford, hired a female detective to snoop around the Alexandria Hotel where the First National Exhibitors Circuit was holding a convention in January 1919. The detective reported back that "a forty million dollar merger" was in the works. Chaplin recalled: "They intended putting the industry on a proper business basis, instead of having it run by a bunch of crazy actors getting astronomical salaries."

Next, Chaplin's brother and business manager, Sidney, called a meeting with an impressive list of attendees that included top names in the shaken film industry: actors Charlie Chaplin, Douglas Fairbanks and western star William S. Hart along with legendary director D.W. Griffith whose Triangle Films had been taken over by Zukor. Last, but hardly least, queen mother Charlotte Pickford was called upon to represent her daughter who was down with the flu.

The very next day, the Big Five, as they were called, publicly announced their intentions of producing their own films and releasing them through their very own new company, United Artists Corporation, with the following statement:

> We believe [United Artists] is necessary to protect the exhibitor and the industry itself, thus enabling the exhibitor to book only pictures that he wishes to play and not force upon him . . . other program films which he does not desire . . . We also think that this step is positively and absolutely necessary to protect the great motion picture public from threatening combinations and trusts that would force upon them mediocre productions and machine-made entertainment.

By removing themselves from the major movie companies that employed them, Hollywood's Big Five gained control of their films, as well as the profits. Hollywood spun into a certified tizzy. What were these hell-raisers thinking?! What could an artistic gang of rebels possibly know about business? Industry chiefs were outraged at such a display of audacity and afraid that their own movie empires might be heading for trouble, as the average movie-goer cared about actors and actresses—the faces they saw on-screen, not the producers, directors or studio heads they didn't see. Even worse, what would prevent other artists from becoming defiant independents?

Ignoring the uproar, the Big Five went about their business. They brought in the current Secretary of the Treasury and son-in-law of U.S. President Woodrow Wilson, William Gibbs McAdoo, as their general counsel. Oscar A. Price, who had previously worked with McAdoo, took the job of president. William S. Hart, however, soon dropped out claiming he didn't want to commit to the three-year time period that the other partners agreed to. His departure brought Hollywood's Big Five down to four.

The new company had a slow start due to prior contractual obligations of the partners, but once they were free to make their own films, UA grew into a force of its own. While all of the partners enjoyed success under their new banner, Fairbanks, true to character, made the most noise. The first feature released through UA, *His Majesty, The American* (1919), cast Fairbanks in the title role of Bill Brooks, a misplaced prince. It was typical Fairbanks folly as he bounced across the screen in full throttle. Next came D.W. Griffith's dynamic drama *Broken Blossoms* (1919) starring Lillian Gish and Richard Barthelmess—United Artists' first major box office hit.

All the while, Pickford, still seeing the now-divorced Fairbanks, remained married to Moore until Fairbanks finally made her choose—divorce Moore or end their affair. Pickford traveled to Nevada and obtained a divorce after which she publicly apologized to her fans assuring them that she would never marry again. She had a quick change of heart, however, when Fairbanks proposed. The couple married in a secret ceremony on March 28, 1920—just a few weeks after her divorce.

When the newlyweds finally came forward about their marriage, they anxiously awaited the fallout. While the media frowned, the public surprised everyone with their hearty approval. As journalist Alistair Cooke put it:

> Douglas Fairbanks and Mary Pickford came to mean more than a couple of married film stars. They were a living proof of America's chronic belief in happy endings.

But it wasn't just America. Fans worldwide cheered the famous two-some as they honeymooned throughout Europe. In London, the celebrated pair even caused a riot when an enthusiastic crowd of fans snatched the petite Pickford from an open Rolls Royce. With a little help from police officers on the scene, Fairbanks rescued his stunned bride. For Pickford, the fervent attention was overwhelming, but her husband thrived on all of the hoopla. The couple may not have sported crowns, but they were as close to royalty as Americans would ever be.

Once home from their extended honeymoon, Fairbanks was about to take his biggest professional gamble. His romantic comedies were standard fan favorites as he whirled and twirled his way through each scene in that sparkling Fairbanks fashion. Complacent with his success, Fairbanks felt secure in the macho image he projected until he acquired the rights to a historical novella set in Spanish-controlled California—Johnston McCulley's *The Curse of Capistrano*. Fairbanks was at first reluctant to make a period picture that required him to wear an outlandish cape and silly mask, but he went ahead with it anyway under the smart direction of Fred Niblo. As the outlaw Zorro, Fairbanks launched the second and most brilliant phase of his already unparalleled movie career, creating a new kind of film with a new kind of hero.

Released on December 5, 1920, *The Mark of Zorro* not only catapulted Fairbanks into a whole new dimension of popularity, but also defined the term "swashbuckler." Making his first entrance as the foppish Don Diego, Fairbanks later emerged as Diego's alter ego, Zorro. Once he brandished a sword and marked his enemies with that famous "Z," Fairbanks never looked back. Instead, he took control.

From Zorro on, he wrote the scripts, chose the cast and handpicked his directors. Fairbanks supervised all aspects of production including set construction and costume design. He surrounded himself with people committed to maintaining his dynamic image. Even his engineer brother, Robert, took care of set logistics and special effects such as slow motion, double exposure and some early animation. He may have sought advice from his production crew, but it was Fairbanks who made all final decisions.

If he had any doubts about Zorro, Fairbanks went full speed ahead with *The Three Musketeers* (1921), playing the daring role of D'Artagnan—his favorite literary character. He even grew his trademark mustache for the film and continued sporting it for the rest of his life. Fairbanks would not settle for anything less than authenticity down to the last detail. The magnificent French sets were based on historic sketches, as were the costumes. It was also the film where the thirty-eight-year-old actor made what is widely considered his riskiest stunt—a perfect one-handed handspring while balancing on a dagger.

The infamous *Robin Hood* (1922) came next at a time when Hollywood had recently generated some bad press from the "Fatty" Arbuckle scandal to the William Desmond Taylor murder and movies were rapidly falling from public favor. Things were so tough that Fairbanks bankrolled the movie himself. When filming began, he modestly claimed that the oversized sets were too much for him. He couldn't compete with such an enormous castle and gigantic drawbridge, but of course he could—he was Fairbanks—and the mammoth sets were his idea to begin with. Scaling the steep castle walls and gliding down the lengthy drapes (with the help of a hidden slide) was natural for him.

While Fairbanks took charge of saving the populace, Pickford made her own contributions to UA, but not until her contractual obligations to First National were met. Pickford's first film released through UA was *Pollyanna* (1920). Once again, the now twenty-eight-year-old actress played the ever-optimistic adolescent. Her turn in *Little Lord Fauntleroy* (1921) finally gave her a chance to grow up—sort of. Pickford, playing the dual roles of the little lord complete with curls, as well as his widowed mother, triumphed at the box office.

With three of the Big Four pulling their weight at UA, Chaplin lagged behind. Still under contract to First National, his smash hit *The Kid* (1921) with child actor Jackie Coogan and featuring "The Tramp" at his best to date, could not be released through UA. Chaplin wasn't free to work for United Artists until 1923 when he wrote and directed, but did not star in, *A Woman of Paris: A Drama of Fate*. Unfortunately, the very artsy film did not do well financially. Disappointed fans wanted "The Tramp," which Chaplin didn't deliver.

Fairbanks was still riding high on his swashbuckling wave when he filmed the magical *The Thief of Baghdad* (1924). With Raoul Walsh directing, flying on a steel-framed magic carpet suspended by six steel piano wires wasn't enough. A fairy tale city was also created covering six and a half acres. To complete the fantasy, domes and minarets were erected for the flying carpet to glide over. And just to add a splash of realism, a large fan blew against the carpet's eight-inch fringe providing an even greater sense of motion. It was Fairbanks at his grandest. When the movie was released, *Photoplay* magazine reported: "Here is magic. Here is beauty. Here is the answer to the cynics who give the motion picture no place in the family of art." They also gave Fairbanks, now in his forties, much of the credit.

For Walsh, who had been under contract with Fox until 1920, *The Thief of Baghdad* was one of his greatest silent film achievements and came at a time when he sorely needed a winner to put him back in the game. Striking out on his own after his Fox contract ran out, he filmed several less than stellar vehicles. Mediocre movies like *The Deep Purple* (1920) and *The Oath* (1921) starred his wife, Miriam Cooper, and were panned by both critics and spectators.

Whenever he could, Walsh preferred taking his show on the road. Location shooting not only provided authentic backgrounds and scenery, but it also gratified the director's wandering ways. Walsh swore that while filming the pirate movie *Lost and Found on a South Sea Island* (1923) in Tahiti, he tipped too many bottles and came away with a nose piercing. *Photoplay* magazine described the film as "the same old melodramatic hokum . . . before a Tahiti backdrop." After riding Fairbanks' magic carpet, however, Walsh was back on top and Paramount wanted him.

By 1924, UA had released several big box office films, but the independent studio was struggling. UA did not provide financial backing for its films. Hollywood's Big Four were each responsible for obtaining funds for their own projects. Therefore, UA's film output was far less than the major studios who churned out movies at an accelerated pace with a combined bankroll. In addition, UA didn't own any theaters and their films couldn't play in the first-rate movie houses owned by other studios. That meant UA films often ran in substandard establishments with lower ticket prices.

In order to remain solvent, the Big Four realized they needed someone in charge who not only understood moviemaking, but also high finance and talent. They called on independent producer Joseph M. Schenck who was currently the head of United Studios, as well as president of the MPPDA. Schenck had more than just business smarts, he had famous family under contract—his wife, actress Norma Talmadge, his sister-in-law, comedienne Constance Talmadge, and his brother-in-law, the deadpan funnyman, Buster Keaton. All were top stars that equated to very big box office.

Schenck was brought in as a partner and named UA's first Chairman of the Board in 1924. His renowned kinfolk tagged along and so did one Latin lover, Rodolfo Alfonzo Raffaele Pierre Filibert Guglielmi di Valentino d'Antonguolla, also known as Rudolph Valentino or just plain Rudy to his friends. Schenck went straight to work reorganizing the company and establishing the Art Cinema Corporation, for the purpose of bankrolling UA films. Now more films could be made, boosting UA's earnings. He then formed the United Artists Theater Circuit, which would acquire or build first-run theaters nationwide for the exclusive showing of UA films.

While Schenck was saving UA, however, he also had his hand in several other endeavors. He was president of the Hotel Holding Company of Hollywood, which was responsible for building the 2.5 million dollar Roosevelt Hotel at the corner of Hollywood Boulevard and Orange Drive.

He also sat on the advisory board of a Los Angeles branch of the Bank of Italy and controlled two-thirds of the Federal Trust and Savings Bank at Hollywood and Highland. And of course, there was still that old amusement park business back in New Jersey.

While Schenck brought in actress Gloria Swanson and producer Samuel Goldwyn (formerly Goldfish), who had been running his own production company, Fairbanks reprised his role of masked crusader. Since the original *Mark of Zorro* (1920) had been so popular, Fairbanks, in true Hollywood fashion, decided on a sequel. *Don Q Son of Zorro* (1925) found Fairbanks playing two roles—the original Zorro, as well as his son. He even used flashbacks from the first Zorro movie for continuity and fought side-by-side with himself. To prepare for the role, Fairbanks had to learn how to crack an Australian stock whip. Always a quick study, he could soon whip-snatch a cigarette from the mouth of some brave soul who stood smoking several feet away.

Next up, Fairbanks was a buccaneer in *The Black Pirate* (1926) where he slashed the sails of an enemy pirate ship. Starting at the top, he plunged his dagger into the sail and while clutching the knife, he descended downward slicing the sails in half as he went. It was a spectacular way to cripple his adversaries, but by now audiences expected no less from the fearless Fairbanks. He also used a new two-tone negative process making *The Black Pirate* the first silent feature filmed entirely in Technicolor.

Scenes were shot on Catalina Island with four of the seven Technicolor cameras in use at that time under the watchful eye of Joseph Arthur Ball. Ball and his wife, Isabel, were now living in California where he headed up Technicolor's west coast facility. Color, however, remained controversial. Some still contested it was bad for the eyes, but that didn't stop Fairbanks. If new technology resulted in better pictures, he was all for it.

The color process itself was somewhat improved, but just as before, included only red and green. Blue was still out of the picture, but Ball and his team continued working on it. The Technicolor film itself posed another problem since its thickness was uneven. It sometimes buckled and often broke as it ran through the projector. At the very least, it caused a fuzzy picture. Replacement reels were in constant demand by the exhibitors and Technicolor employees were left to iron out the kinks—literally. The application of heat would smooth out any unevenness in the film.

In between Fairbanks' last two swashbucklers, the lagging Chaplin finally hit his own bases-loaded homerun for UA with *The Gold Rush* (1925) depicting "The Tramp" and his gold-searching adventures in Alaska. The silent film, famous for its scene featuring "The Tramp" dining on his boot, was one of Chaplin's, and UA's, all-time biggest moneymakers. The partners could no longer accuse Chaplin of not pulling his weight.

With Schenck leading the way for Griffith's edgy dramas, Fairbanks' daring adventures, Chaplin's funny business and Pickford's youthful innocence, UA remained a solid force in an industry where being major didn't always equate to being better.

Not bad for a bunch of lunatics.

Chapter Fourteen

IN THE ZOO

Junk dealing was part of Louis B. Mayer's past and he wanted to keep it there. Married with two young daughters, he was now the established owner of the upscale New Orpheum Theater tucked neatly inside the boundaries of Haverhill, Massachusetts. Mayer, however, was satisfied with neither his current place of business nor his good standing in the community. He wanted class and long-lasting respect that teetered on worship. When Louis B. Mayer wanted something, he went after it like a hound focused on a foxhunt. By 1911, he had obtained the backing of several local businessmen and built a grand theater that far surpassed the New Orpheum.

The Colonial Theater was presented to the public on December 11, 1911 at a black-tie event. For the first time, tuxedoed patrons experienced the opulent ninety-five-foot lobby that boasted artwork on every wall including one prophetic painting that captured a lion at rest. Awed by the rosewood trimmings that surrounded them, as well as the plush carpeting that cushioned their well-heeled feet, guests ascended an imposing marble stairway that led to the 1,500-seat interior. An eye-catching proscenium arch dominated the main room where a large stage and live orchestra greeted the crowd. Ever the showman who could work a room better than most actors, Mayer took the spotlight in an emotional speech with just the right mix of gratitude, humility and tears—a practice he continued throughout his life, whether standing before a league of cheering fans or an audience of just one disgruntled movie star.

With his professional reputation on the upswing, Mayer booked the Boston Opera Company to play at his new theater. He worked hard bringing in popular Broadway plays with big names like entertainer extraordinaire George M. Cohan. A few new and upcoming performers such as Milton Berle and George Burns also graced The Orpheum's marquee. He even formed his own stock company to ensure his theaters had quality shows to book. A sincere patriot, Mayer also swore allegiance to the United States, becoming a proud American citizen in 1912. All the while, Mayer, who opened several more New England theaters, still kept an eye on the growing movie industry.

His business worries, however, fell from the forefront during October 1913, when Mayer's beloved mother, Sarah, grew ill from a bad gall bladder. Mayer immediately took his wife, daughters and personal physician back to St. John. He even brought in one of Canada's finest surgeons. Despite his best efforts, Sarah died. Mayer, feeling like he failed her, was crushed. He carried Sarah's picture with him every single day for the rest of his life and often showed an unusually high level of empathy, for an otherwise aloof man, toward anyone caring for their dear, old mom.

Mayer's good movie fortune began from the distributing end of the business. In early 1915, he joined Pittsburgh millionaire Richard Rowland to form Metro Pictures Corporation, a film distributor for early production companies like Quality Pictures and Tiffany Film Corporations. Their biggest coup came from D.W. Griffith's cutting-edge film, *Birth of a Nation* (1915). The group obtained the regional distribution rights to the much-ballyhooed Civil War drama. Taking advantage of the notorious buzz surrounding the film, Mayer claimed to have invested $55,000 (which equates to over one million dollars today) and earned at least ten times that amount.

After this windfall, Metro Pictures was ready to make films of its own. They signed on popular leading man Francis X. Bushman and the young Mary Miles Minter. Situated in Manhattan over a garage, the studio quickly churned out dozens of movies including Mayer's first personal attempt at producing an 18-episode serial, *The Great Secret* (1917), starring Bushman. Unfortunately for Mayer, the married Bushman, a father of five, conducted an unsavory affair with his leading lady, actress Beverly Bayne. The blissless Bushmans soon separated and suffered a hate-filled divorce complete with public name-calling. Partly due to the ugly Bushman break-up, the not-so-great action adventure series bombed. Mayer never forgave the high-maintenance actor for his obnoxious indiscretions.

Mayer did, however, learn that the role of moviemaker was more to his liking than movie exhibitor. Realizing that the best place for his future film endeavors was the west coast, he took over the troubled Selig Studios on Mission Road in Edendale, California in 1918—right in the middle of the Selig Zoo and across the street from two animal farms, one raising alligators and one hatching ostriches. There, he established Louis B. Mayer Productions. Working in the zoo was good practice for the future, but when the monkeys escaped from their cages, nothing was safe as they pillaged the place. Columnist Hedda Hopper, who once worked for Mayer as an actress, recalled those early days:

> Louis B. chose the Selig Zoo because it was the cheapest place in town. That was a funny lot, with wild animals roaming around just like the actors. The lions and tigers were toothless and tame, but if you didn't know that, it was rather frightening, coming 'round a corner and suddenly running into one.

After settling in at the new facility and adjusting to the beastly neighbors, Mayer tapped the services of attorney Edwin J. Loeb who, in addition to his legal advice, offered Mayer his friendship and ultimately his secretary. By the time Mayer arrived in California, Loeb's good nature and professional expertise were well known throughout the film community. The popular attorney now had a long list of movie clientele whom he also included in his social circle. Film folks from actors to writers to producers to studio heads called upon Loeb when they encountered legal concerns, complex contracts, tricky negotiations or even when they just felt like a good game of poker.

Loeb and his wife, Bessie, had been married for eight years and, much like the Mayers, were raising two young daughters. Prominent members of their community with strong family ties to Los Angeles history, newcomers appreciated the Loebs' hospitality. With an air of grace, Loeb even gave up his skilled secretary, Florence Browning, when Mayer asked her to work directly for him. The movie man's explanation was simple: "That's the kind of people I want working for me. I want high-class people."

At work, Mayer immersed himself in everyday studio business. Instead of staying inside his small office closing deals, he roamed the premises watching and absorbing the mechanics of movie making. He spoke with cameramen, set builders, actors and writers. Driven by a deep inner fear of failure, Louis B. Mayer was determined that one day, his would be the most recognized name in the motion picture industry. Like the lion sporting his unchallenged crown in the jungle, Mayer sought respect.

With a couple of motion picture notches in his California belt, Mayer dissolved his business interests on the east coast. By 1920, he was fully committed to making west coast films and hired successful director John M. Stahl to help him. The ever-particular Stahl and his slow methodical manner of movie making often annoyed the impatient Mayer who preferred immediate results. Stahl's painstaking care of pre-production details paid off in the end, however, when his films came in on time and within budget. Mayer's irritation was usually countered by his satisfaction with Stahl's final products. The director's morally upright movies were always in line with Mayer's vision—wholesome entertainment with just the right amount of sentiment tossed in. Stahl echoed Mayer's standards when he shared his own thoughts:

> To me, the ideal picture would be the true life of a young man [or] woman, from the time of their meeting until later life. Their courtship, marriage, and trials and tribulations of wedded life. . . . The result, though, should be a masterpiece, one in which humanness would be the predominating element. . . .

Mayer hired another experienced director, Fred Niblo, who recently worked with Douglas Fairbanks on his swashbuckling adventures, *The Mark of Zorro* (1920) and *The Three Musketeers* (1921) at United Artists. Not just impressed with Niblo's work, Mayer also noted his self-confidence and polished image. The director definitely had that "class" factor Mayer was always after. Nor did it hurt that both men shared a passion for classical music. Niblo, now married to second wife, actress Enid Bennett, had an infant daughter, Loris. He also had a son, Fred, Jr. from his first wife, Josephine Cohan, who died in 1916. Cohan, the sister of theatrical great George M., was one of the famous Cohan family members who performed throughout the world.

The Niblos lived in an upcoming area called Beverly Hills. In 1923, many major Hollywood players also populated the new community. As more people poured into the area, the utility company couldn't keep up with the influx. Water became an issue. Beverly Hills was threatened by annexation to Los Angeles in order to tap into the larger city's water supply. Many influential residents who worked in the movie business banned together protesting the takeover. A vote was held and the annexation was defeated 507 to 337. Beverly Hills remained independent and, in 1924, the city funded the drilling of additional wells. Today a "Monument to the Stars" stands at Beverly Drive and Olympic Boulevard honoring

Fred Niblo and the seven celebrities who fought back: Douglas Fairbanks, Mary Pickford, Will Rogers, Conrad Nagel, Tom Mix, Harold Lloyd and Rudolph Valentino. Not bad company to keep.

As Mayer continued churning out his moderately successful pictures, the money he made from one film was usually put right back into his next production. When bill collectors appeared at his office door, he often collapsed in front of them in the dramatic grip of a well-timed "heart attack." The dismayed moneymen would almost always back off for a bit, only to return again when Mayer was feeling "better."

By 1923, Mayer needed help running his studio. He wanted someone qualified to produce pictures, assist with the business, make sound decisions, and have the solid backbone to deal with the multiple personalities on the lot—not to mention the critters. Mayer's good friend Edwin Loeb knew just the man. Loeb's best buddy was currently running Universal Studio, but the young man was no longer satisfied working for "Uncle" Carl Laemmle, and wanted out. Loeb arranged a meeting between Louis B. Mayer and the very young and talented Universal executive, Irving Thalberg.

Thalberg's confidence and authoritative demeanor, combined with his boyish looks, intrigued Mayer. Besides, Thalberg's earlier showdown with director Erich von Stroheim had left Hollywood atwitter. When Mayer met Thalberg for the first time, Mayer shared his concerns about a film that was currently in production at his studio. The director intended to shoot several scenes depicting naked women, which went against the wholesome image that Mayer envisioned. He asked how Thalberg would handle the situation. Without hesitating, Thalberg declared that at Universal, there would be no debate. *He* was the producer and *his* decisions were final—not the director's or anyone else's. Mayer liked his answer and his self-assurance. No doubt, he also glimpsed that "class factor" he so valued. After their meeting, Mayer asked Loeb to relay a message to the youthful producer: "Tell him if he comes to work for me, I'll look after him like my own son."

And so, on February 15, 1923, one of Hollywood's most remarkable love-hate relationships began. Mayer had just one rule—his daughters were off limits to Thalberg. Well aware of the young man's unstable heart, Mayer made no secret of the fact that he didn't want a widowed woman on his hands. Once this matter was understood, thirty-seven-year-old Mayer and twenty-three-year-old Thalberg were inseparable. Despite their differences, they made a dynamic team. Mayer cut a hardy figure compared to Thalberg's fragile form. Mayer relished the spotlight while Thalberg shunned it. Mayer was flamboyant, Thalberg modest. Together, however, they were potent as Mayer was content running the business while Thalberg oversaw production.

When Marcus Loew, owner of Loew's Theaters and Metro Pictures, bought out Goldwyn Pictures, he needed a responsible man in charge. His lawyer recommended Mayer for the job. After intense negotiations, Louis B. Mayer Productions merged with Metro Pictures and Goldwyn Pictures to form Metro-Goldwyn-Mayer (MGM). With Mayer officially named First Vice President, Loew wanted to put his son, Arthur, in charge of production. Mayer demanded Thalberg and refused to budge on the issue, and so Thalberg stayed on as Second Vice President and Supervisor of Production. Arthur Loew was out before he even got in.

Mayer also persuaded the successful Head of Production at Warner Bros., Harry Rapf, to join them. The men shared a similar philosophy—movies were meant to entertain. Rapf was the driving force behind most of the Warners' successful movies from 1920 to 1924. It was Rapf's discovery of Rin Tin Tin that saved the brothers from bankruptcy. The "triumvirate," as the press dubbed MGM's big three, were charged with turning a profit and providing Loew's Theaters across the country with first-rate movies. The mega-merger was reported in the *L.A. Times* on April 18, 1924:

> The merger greatly increases the already vast number of theaters owned, controlled or operated by Marcus Loew. The Capitol, New York, the California and Miller's theaters in Los Angeles, the Ascher

Circuit of twenty theaters in Chicago and houses in Seattle, Tacoma, Washington and Portland, Oregon all of which were controlled or operated by Goldwyn, are now added to the Loew chain. This makes Marcus Loew the director of approximately 350 theaters in all parts of the United States.

MGM moved into the former Goldwyn studio located on Washington Boulevard in Culver City. Originally built by producer Thomas Ince in 1915, the complex sat on more than forty acres. MGM also inherited the Goldwyn trademark—a roaring lion surrounded by a banner emblazoned with the words "Ars Gratias Artis" or "Art for Art's Sake." Publicity man Howard Dietz had come up with the logo in 1921. A Columbia University graduate, he was inspired by an image of a lion, the university's mascot, which appeared on the cover of *The Jester*, a school publication. He then incorporated the Latin phrase, something one of his professors liked to write on the blackboard. Of course, no one actually heard the lion roar until the advent of sound.

MGM formally opened its doors on April 26, 1924. The official ceremony took place on the studio's front lawn with all the pomp and circumstance that Mayer, along with the U.S. Army and Navy, could muster. As Fred Niblo hosted the event, planes flew overhead showering flowers on the crowd that included over 300 military men in uniform. Congratulatory telegrams came from U.S. President Calvin Coolidge and the current Secretary of Commerce, Herbert Hoover. Even Harry and Jack Warner sent their good wishes. Mayer, flanked by his assistants Rapf and Thalberg, took center stage, which was bedecked in the patriotic red, white, and blue. In his melodramatic fashion complete with tears, the new headman promised the group: "This is a great moment for me. I accept this solemn trust, and pledge the best that I have to give."

Mayer's good friend and poker partner, Edwin J. Loeb, along with newly hired Loeb attorney George Washington Cohen, assisted with legal matters surrounding the new company. The twenty-nine-year-old Cohen and his wife, Carolyn, had recently welcomed their first son, Donald. Loeb soon introduced Cohen to the legalities of moviemaking. Cohen kept one foot in the law firm and the other in Hollywood for the next twenty years.

With Mayer holding the title of first vice-president, he earned $1500 per week. His associates, Thalberg and Rapf, each pulled in $650. There was one difference, however. While Mayer and Thalberg were allowed 20 percent of the overall profits, Rapf was given 25 percent of the profits from just three of his films. Thalberg and Rapf had adjoining offices identical in size. They shared a projection room and their secretaries worked together in the same office space. In the beginning, the two were very much equals and worked as a team to launch MGM.

Mayer, Thalberg and Rapf hired writers, directors, actors, cameramen, set designers, and prop men. They established entire departments for make-up, wardrobe, and publicity. Mayer controlled the budgets, handled the politics and basked in the hype. Thalberg, with his flair for storytelling, supervised day-to-day production from start to finish. He often worked more than sixteen hours each day, cramming all he could into every moment. Rapf also oversaw daily production and continued flushing out major new talent like Lucille Fay LeSueur and Maria Guadalupe Velez de Villalobos, soon to be known as MGM royals Joan Crawford and Lupe Velez, respectively.

Mayer retained the services of Goldwyn's prized art director, Cedric Gibbons—another "classy" employee. The well-educated Gibbons, with his striking good looks, was as debonair as any actor he might have mingled with. During his tenure with Goldwyn, his reputation as a cutting edge set designer flourished. As head of MGM's Art Department, he became a celebrity in his own right; his contract allowed him credit on all of the new studio's major productions. From MGM's beginnings until he retired thirty-two years later, his name was listed on over 1500 films.

Gibbons, who revolutionized the way movies looked with his sleek yet elegant Art Deco style, is often credited with bringing three-dimensional sets to the movies, effectively replacing painted backdrops. In deference to those early film actors who, after taking off their gloves, pinned them to the canvas scenery, Gibbons was sometimes referred to as "the man who put the glove on the mantelpiece." Now, he was about to stamp his own brand of glamour on MGM films making them stand out with panache and style—just the kind of "class" Louis B. Mayer was looking for.

Gibbons wasn't the only employee acquired through the merger. The overworked matinee idol Conrad Nagel enjoyed great success at Goldwyn's. His popularity kept him working on back-to-back films with hardly any breaks. At six feet tall with blonde hair and blue eyes, his timeless goods look and matinée idol status assured him a spot at MGM. The married actor and father, who enjoyed tennis and swimming, had a wholesome image that appealed to Mayer's penchant for refinement. Nagel was also known around the Goldwyn lot as a connoisseur of pretzels. He liked them so much that he set up a pretzel box in the studio's cafeteria. Nagel enjoyed a good crunch and all employees were encouraged to help themselves at the actor's expense. No doubt, MGM was anxious to retain his services and perhaps his pretzel box, too.

Like Gibbons and Nagel, writer Carey Wilson was also a Goldwyn alumnus. He penned several successful films for the studio and was recognized as one of their top writers. Outside of work, Wilson had once rented a house with two of his buddies, fellow Goldwyn writer Paul Bern and a young actor named John Gilbert, who had recently split from his second wife, actress Leatrice Joy. By the time Wilson joined MGM, however, he was a married man with a family. He and his wife, former dancer Nancy Everett, had a daughter, Nancy Hope, born in 1921.

A dedicated stamp collector and avid reader, Wilson subscribed to over 150 monthly publications and owned over 10,000 books. In addition, he liked to tinker in his own machine shop located right behind his house where he especially liked to build radios. He also enjoyed photography, woodcarving and clay modeling. He was once described as a "gadgeteer" by the press: "Carey's the kind of guy who, when you ask him the time will tell you how to make a watch."

One of Wilson's future writing partners, Benjamin Floyer Glazer, was also hired by MGM after an earlier success, *A Trip to Paradise* (1921), which was written for Metro Pictures. Prior to the merger, Glazer worked for Louis B. Mayer Productions. Impressed with Glazer's ability to translate European classics for American audiences, as well as his past theatrical experience, Mayer brought him into the MGM fold. Still married to Alice, the couple had no children.

Wilson and Glazer teamed up to write the romantic drama *Sinners in Silk* (1924), an early MGM film featuring Conrad Nagel. This romantic drama whose tagline proclaimed, "here is the truth about today's flappers and lounge lizards!" also featured future gossip doyenne Hedda Hopper. Glazer then adapted another Molnar work, *Fashions for Men* which turned into *Fine Clothes* (1925) starring Lewis Stone under the direction of John M. Stahl. Next, he teamed up with the Hungarian-born Erich von Stroheim and co-wrote *The Merry Widow* (1925) starring silent megastar John Gilbert who became one of Glazer's closest friends.

In 1926, Glazer wrote a sizzling photoplay based on Hermann Sudermann's novel *The Undying Past*. John Gilbert was cast to star as Leon von Harden with Lillian Gish as his leading lady. Instead of the highly paid Gish, however, a newly signed contract player from Sweden took on the role of Felicita. When Greta Garbo cozied up to John Gilbert for the first time in *Flesh and The Devil* (1926), the cameras caught the earliest sparks of a fiery love affair that spread into their personal lives. When director Clarence Brown yelled "Cut!" the lovebirds continued nuzzling even when the cameras stopped rolling causing many embarrassing moments for the rest of the cast and crew. The couple's steamy chemistry, candid passion and smoldering clinches sent spectators swooning, even though in real life, Garbo stood a shattered Gilbert up at the altar. Although Garbo never married, Gilbert took two more wives, but divorced each one.

As the new studio took shape, Thalberg and Rapf presented two very different leadership styles. Where Thalberg was poised and polished, Rapf was rough and rude. The twenty-something Thalberg charmed the staff with his good sense of humor while the forty-something Rapf often growled out his orders. Thalberg displayed a gentle side; Rapf protected his tough-guy image, afraid a little tenderness might be mistaken for weakness. Before long, Thalberg became the favored producer despite the irritating way he jingled pocket change or bounced a gold coin off his desk during meetings.

Thalberg immersed himself in MGM moviemaking from pre-production to post-production. He reviewed scripts with writers; he approved costumes and sets; he had the final word on casting and was a master at editing. No detail escaped his attention. Thalberg demanded perfection—or at least as close as he could get to it. Writers, directors, actors, everyone sought his advice on everything from sets to scenes to editing, making him notoriously late for appointments. Director Clarence Brown claimed it was always worth the wait:

> You would be working with your writer, and you would come to this scene in the script. It didn't click. It just didn't jell. The scene was no goddam good. You would make a date with Irving, talk to him for thirty minutes, and you'd come away with the best scene in the picture.

Thalberg also inherited his share of headaches resulting from the multiple mergers. His old nemesis whom he had fired at Universal, director Erich von Stroheim, was back—this time with a nine-hour drama, *Greed* (1924) based on the novel *McTeague, A Story of San Francisco* written by author Frank Norris and originally published in 1899. Throughout filming, von Stroheim carefully followed the book making sure to include every detail, which resulted in the extremely long film. Mayer and Thalberg would not release a movie that required patrons to pack a lunch.

Already on the wrong side of Thalberg, von Stroheim reluctantly pared the movie down to what he deemed a more acceptable three hours and forty minutes, but his new cut wasn't good enough. Neither Mayer nor

Thalberg was happy with von Stroheim or his still-too-long film. They called in their top title writer, Joseph Farnham, known for his brevity.

Farnham was instructed to maintain the storyline through title cards and cut the footage down to a more acceptable length. Farnham did as he was told and chopped the movie to ten reels. The problem being—Farnham never read the book and von Stroheim's epic was decimated. The outraged director reportedly stated: "The only thing [Farnham] had on his mind was his hat!" The film slashing did nothing to improve relations between von Stroheim and Thalberg.

The driven Thalberg continued supervising the studio's major productions including *Ben-Hur: A Tale of the Christ* (1925), another troubled movie that was already in process under Goldwyn when the MGM merger occurred. Under the old regime, filming of the biblical epic began in Rome with disastrous results. Two hundred reels of film were useless. Mayer's most prized writers, Carey Wilson and Bess Meredyth who previously worked for Mayer at his production company, replaced scenarist June Mathis. The bible-sized script was rewritten. Ramon Novarro supplanted the movie's original star, George Walsh—director Raoul's brother. Fred Niblo was dispatched to take on the role of director from Charles Brabin. Shooting started over. Costs ran high. Cultural differences between American and Italian filmmakers only added to the difficulties.

Mayer, along with his family, personally traveled to Rome leaving Thalberg and Rapf to run the California studio. More irritable than usual, Mayer wasn't well. He hadn't been to a dentist in years and was in agony due to abscessed teeth. He finally collapsed in Italy where doctors deduced that toxins had spread throughout his body. With antibiotics not yet available, his only chance at survival was to have all of his teeth removed. As each tooth was extracted one by one inside his hotel room, Mayer hung on for his life throughout the pain. Daily wires flew back and forth between Los Angeles and Rome as Thalberg anxiously awaited word on Mayer's condition. After several nerve-wracking weeks, Mayer improved and eventually stopped production of *Ben-Hur*. The disheartened group returned to California.

Thalberg had no intention of scrapping the movie. Instead, he ordered Cedric Gibbons to rebuild ancient Rome, complete with a new Circus Maximus, on the studio's back lot. Thalberg spent weeks poring over every detail of the movie's famous chariot race. He wanted close-ups of his stars as well as the running horses and the spinning wheels. To capture all of the action, dozens of cameras were placed around the set. A pit was even dug into the ground and a camera positioned inside it so the racing chariots could be filmed from below.

The day of the race, 3,900 toga-wearing extras were camera-ready. Thalberg demanded more so another 400 people were brought in from the local neighborhood and added to the crowd. When it was time for lunch, Thalberg refused to stop filming. The production manager protested saying that the extras were hungry and might riot. Thalberg never wavered. "Fine!" he spouted. "That'll add some realism to the scene."

After all the hoopla, it was no wonder that Thalberg's bad heart caught up with him. During November 1925, he collapsed at work and was rushed to the hospital where doctors diagnosed a heart attack. Ordered to stay in bed, Thalberg couldn't rest. He viewed daily rushes projected onto the hospital room's ceiling. He read scripts and held meetings. One month later, he ignored his doctors' advice, as well as his mother's protests, and returned to MGM, but not before *Ben-Hur* premiered to high praise from the critics and loud cheers from the audience. Thalberg was not only credited for saving the production, but for turning it into a masterpiece.

From the exhilarating chariot race to the ambitious battle scenes, the film was one of the new studio's greatest silent triumphs and set the standard for MGM movies to come. Metro-Goldwyn-Mayer had finally arrived on the landscape of movie history along with Louis B. Mayer's long-desired respectability.

Chapter Fifteen

THE REST OF 'EM

Not all of the Academy's founding members were affiliated with major studios. Some were independents with their own show business interests while others were filmmakers who carved a separate niche in the house of Hollywood. Take Sid Grauman for instance. After the San Francisco earthquake, he and his father once again found tremendous success in the City by the Bay. Eventually, they opened several movie theaters and vaudeville houses throughout the area, but that wasn't good enough. The Graumans wanted to be in the center of the newly developing motion picture industry—not in a city north of it. Around 1917, they took a gamble. Sid Grauman met with Famous Players-Lasky Corporation President Adolph Zukor, persuading him to buy all of their San Francisco theaters. He also persuaded Zukor to finance a new theater in downtown Los Angeles.

Together, the father-and-son team converted an office building, located at Third and Broadway, into a magnificent showplace they called the Million Dollar Theater. The Spanish Baroque-style structure was aptly named since it cost over one million dollars to refurbish. With striking statues, detailed murals and ornate carvings, the opulent theater rivaled any showplace that the east coast had to offer. Grauman never settled for plain old run-of-the-mill grandeur, he insisted on razzle-dazzle. For his patrons, attending a movie was not just a temporary distraction—it was an unforgettable event.

When the doors opened on February 1, 1918, William S. Hart's western film *The Silent Man* (1917) was shown after one of Grauman's soon-to-be-famous live prologues set the mood. Among the crowd that night were director Cecil B. DeMille, along with silent screen stars Douglas Fairbanks and Charlie Chaplin. The new theater was such a hit that even with 2,345 seats, Grauman turned away customers night after night.

In 1919, he purchased Quinn's Rialto, a two-year-old nickelodeon. After several weeks of remodeling, Grauman turned the arcade into the New Rialto Theater. Holding approximately 1,000 patrons, The Rialto reopened on November 20, 1919 with DeMille's *Male and Female* (1919), which was adapted for the screen by Jeanie Macpherson and featured former slapstick comedienne Gloria Swanson. Unlike the Million Dollar Theater, which only played movies for one week, the Rialto kept its films for longer engagements.

Grauman's third venture, also located in downtown Los Angeles, was the art deco Metropolitan Theater on Sixth and Hill. It cost approximately four million dollars making it the most expensive and most elaborate theater out west. Always outrageous, Grauman placed a sphinx, topped by a George Washington head, on a pedestal in the lobby with the inscription: "You cannot speak to us, O George Washington, but you can speak to God. Ask him to make us good American citizens." But Sid Grauman wasn't done dazzling. He soon moved on to a suburb just west of Los Angeles called Hollywood.

There, on Hollywood Boulevard at McCadden Place, Grauman's team of architects and designers outdid themselves with the magnificent Egyptian Theater. Resembling the ancient palaces of the pharaohs, it was the first major cinema erected outside of the downtown area. Unlike most theaters of the time, the Egyptian had a courtyard complete with statues of a regal-looking elephant wearing royal garb and an over-sized man with a dog's head who kept an eye on a row of shops that stood along one side. Grauman even paid a fellow to dress like an Egyptian soldier. This employee marched along the roof proclaiming the start time of each show.

Patrons passed through four colossal columns (more than four feet wide and twenty feet high) on their way into the lobby. Inside, the stunning details transported paying customers into another world and time. Egyptian figures stood tall while hieroglyphic-like markings were carved on the walls. A sizeable sphinx along with faux sarcophagi added to the ambience. The theater's focal point, a large golden sunburst poised strategically above the movie screen, created a mystical aura.

Costing a mere eight hundred thousand dollars, the Egyptian had no balcony and sat only 1,770 moviegoers. It opened on October 18, 1922 with the first showing of Douglas Fairbanks's *Robin Hood* (1922). That night, Grauman pulled out all the stops. Searchlights swept the sky, as thousands of movie fans lined the streets to glimpse their favorite stars, decked out in their finery, stroll down a red carpet. The movie premiere in all its glamour and glitz was born, making Sid Grauman a preferred favorite among Hollywood bigwigs.

While Grauman went about building theaters and showcasing films, Fred Beetson tried his best to protect America. As Will Hays' right-hand man in Hollywood and Vice President of the Motion Picture Producers and Distributors of America, he was in charge of censorship issues, but he also watched over the animal actors and helped establish a bureau for the thousands of extras who constantly scrambled for work. He even placated the local ladies when, as a guest speaker, he joined the Women's Club of Hollywood for lunch. He let them know that:

> Our office has nothing to do with the personal conduct of people in the motion picture industry. We are not waiting for laws to guide us

in making better pictures. We are looking for cooperation and suggestions from the women.

In 1926, Beetson was also called upon to support the newly formed Studio Relations Department (SRD)—another Hays effort to combat movie demons. Under the leadership of Colonel Jason S. Joy, a former military man and American Red Cross executive, this group was charged with bringing the various studios together and improving work conditions across Hollywood. The SRD concerned itself with developing work-related recreation such as athletic activities, overseeing the treatment of child actors and organizing lunchrooms where crew members could get decent meals for fair prices.

In addition, Beetson was part of a five-man committee along with producers Joseph Schenck, Jack Warner and Irving Thalberg, as well as First National representative John McCormick. This group reviewed formal grievances submitted by film actors, from stars to extras. If the committee determined an allegation was valid, they ensured that corrective measures were taken and the matter resolved to everyone's satisfaction—without fear of repercussions. If, after an investigation, they deemed an issue as baseless, they clarified their findings making certain that all parties involved understood their position.

As Beetson righted wrongs and tried to keep films smut-free, M.C. Levee continued running United Studios on Melrose Avenue. As studio president, he also thought about movie censorship and took things one step further when he spoke to the press about fiction in general:

> I believe the entire field of modern fiction will soon undergo a radical change. Authors frequently realize more money on the film rights to their books or plays than from any other source. Writers of modern fiction will very shortly begin to realize that unless their stories are without objectionable situations or themes a very lucrative avenue of revenue is closed to them . . . I predict a marked change in the type

of book and play which has seemed so popular during the last year, as a direct result of Mr. Hayes' idea.

By now United Studios had a lot to offer. They housed pre-built sets that included churches, schools, hotels and formal gardens. The studio even had city centers patterned after famous places like Paris, Tokyo and Honolulu. Their props and furniture ran the gamut from Renaissance to Modern with everything from stained glass windows to fireplaces to draperies. United Studios also carried a large collection of musical instruments, oriental rugs and costumes. And if they didn't have something a filmmaker needed, artisans on staff could build it, sew it, paint it or plant it.

In 1924, United Studios, under Levee's direction, kept busy with several major productions including *Lilies of the Field* (1924) directed by John Francis Dillon and French filmmaker Maurice Tourneur's *The White Moth* (1924) starring the popular Barbara LaMarr. Director Frank Lloyd's classic action movie *The Sea Hawk* (1924), featuring silent screen favorite Milton Sills, was also filmed at United Studios. Levee predicted that in 1925 his studio would soon reach maximum production capacity with more and more filmmakers moving permanently to California.

Charles H. Christie was another successful producer during the Roaring Twenties. He worked alongside his brother, Al, at the Christie Film Company. With funnyman Al making the movies, Charles took care of the serious stuff like running the studio. Top filmmakers known worldwide for their comedy features, Christie films played in over thirty countries. The brothers not only worked together, but also lived together. They shared a home with family members including their mother, Mary, and half-sister Anne.

Charles was also committed to the community. He was a member of both the Hollywood Athletic and the Lakeside Country Clubs. He sat on the Hollywood Chamber of Commerce, which was founded in 1921, and assisted in the creation of the Motion Picture Relief Fund along with Mary Pickford. In addition, both brothers took a shine to terriers. They not only raised the pups, but also organized the first dog shows in Hollywood. *The Dog Fancier* magazine reported in November 1922:

> Mr. Charles Christie, finding competition in Bull Terriers not very interesting, has for some time been looking for a breed to which to transfer his fancy, and with the acquisition of the imported Scottie, Taybank Pilot, believes he has found what he wants and will have several Diehards at future shows. His Bull Terrier, Champion Heath-erene Boy, continues to win the specials but, most likely will see his last ring at Hollywood as he is to be withdrawn from all competition thereafter.

Also in 1922, the brothers created the Christie Realty Corporation. Charles even joined together with journalists/editors Albert Shaw and Arthur Brisbane, as well as movie czar Will Hays to buy Innerarity Island near Pensacola, Florida—former hangout of real buccaneer Jean Laffite. The group originally intended to use the place as a real estate investment, but changed their minds and decided to keep the picturesque acreage for themselves.

The very busy Charles also succeeded Joseph M. Schenck as president of the Motion Picture Producers and Distributors of America in 1925. He was elected to office along with First Vice President Irving Thalberg, Second Vice President M.C. Levee and Secretary Treasurer Fred Beetson. That same year, the Christie Brothers purchased the Hollywood Studios located on Santa Monica Boulevard for $250,000. There, the Christies filmed one of their most famous comedies, *Charley's Aunt* (1925), starring Sid Chaplin, the famous Little Tramp's brother, with titles written by Joseph Farnham. The story centers on a young man posing as his aunt, which causes all kinds of unexpected havoc—a cross-dressing theme that still generates laughs.

Spectators enjoyed the long and hearty guffaws that a Christie comedy guaranteed. They also expected the same from Harold Lloyd. Now with his own production company, the bespectacled funnyman meant big business. His first picture under the Harold Lloyd Corporation was *Girl Shy* (1924) with new leading lady, southern belle Jobyna Ralston. She replaced Mildred Davis, who was now Lloyd's wife. Born in Tennessee, she was named after her parents' favorite theatrical actress, Jobyna Howland. Ralston's career began on stage as a youngster and, at twenty-one, she made her Broadway debut. Eventually, she took on minor film roles until producer Hal Roach cast her in several one-reelers. From there, she came to Lloyd's attention when he was hunting for a new actress to play "The Girl."

Girl Shy was another wildly successful vehicle for Lloyd's "glasses character." In this film, "The Boy" tries to save "The Girl" from marrying an undesirable man who already has a wife. In order to stop the deceitful wedding, "The Boy" takes a wild ride, first, as a passenger in an automobile until a policeman on a motorbike pulls the car over. As the policeman asks the driver, ". . .What are you trying to do—run away from your rear tires?," "The Boy" steals the officer's motorcycle. He races through the city streets dodging pedestrians, streetcars and chickens until the bike wipes out. He then continues his exhilarating romp with a two-horse carriage. When a wheel falls away from the carriage, he climbs onto one of the horses. Astride one horse and holding the second one close by, "The Boy" gallops to the wedding just in time to whisk his ladylove away from the underhanded bridegroom.

Lloyd was also a hero in real life when a gas heater exploded in his home. Roused from his bed, he found his chauffeur unconscious and dragged him to safety. He was also one of Hollywood's favorite bosses. Most people who worked for Lloyd stayed with him. He valued his "gag men" and paid them top dollar. Some earned as much as $800 per week—an outrageous amount considering the average worker in 1925 pulled in about $25 each week. Other studio employees were equally important. Lloyd kept many of them on the payroll year-round—whether they were working or not. He often insisted that the workday end at three p.m. to allow his cast and crew some recreational time for a friendly game of handball. He believed that the sport was a great stress reliever and an even better way to keep trim, not to mention the camaraderie and loyalty it fostered.

For all his popularity, Lloyd, who never wore his horn-rimmed glasses off-screen, was rarely recognized in public. He once recalled:

> I'd be with Doug Fairbanks and Mary Pickford and heck, I'd get pushed out of the way. The people wanted them, not me. Without the glasses, no one ever recognized me.

Inspiration Pictures, founded by New York attorney Charles H. Duell along with Director Henry King and his actor-partner Richard Barthelmess, was another production company that claimed its own success. Their hit film *Tol'able David* (1921) won several international awards and set a precedent for Inspiration movies to come. King didn't disappoint. He delivered when he took on *The White Sister* (1923), which was based on a novel by writer Francis Marion Crawford. Crawford's story takes place in Italy where the heroine is engaged to a military man whom she believes has been killed. In sorrow, she joins the convent, but after taking her final vows as a sister of God, her fiancé makes a shocking return.

King cast experienced actress Lillian Gish in the lead role, but for the part of the soldier, he spotted a newcomer—British stage actor Ronald Colman. A former soldier himself, Colman was seriously wounded in World War I and discharged from the service before becoming an actor. King, however, wanted a little more edge to his leading man. He is credited with penciling a thin mustache along Colman's stiff upper lip giving the character his dash. The mustache was such a hit that Colman grew a permanent one.

For filming, King took his company to Rome. His art director, Robert Haas, designed a set with French windows. King tried to tell him that there were no French windows in Rome. The disbelieving Haas and the insistent director took a ride through several Roman neighborhoods to find that no one in the city had French windows. The set was redesigned and the French windows removed.

King even called upon the Catholic Church for assistance with the secular ceremony in which Gish becomes a nun. The director later described "a short, fat little priest" who came to the set carrying a script. Through an interpreter, the man of God staged the ceremony over the next eleven hours, careful to include every celebratory detail. The next morning King shot the scene. Only later did he discover that the rotund clergyman was the Vatican's head ceremonial director—an expert's expert.

The movie's finale involved a dramatic eruption of Mt. Vesuvius. For this scene, King went to the mountain. He, along with a guide, a cameraman and other crewmembers, rode by horseback to the top of the volcano hoping to capture some of nature's dramatics on film. Recalled King:

> Well, we carried on up the side of the main crater and I wanted to look inside it. The hole in the top was about sixty feet across and it was banked up with ashes. I had a Leica. I gave it to the cameraman and told him to photograph me when I reached the edge. Well, the heat was so intense I couldn't stand it. It singed my eyebrows and my hair. When I came back my face was blood red and the guide was lying on his stomach, praying. I asked him what the matter was. "Only one other man ever did that," he said. "The bank of ashes gave way and he went right on in." I never thought of that; I was just being stupid. That little expedition took twelve hours—but we got our film. . . .

King's partner at Inspiration Pictures, Richard Barthelmess, was one of the silent screen's favorite sons. While he continued making crowd-pleasing movies for the company, including several directed by King, Barthelmess' private life took a colorful turn. In early 1925, he returned from Guantanamo, Cuba on board a Navy battleship where he was researching his role as a sailor in *Shore Leave* (1925). Back in New York, he was briefly hospitalized for treatment of an abscess amidst a swirl of rumors concerning his five-year-old marriage to entertainer Mary Hay.

By now, Hay, a former Ziegfeld girl, had discovered a new dance partner, Clifton Webb. The energetic stage couple was featured regularly at Ciro's, a popular New York nightclub—until the place got padlocked for serving illegal hooch. After the Volstead Act violation, Hay and Webb hit the vaudeville circuit, taking the nine-man band from Ciro's with them. Their comedic dance routines could always be counted on to please the crowd.

By mid-May, Hay admitted that she and her husband were separated, but denied that they were divorcing. She blamed their separation on business—she and partner Webb were committed to dancing in Europe while Barthelmess had contractual duties in the States, forcing them apart. That didn't explain why Barthelmess moved into New York's Algonquin Hotel the month before. Their toddler daughter, Mary, born in 1923, was to remain with Barthelmess during Hay's absence. More permanent custody arrangements would be worked out upon the dancer's return to California. But no one was talking about a divorce.

Later that same month, Barthelmess was the only passenger on a short flight from Norfolk, Virginia to Anacostia. A Navy man, Lieutenant Teneyck Dew Veeder, piloted the small plane. The officer was suddenly stricken with what was believed to be a heart attack just as he prepared to land the plane. Once the plane stopped on the runway, Veeder lost consciousness. When he failed to turn off the engines, Barthelmess tried to get the ailing man's attention, but there was no response. Emergency workers were brought in. They tried to revive him, but Veeder died at the scene—a hero for bringing his plane and his passenger down safely despite the medical emergency that proved fatal.

Regardless of his ongoing personal mishaps, Barthelmess maintained his matinée idol cool and continued to be one of Hollywood's top box office draws. From the drama of *The Enchanted Cottage* (1924) to the comedy of *Shore Leave* (1925), the handsome actor stayed in his audience's good graces. Of course, the ladies might have admired him just a little more now that he was raising a daughter alone.

Director Frank Lloyd also had a daughter, Alma, whom he often cast as an extra in many of his top-grossing films. Lloyd not only liked romance and drama, but he also took pride in getting things right. By 1924, when he helmed the swashbuckling epic *Sea Hawk,* based on the novel by writer Rafael Sabatini, his reputation for fine work was established. The seafaring adventure starred actor Milton Sills. He played Sir Oliver Tressilian, a British knight who later turned into Sakr-el-Bahr, a Sea Hawk, or pirate. The film employed thousands of extras and called for elaborate sets, as well as detailed period costumes.

Four sixteenth century-like ships measuring over 100 feet in length were built, along with a pier, on the northeast end of Catalina Island. Set builders also constructed a three-story Algerian slave house complete with a minaret as well as three other similarly themed structures. *The Los Angeles Times* also reported on the vast amount of props used for the film:

> . . . There were 213 cannon made especially for the production, of three different types, Spanish, English and Moorish . . . There were 400 Spanish muskets, 200 English muskets and 400 Moorish rifles of the sixteenth century. Five hundred spears and 300 battle axes. Six hundred brass shields, several hundred helmets of three styles, hundreds of bows and arrows, 150 cross bows . . . powder horns, ancient water buckets, barrels, ammunition kegs, casks, blankets, scimitars, dueling swords . . . sabers, cutlasses, lanterns . . . candles, rum bottles (entirely empty) . . .

Working more than 65 miles from the studio and forty miles from the nearest harbor in San Pedro made a daily commute impossible. Crewmembers erected over 100 tents for workers to live in, plus a dining hall, a barbershop, a bathhouse and an executive office. Dubbed "Camp Lloyd," supplies arrived daily by boat and, every other day, an aeroplane dropped off new film and returned negatives to the main studio for processing. To alleviate boredom, nightly entertainment consisted of boxing matches, band concerts and whatever else the group could muster.

Lloyd also took pride in righting wrongs. The California State tax law imposed a three-cents-per-gallon gas tax for gasoline used on the highways. Lloyd complained to the State Treasurer's office because he paid this tax on gasoline purchased for the film's four ships. He pointed out that his ships never once entered a public road. The state presented Lloyd with a $252 check—the first refund given since the tax law took effect the year before.

It was no wonder that Lloyd's doctors advised him to rest once filming ended. He packed up his family and headed to Japan, China and Hawaii for several months in the fall of 1925. Shortly after his return, Lloyd was hospitalized and required surgery after an attack of appendicitis.

By the time *Sea Hawk* wrapped, its star, Milton Sills, was at the top of his professional game. Prior to his huge success as Sakr-el-Bahr, Sills freelanced, working at several major studios. He filmed *Dangerous to Men* (1920) with Viola Dana for Metro Pictures and appeared opposite Lois Wilson in *Lulu Bett* (1921) for Famous Players-Lasky. By 1924, he was ready to settle down professionally and signed a long-term contract with First National where he starred in *Sea Hawk*, after which his career soared even higher. Now more than just a handsome and sophisticated matinée idol, Sills was a super hero.

At home, super hero status did not apply. In the fall of 1925, his wife, Gladys, filed for divorce claiming desertion. She stated that her husband permanently left her on August 11, 1924. In a letter, Sills wrote: "Close and sealed forever, any possibility of my ever living again under the same roof with Gladys. I shall never again go back to Hollywood and the old home or let her come to New York to live with me."

Their divorce was final on October 11, 1926 with Gladys, who never remarried, given full custody of their daughter, Dorothy. The very next day, Sills married actress Doris Kenyon, one of his previous costars. The couple wed in a quiet ceremony overlooking Silver Lake in the Adirondacks near Ausable Forks, New York where Kenyon owned a summer home. It was reported that the bride had been quite ill; therefore, the guests were limited to immediate family. According to Sills' daughter, Gladys tried to commit suicide that same day.

After their honeymoon, Sills and Kenyon returned to Hollywood. Still considered one of the most intelligent and well-read actors in the business, the serious-minded Sills often drove reporters batty. During interviews, he liked to discuss the distance between stars, the speed of light or the joys of growing phlox divaricata in his garden. Philosophy, along with the meaning of Shakespeare, was also among his favorite topics. Interviewers were always relieved when the conversation turned to the movies and Sills' current film. One reporter affectionately referred to the actor as "filmdom's pet highbrow."

Whether they worked for a major or minor studio, or simply struck out on their own, Hollywood heavyweights took command. Directors, actors, exhibitors and producers shared one common goal—the continued success and growth of the motion picture industry.

Chapter Sixteen

THE GANG'S ALL HERE

A mention of the Roaring Twenties conjures up images of short-skirted flappers, serious marathon dancing and illegal speak-easies where horn-blowing bands showcased a new, controversial sound called jazz. But there was more to this decade than a quick-kicking Charleston and a long raccoon coat. It was a time of rebellion, a time of cultural change and a time for risk takers to act.

European borders shifted as various treaties were signed following World War I. Germany, still recovering from The Great War, found new interest in a young Nazi leader. "Il Duce," Italy's current prime minister, was putting the squeeze on his country's king, Victor Emmanuel. King Tut's tomb was discovered near Luxor. Catholic Pope Benedict XV proclaimed the young French heroine Joan of Arc a saint. Mexico was absorbed in its own violent rebellion while a powerful earthquake terrorized Japan. Toronto scientists discovered how to extract insulin from dogs giving hope to diabetics.

In America, country folk were deserting the farm for the big city. Women, seeking independence, finally gained the right to vote while Native Americans were promoted from their tribal ranks to U.S. citizens. Congress passed the Emergency Quota Act limiting the number of incoming immigrants in an attempt to appease Americans who now feared the influx of foreigners. Boston baseball hero Babe Ruth moved out of the Red Sox dugout and into New York. Names like Al Capone, Charles Darwin and Lucky Lindy made the news.

Henry Ford revolutionized life in the factories with his forty-hour workweek and assembly-line approach to manufacturing. His affordable Model Ts were quickly becoming part of the landscape that now included concrete roads and gas stations. Families gathered around the radio for in-house entertainment and mother used a telephone when she needed to catch father at work. Flying remained mostly for thrill-seekers, but barnstormers still drew wide-eyed crowds who preferred to watch while keeping their own feet on the ground.

Flickers had turned into features and larger studios were replacing many of the smaller production companies. During the 1920s, Hollywood's Big Five Studios rose to prominence: Warner Bros. Pictures, Paramount Pictures (formerly Famous Players-Lasky Corporation), Radio-Keith-Orpheum (RKO) Pictures, Metro-Goldywn-Mayer and Fox Film Corporation. In addition, three smaller studios also evolved: Universal Pictures, United Artists and Columbia Pictures. The major difference? The Big Five owned their own theater chains while the Little Three had none.

In order to sell movie tickets, the studios needed stars. Producers competed by offering higher and higher salaries to those bankable stars that guaranteed big box office. Eventually, those high dollars drew public criticism that claimed these extravagant salaries were decadent and made the film industry look bad. Reformers who belonged to church groups, ladies' clubs and other civic-minded organizations had already won their battle with the bottle. Now, they targeted Hollywood where they believed fast cars and even faster women prevailed. For highly paid stars that lacked discipline, the "easy" money came too quickly and gave way to evil excess. Their palatial homes were too large; their fancy clothes too garish; their lavish spending too wasteful. Morality was tossed aside as divorce, adultery and drug use took precedence setting shameful examples for Christian-raised youth. "Sin City" and its inhabitants must be cleaned up—much like the booze factor was a few years before with the start of Prohibition.

In Hollywood, there was no common ground where decision-makers could meet to ward off these accusations. Instead of being proactive, authority figures reacted, one voice at a time, to all of the bad press. Lacking industry standards and guidelines, Hollywood also faced its own unrest. Infighting between the various factions was another problem; directors, producers, actors, writers and technicians often played the blame game when things went wrong—or even when they didn't. As a result, these individual groups were gaining strength with talk of union- izing. In addition, technology was advancing faster than anyone was prepared for; sound was coming and bringing with it a complete overhaul of "business as usual."

As 1926 turned into 1927, MGM headman Louis B. Mayer was troubled by this unstable climate that threatened the continued success of the film industry. Something had to be done, but he couldn't do it alone. In early 1927, Mayer invited Fred Niblo, Conrad Nagel and Fred Beetson to dinner at his Santa Monica beach house—all men he respected for their ability to get things done. The foursome discussed the many woes that currently faced the motion picture industry and they came to one conclusion— Hollywood lacked unity and it was time to regroup. Niblo, Nagel and Beetson all had past experience with various work-related organizations and it was only natural for these particular men to think along these lines. Mayer heartily agreed.

Now, more than ever, they felt that Hollywood needed a single authori- tative voice to speak out on its behalf. Stand alone and go down with declining ticket sales or present a united front and move forward with a positive spin. If they could establish a single organization made up of Hollywood's finest writers, producers, actors, directors, and technicians, they might be able to ward off an angry public, clean up their tarnished image, promote their good works and resolve their own inner conflicts. And with any luck, they might even be able to pave the way for the next generation of filmmakers.

Inspired by their dinner conversation and believing they could make a difference, Mayer, Niblo, Nagel and Beetson each contacted a cross-section of those industry leaders who, in 1927, were at the top of their game. They explained their idea of organizing a single group to represent them all, and their plan was well received. Encouraged by the positive feedback, Mayer arranged for a banquet to be held at Los Angeles' Ambassador Hotel on January 11, 1927. There is no official record of who was actually invited to dinner that night, but the following men and women stepped forward, prepared to take action:

THE PRODUCERS

- **Charles H. Christie**—Considered one of the first movie moguls, Christie ran the internationally known Christie Film Company, which specialized in comedies, along with his younger brother Al. The two men also established the Christie Realty Corporation. Aside from his movie work, Christie was very influential around town. He was heavily involved in various Hollywood organizations and community efforts ranging from dog shows to chamber of commerce initiatives. The Christies were also looking for new property in the San Fernando Valley hoping to expand their production facilities. Most recently, partner-brother Al was in a serious auto accident that killed actress Marie Prevost's mother.
- **Milton E. Hoffman**—Back from Britain where he opened a studio for the Famous Players-Lasky Corporation, Hoffman was now the company's executive manager on the West

Coast. The studio had recently moved from the old Vine Street location to Melrose Avenue. Highly respected for his efficiency, hard work and many years associated with the film business, he was soon to take on his greatest challenge as president of the Central Motion Picture District—an organization responsible for the development of movie studios in and around Los Angeles. The group was about to invest $20,000,000 in the construction of a new film center called Studio City.

- **Jesse L. Lasky**—Now Adolph Zukor's partner and head of production at Famous Players-Lasky Corporation, Lasky was in charge of one of the world's largest motion picture companies. Their groundbreaking movie, *It* (1927), starring ultimate flapper Clara Bow, was about to be released and make Bow Hollywood's very first "It Girl." At home, the forty-six-year-old Lasky was the father of three—two sons and a daughter. His elaborate Hollywood estate was one of the first to have a tennis court and swimming pool built on the premises. The press reported that Lasky was worth about $20,000,000 and that he carried a life insurance policy valued at $5,000,000.

- **M.C. Levee**—In 1926, Levee sold his impressive United Studios to Famous Players-Lasky. He then accepted a position as General Executive Business Manager at First National. With the many department heads reporting directly to him, Levee took care of the company's business side. Well respected for his keen insight into studio mechanics, he also supervised the construction of First National's new $2,000,000 studio. Located on Olive Avenue in Burbank, the original site covered almost eighty acres that included a hog farm. After its completion, the sprawling facility boasted thirty buildings with four enormous stages and a restaurant.

- **Louis B. Mayer**—The headman in Metro-Goldwyn-Mayer's triumvirate, Mayer reported directly to Marcus Loew, owner of Loew's, Inc., MGM's parent company. Although Loew expected fifteen films to be completed annually, Mayer and his team delivered over forty. MGM was now the industry's top profit-maker and boasted stars like Conrad Nagel, John Gilbert, Greta Garbo and Lionel Barrymore—none of them more dramatic than Mayer himself. The studio chief and his family had recently moved into a newly built home on the beach at Santa Monica. The four-bedroom Spanish-style house with its thirteen bathrooms cost $28,000. Neighbors included Jesse L. Lasky and Samuel Goldwyn.

- **Harry Rapf**—After making Rin Tin Tin an international star for Warner Bros., Rapf became an important part of the MGM triumvirate under Louis B. Mayer. Still in charge of many MGM productions, but taking a back seat to Thalberg, he never stopped looking for talent on-screen or off. Rapf's latest find was a wordy young man named David O. Selznick, son of Lewis J. Selznick, Rapf's former boss at Select Pictures. The future producer first worked as a reader who greatly annoyed Mayer with his many long-winded communications. Rapf often kept family and friends on the payroll, as well. While running the wardrobe department, his brother, Joseph, made Rapf a new uncle.

- **Joseph M. Schenck**—The man in charge of United Artists was a first class Hollywood high roller. Schenck had just established the United Artists Theater Circuit, Inc. and was now scouting building sites in several major cities such as Detroit and Chicago. Still married to popular actress Norma Talmadge, Schenck was a powerful man who also had a hand in banking and real estate. He recently weathered the untimely death of thirty-one-year-old Rudolph Valentino who suffered an infection after undergoing surgery for acute appendicitis and perforated gastric ulcers. Schenck, along with Valentino's trusted manager, S. George Ullman, kept vigil at the stricken actor's deathbed. It was a shaken Schenck who broke the shocking news of Valentino's death to reporters, setting off an unprecedented public frenzy.

- **Irving G. Thalberg**—At twenty-six, Thalberg was the Academy's youngest founding member and the most seriously ill. Part of the MGM triumvirate along with Louis B. Mayer and Harry Rapf, the driven Thalberg was quickly distinguishing himself as the studio's favored producer despite a serious heart condition. His underlings often tapped into his uncanny genius for story telling whenever they needed help. One of Hollywood's most eligible bachelors, he squired around his favorite date, Constance Talmadge. This past New Year's Eve, however, he brought MGM actress Norma Shearer to Mayer's house party. Girlfriends aside, it was his zealous mother who tucked him in at night and doled out his meds.

- **Harry M. Warner**—As top man at Warner Bros., Harry had his share of headaches. The studio took a financial hit when their first major foray into sound with Barrymore's *Don Juan* (1926) didn't pull in enough profits to cover its cost. Teetering on bankruptcy, Harry nixed any future attempts at making silent movies heard. Brother Sam, a motivated sound advocate, was so disgruntled he accepted a position under Adolph Zukor at Paramount. When the family ganged up on him, however, Sam relented, remaining with his brothers and their financially troubled studio. He soon convinced Harry to take a half-million-dollar gamble, which would ultimately save the studio and turn the film industry inside out.

- **Jack L. Warner**—The youngest Warner Brother and Vice President in Charge of Production, Jack remained at odds with Harry over the running of their studio and anything else he could think of. Closest to his brother Sam, the two men often teamed up on their filmmaking projects. It was Jack who signed stage actor George Jessel for the lead in Sam's new talking picture. When the actor demanded more money for singing on-screen, Jack let him go and turned to entertainer Eddie Cantor who refused the part. The four battling brothers managed to unite momentarily in the summer of 1926 in honor of their parents' golden wedding anniversary—it would be the four men's last official celebration together.

THE DIRECTORS

- **Cecil B. DeMille**—One of Hollywood's most highly regarded directors, DeMille was just finishing up work on another biblical epic, *King of Kings* (1927) written by Jeanie Macpherson. By now, he had left Paramount and the tight-fisted Zukor to establish his own production company, DeMille Pictures Corporation. His brother, William, soon joined him. Sinking $2,500,000 into the *King of Kings*, DeMille was once again accused of flagrant spending. As his company struggled to meet its financial obligations, the private DeMille juggled three women—his wife, Constance, who continued to immerse herself in charity work, and his two main mistresses, the ever-faithful Macpherson and actress Julia Faye.
- **Henry King**—The director who once risked a climb to Mt. Vesuvius was now working for producer Samuel Goldwyn. King's first film with Goldwyn was the classic mother-daughter drama *Stella Dallas* (1925) featuring Belle Bennett who supposedly gained weight for the role. Just released under the Goldwyn banner was another one of King's major films, *The Winning of Barbara Worth* (1926) with the now popular mustachioed man, Ronald Colman. Shot on location

in northern Nevada's Black Rock Desert, the company built a town for filming purposes and set up tents to accommodate living arrangements for more than 1,000 people. The group affectionately referred to their new settlement as "Barbara Worth."

- **Frank Lloyd**—The Scottish-born director was currently working at Paramount with flapper Clara Bow on the romantic drama *Children of Divorce* (1927). In addition to making movies, he had recently been in charge of an elaborate Fourth of July pageant that took place the summer before. He worked with members of the Chamber of Commerce to stage the celebration at Los Angeles's Coliseum where famous people and moments from U.S. history were remembered. An outdoorsman, he also enjoyed flying, golfing, hunting, fishing and horseback riding. When his good friend actor Wallace Beery married actress Aleta Gillman, the nuptials took place at Lloyd's home with the director giving away the bride.

- **Fred Niblo**—The former world traveler and theatrical entertainer had some pretty impressive films under his directorial belt—*The Mark of Zorro* (1920) and *The Three Musketeers* (1921) both with the swashbuckling Douglas Fairbanks, as well as *Blood and Sand* (1922) starring the late lover Rudolph Valentino. He also helmed MGM's first epic, *Ben-Hur: A Tale of the Christ* (1925). A Mayer favorite, Niblo was also known for his fine public speaking skills. A much-sought-after master of ceremonies, he hosted many high-profile Hollywood events like the official opening of Sid Grauman's Egyptian Theater. Niblo and his actress wife, Enid Bennett, recently added son Peter to their still growing family.

- **John M. Stahl**—The MGM director's latest release was a romantic drama called *The Gay Deceiver* (1926). The movie starred actor Lew Cody as a French matinée idol surrounded by scandal. Several weeks later Stahl dealt with his own personal drama. His wife of twelve years, Irene, collapsed in early November 1926 at the Ambassador Hotel where the couple lived. One week after undergoing surgery, she unexpectedly died in the hospital. The widower would soon leave Mayer and MGM to start his own production company with Tiffany Pictures. The company would be renamed Tiffany-Stahl as the director temporarily traded in the megaphone for a producer's hat.

- **Raoul Walsh**—Back at Fox, Walsh's classic war drama *What Price Glory* (1926) was now playing to enthusiastic audiences. The realistic battle scenes complete with teeth-rattling explosions so disturbed the neighbors during filming that, on several occasions, they called the police. According to Walsh, an assistant would take the blame and then be arrested. Once the fall guy was carted off to jail, Walsh would resume working. At least one man, twenty-five-year-old actor Jack Fay, died from injuries received during filming. Walsh's private life was just as chaotic. He and his wife, actress Miriam Cooper, were in the midst of a bitter divorce. She claimed that her wayward husband admitted "he never should have married."

THE ACTORS

- **Richard Barthelmess**—Despite his insistence that his marriage was not over, Barthelmess' wife, dancer Mary Hay, filed for divorce once she got to Paris. The marriage officially ended on January 15, 1927. Custody arrangements for their daughter, Mary, stated she must spend six months of the year with each parent. At the moment, however, the two-year-old girl was living with Barthelmess while her mother was away. Despite the scandal, Barthelmess remained one of the public's favorite matinée idols. He was soon to be seen on-screen in one of his best films, *The Patent Leather Kid* (1927), which explored the world of boxing—both the good and the bad.

- **Douglas Fairbanks**—Everyone's favorite sword-wielding swashbuckler was between pictures. Fairbanks's last release was *The Black Pirate* (1926) with actress Billie Dove. His next film would be *The Gaucho* (1927), which placed him opposite sizzling teen Lupe Velez. At the studio, he worked out in a private gymnasium that boasted the latest exercise equipment, as well as a personal trainer. He also relaxed in his own Turkish bath where he entertained guests, such as Chaplin, Barrymore and even the King of Thailand. Married to "America's Sweetheart," Mary Pickford, for the past seven years, the actor and actress were Hollywood's first super couple and treated like royals wherever they went.

- **Jack Holt**—Brawny star of the silent saddle, Holt was riding high at Paramount. Starring in several adaptations of author Zane Grey's western novels, he epitomized the Hollywood cowboy and was known off-screen for his highly skilled polo playing. Due to his energetic approach to the game, he often took spills from his horse causing his friends to rib him about wearing a parachute while he played. He recently finished filming *The Mysterious Rider* (1927) starring in the role of Grey's Western hero, Bent Wade. At home, Holt was still married to Margaret, his wife of ten years, and raising three children, stepdaughter Imogene, seven-year-old son Charles John, Jr. and daughter Elizabeth, six.

- **Harold Lloyd**—The man with the glasses was one of Hollywood's highest paid actors pulling in about $40,000 per week, or $2,000,000 each year. His just-released comedy, *The Kid Brother* (1927), proved to be Lloyd's favorite of all his films and his last motion picture with his popular leading lady, Jobyna Ralston. After losing two directors, one to other contractual obligations and another to illness, Lloyd took over directing responsibilities along with his brother, Gaylord, who acted as his assistant. Now a member of the Masons, Lloyd and his wife, former actress Mildred Davis, were building a home in Beverly Hills. The lavish estate, eventually known as Greenacres, would include a dozen gardens with as many fountains.

- **Conrad Nagel**—The handsome blue-eyed, blond actor was one of MGM's busiest leading men. In 1926, he starred in six features beginning with *Dance Madness*, which was released on January 4, 1926, and ending with *Tin Hats*, which hit theaters on November 28, 1926. Nagel was just as hardworking in 1927. Currently filming *Heaven on Earth*, the movie was slated to begin its run on March 5, 1927. He starred in five more productions that same year. His last film released in 1927 was a Warner Bros. feature, *If I Were Single*, costarring actress Myrna Loy. The tired actor lived in Beverly Hills with his wife, Ruth Helms, and six-year-old daughter Ruth Margaret.

- **Mary Pickford**—The most powerful woman in Hollywood, Pickford continued acting in and producing films for United Artists. Her latest movie, *Sparrows* (1926), in which the thirty-five-year-old actress played yet another impoverished child, proved to be a classic. At home, she and Douglas Fairbanks lived a hectic life on their eighteen-acre Beverly Hills estate, Pickfair. Second in popularity only to the White House, their magical home drew VIPs from around the world including lady flyer Amelia Earhart, scientist Albert Einstein and Sherlock Holmes creator Sir Arthur Conan Doyle. Kings and queens, dukes and duchesses, lords and ladies from Alba to Vienna came calling on America's favorite couple.

- **Milton Sills**—A newlywed, Sills had just divorced his first wife, Gladys, in a California court and, the very next day, married actress Doris Kenyon in Ausable Forks, New York. Following their honeymoon, Sills had recently returned to Hollywood where he was building a home in Brentwood Heights. The new Mrs. Sills would soon leave for New York due to her pregnancy. On-screen, Sills' film *The Silent Lover* (1926) was currently in theaters while his next movie, *The Sea Tiger*, was scheduled for release on February 27, 1927. The drama, written by Carey Wilson and based on a novel by author Mary Heaton Vorse, paired up the scholarly actor with leading lady Mary Astor.

THE WRITERS

- **Joseph W. Farnham**—One of the top nine title writers in the film industry, Farnham was the wordsmith behind many of Hollywood's greatest films such as *Charley's Aunt* (1925) and *The Big Parade* (1925). His most recent titles were featured in the comedy *Tell It to the Marines* (1926) starring Lon Chaney. In one scene where Farnham described a newly enlisted private named George Robert "Skeet" Burns, he wrote: "The greatest public improvement ever made to Kansas City was when George Burns left to join the marines." Farnham, a former newspaperman, recently signed a contract that reserved his pen exclusively for MGM films. He even had a sandwich named after him in the studio commissary.

- **Benjamin F. Glazer**—Another MGM writer who had been with Mayer before the merger, Glazer had recently finished penning those sweltering love scenes between actor John Gilbert and his leading lady Greta Garbo in her breakout role as Felicitas in *Flesh and the Devil* (1926). With a big box office hit to brag about, Glazer was now recognized as one of the motion picture industry's finest photoplaywrights. His most recent credit, just released on New Year's Day, was *The Lady in Ermine* (1927). He was now working on *7th Heaven* (1927), which would soon prove to be one of his greatest efforts. It wouldn't be long, however, before he dropped his pen and plunged into the hectic role of producer.

- **Jeanie Macpherson**—Still working and cuddling with DeMille, the pretty Macpherson's current project was *The King of Kings* (1927), scheduled for an April release date. Highly paid for her writing services, she was also in charge of DeMille's scenario department where she not only developed photoplays, but also worked on the set alongside the intimidating director. Macpherson recently told the press: "It is on the sets, as production on a picture progresses, that the photoplay is completed and made to faithfully cling together. It is there that director, supervisor, star and scenarist get together in informal confab to thrash out the various situations of a picture."

- **Bess Meredyth**—One of several women leading the writing pack in Hollywood, Meredyth was a top scenarist at Warner Bros. After working in Italy on MGM's spectacle, *Ben-Hur: A Tale of the Christ* (1925), she signed a lucrative contract with Warner Bros. There, she recently penned the soon-to-be released *Don Juan* (1926) featuring the dashing and bottle-bearing John Barrymore. Her next film, *When a Man Loves* (1927), was another historical romance with Barrymore once more the lover and hero. Newly divorced from actor-husband Wilfred Lucas, and raising her son, John, Meredyth had just met someone new—Hungarian director Mihály Kertész who was also employed by Warner Bros.

- **Carey Wilson**—Now working as a scenarist for First National, Wilson's latest feature, *The Sea Tiger* (1927), starred highbrow actor Milton Sills. Wilson believed that a good photoplay included five important pieces—a solid theme; story advancement through pantomime; a good plot that depicts the theme by manipulating the characters and storyline; characters with individuality that demonstrate the human touch; and finally, development as the story builds from the beginning to its climax or crisis. At home, the writer was still married to wife Nancy. In addition to their six-year-old daughter, Nancy Hope, the couple recently welcomed a new son, Carey Anthony, Jr.

- **Frank E. Woods**—At sixty-six years old, Woods was the Academy's oldest founding member. In 1922, he had resigned from his position with Famous Players-Lasky to team up with two other writers, Elmer Harris and Thompson Buchanan. The three men established their own production company, Associated Authors. Their films would be released through the Allied Producers and Distributors Corporation, a subsidiary of United Artists where Woods' old boss, D.W. Griffith, was a partner. Woods' brother, Arthur, was now a research director for Douglas Fairbanks and had worked on several of the swashbucklers including *Robin Hood* (1922) and *The Thief of Baghdad* (1926) ensuring their historical accuracy.

THE GUARDIANS

- **Frederick W. Beetson**—As secretary of the MPPDA, Beetson had recently returned from New York where negotiations concerning open versus closed union shops were started, averting a strike by studio craftsmen. The Central Casting Corporation was celebrating its first anniversary and, for the month of January 1927, placed over 30,000 extras in the movies. Beetson also faced censorship issues. He, along with major producers, soon pledged that movies would no longer contain profanity, disrespect clergymen or deride the U.S. Constitution—in particular the prohibition amendment. The group also promised to clean up their billboards. The "Don'ts and Be Carefuls" were about to kick in.

- **George W. Cohen**—By now, Cohen had been with the law firm of Loeb and Loeb for almost three years. Married and the father of a two-year-old son, Cohen had become firmly entrenched in the legal wranglings of the motion picture industry. Louis B. Mayer called upon his trusted lawyers, Loeb and Cohen, to develop a solid constitution and practical by-laws for the organization he envisioned. The attorneys worked closely with the Academy's original founders clearly documenting their intent, duties and responsibilities, officer election guidelines, membership rules and a formal method for conducting meetings, as well as creating amendments. They then submitted the completed paperwork to the state of California.

- **Edwin J. Loeb**—The law firm of Loeb and Loeb counted among their clients Sam Goldwyn, Carl Laemmle, Charlie Chaplin, Mary Pickford and Douglas Fairbanks. They also represented Louis B. Mayer and Irving Thalberg and assisted with the legalities concerning the establishment of MGM. Loeb and his wife, Bessie, were parents of two girls, thirteen-year-old Marjorie and ten-year-old Virginia. Loeb had recently handled a case for B.P. Fineman, general manager of Film Booking Offices (FBO) Studios, Inc. Fineman was embroiled in a lawsuit with actress Peggy Udall who charged him with "overfriendliness." He countered by saying Udall tried to force him into giving her a contract. Another case of Hollywood "he said . . . she said."

THE TECHIES

- **Joseph Arthur Ball**—In early 1927, Ball and his team of color engineers were still attempting to capture on film that mulish blue hue. The current two-color (red and green) process was workable, but could be much improved upon by adding a third color. The high cost of color film and its quality also remained problematic for filmmakers. After completing his work on *The Black Pirate* (1926) featuring Douglas Fairbanks, Ball was back in the lab attempting to improve the film itself. His team perfected a new dye-transfer process, which involved the use of specially prepared gelatin, preventing the film from buckling. At home, the thirty-two-year-old Ball and his wife were soon expecting their first child.

- **Cedric Gibbons**—Brought in by Louis B. Mayer to head MGM's Art Department, Gibbons ran his sector like an architectural office. Many of his staff members were actual architects and draftsmen that were organized into several distinct groups. A supervisor who reported directly to Gibbons ran each area. While he encouraged imaginative sets, accuracy was also important. Gibbons established an extensive library at the studio that included detailed books on art and architecture from around the world. Now in his mid-thirties and recently divorced from first wife Gwendolyn, Gibbons was an uncle to his sister's teenage daughter, Veronica, whom everyone called Rocky.

- **Roy J. Pomeroy**—With his knack for working on-screen magic, Pomeroy was an all-important figure at Paramount. As a result, he was appointed chairman of a special committee formed by several major studios, including Paramount and MGM, to analyze different sound systems. In addition, he would soon be working on one of Paramount's most important features, *Wings* (1927), starring Clara Bow. The Great War drama, directed by former World War I aviator William Wellman, realistically depicted aerial battle scenes. Thanks to Pomeroy, the buzzing planes and booming explosions were recorded and played back by technicians who synchronized the sound as the movie played.

A LITTLE SUNSHINE

- **Sid Grauman**—They didn't call Sid Grauman "Little Sunshine" for nothing. Small in stature and always smiling, he was one of filmdom's most prominent figures. His lavish theaters were now focal points for the evolving movie industry. Stars, directors, producers, all sought his favor. Everyone wanted their films premiered at one of his over-the-top establishments. In addition to being President of United Artists Theater Chain, the always upbeat Grauman was busy with the construction of yet another theater. This new movie palace was located on Hollywood Boulevard a few blocks down from the Egyptian Theater. Grauman's Chinese Theater was destined to become his most memorable.

These 36 men and women realized that a daunting challenge was before them as they came together at the Ambassador Hotel. The industry they had shaped from novelty to art form was in trouble.

All together now, it was show time!

Chapter Seventeen

LET'S GO ON WITH THE SHOW!

L os Angeles' Ambassador Hotel was only six years old in 1927, and considered a favorite Hollywood hotspot. Situated on Wilshire Boulevard between Catalina and Mariposa, the hotel was also home to a world-famous nightclub, the Cocoanut Grove, where nimble-footed celebrities often danced the night away. Frequented by the rich and famous, Louis B. Mayer knew the importance of location. He shrewdly chose the popular venue for the banquet he organized on January 11, 1927. Always concerned with that "class factor," he could count on the Ambassador to provide not only an elegant backdrop, but an outstanding meal as well. His guests would be in a receptive mood that night and open to his ideas.

Mayer needn't have worried. The enthusiastic group was already in tune with what was being proposed. After impassioned speeches by Mayer, Nagel and Niblo, each guest was given a chance to talk about their personal vision of this organized entity, as well as their own interests and any specific activities that they each might support. These 36 individuals, now joined together as founders of the Academy, unanimously agreed to continue meeting informally in the coming months to develop further details, as well as a constitution and by-laws. It is believed that Nagel, either at this meeting or one that soon followed, also suggested the name "International Academy of Motion Picture Arts and Sciences" for the new association.

Following some discussion, the founders agreed to the title, but only after dropping the word "International." According to Pierre Norman Sands who documented those early years:

> . . . the title "Academy of Motion Picture Arts and Sciences" reflected their convictions that the organization should represent all facets of motion picture production both in the arts and sciences. They also believed that this particular title would properly reflect the dignity and honor of a profession considered by them to be the equal of other creative fields of endeavor.

By May, the industrious group had been officially recognized by the State of California and was planning another banquet—this time at the Biltmore Hotel. Located in Pershing Square in downtown Los Angeles, the luxury hotel opened in 1923. It was the largest hotel west of Chicago at that time and another favorite gathering place of Hollywood's elite. The founders invited a cross-section of 300 men and women from the motion picture industry to the Biltmore on May 11, 1927 to discuss the Academy and what they hoped to achieve within the industry. According to the invitation:

> If we producing workers, actors, directors, technicians, cinematographers and producing executives who have the future progress of this great universal entertainment at heart, will now join unselfishly into one big concerted movement, we will be able to effectually accomplish

those essential things which we have hitherto neglected. We can take aggressive action in meeting outside attacks that are unjust. We can promote harmony and solidarity among our membership and among our different branches. We can reconcile any internal differences that may exist or arise. We can adopt such ways and means as are proper to further the welfare and protect the honor and good repute of our profession. We can encourage the improvement and advancement of the arts and sciences of our profession by the interchange of constructive ideas and by awards of merit for distinctive achievements. We can take steps to develop the greater power and influence of the screen.

That night, the founders stuck together. They all sat side-by-side at one very long table that stood in the front of the room. Guests were seated at much smaller round tables, each adorned with a colorful flower arrangement, set up throughout the banquet hall. Under the direction of the Academy's first President Douglas Fairbanks and Vice President Fred Niblo, the founders made it perfectly clear that the attendees were invited as their guests and under no pressure to join that day. They were simply there to enjoy a meal and hear about the newly formed group. Speakers included Cecil B. DeMille who reminded all present of the considerable power and influence they wielded. The founders must have made a strong impression. Of the 300 that attended, 231 signed up on the spot and paid their $100 dues to M.C. Levee, the Academy's first Treasurer while Secretary Frank E. Woods took notes.

Enough money was collected to fund the Academy's first offices on Hollywood Boulevard. By the following November, their headquarters were ensconced down the street at the brand new Roosevelt Hotel that had just opened its doors six months earlier. The Spanish-style building was named after President Theodore Roosevelt and financially backed by a group of investors that included Mary Pickford, Douglas Fairbanks and Louis B. Mayer.

Multiple committees were also established to accomplish specific goals. With writer Frank E. Woods actively involved, the Conciliation Committee was formed to settle disputes. Scholarly actor Milton Sills headed up the Committee on College Affairs and worked with members including Cecil B. DeMille, Irving Thalberg, Joseph Arthur Ball and Roy Pomeroy to ensure future filmmakers would have the advantage of a formal education. The Standards Committee was tasked with identifying industry-wide policies and practices. A committee chaired by Cedric Gibbons was also formed to design the Academy's Award of Merit Program; Sid Grauman, Bess Meredyth, Richard Barthelmess and Henry King were also part of his team.

And as if tackling all of these initiatives wasn't enough, by the fall of 1927, the Warner Brothers premiered *The Jazz Singer*, the first feature-length film with synchronized dialogue spoken in between songs that were sung by entertainer Al Jolson. When audiences heard Jolson ad lib: "Wait a minute, wait a minute! You ain't heard nothin' yet!," they hung on every audible syllable.

After *The Jazz Singer*, the expressive silent pictures seemed stiff and outdated. Spectators were no longer content to simply watch—they wanted to listen. Sound, however, meant industry-wide changes and many of Hollywood's top leaders like Jesse Lasky and Irving Thalberg maintained that "talkies" were no more than a temporary whim. People would soon tire of hearing their favorite players speak and filming would return to the silent norm of business as usual. Within a matter of months, these same men had to face facts: sound was here to stay and there was no going back.

Sound, however, meant a whole new way of doing business. Sound-proof stages had to be built to keep out unwanted noises while filming. Stationary microphones were now planted among flowers or concealed behind various props around the sets. Actors had to remain within range or their lines would be inaudible. Cameras stood still as they were enclosed inside soundproof booths causing many a cameraman to swelter. A new employee called a "sound mixer" sat in a small room behind glass listening to every line of dialogue on a headset. If the talking didn't meet his approval, he spoke up causing many delays and limitless irritation for the directors.

Wardrobe had to alter costumes making sure to use material that wouldn't rustle. Set directors had to re-evaluate their construction to minimize echoes and extraneous sounds. Directors could no longer use their megaphones or give pertinent pointers while the cameras were rolling. Writers had to rethink their screenplays adding dialogue where once pantomime sufficed. Even film editors had to learn how to work with dialogue so they didn't cut important lines. Nervous actors either learned to talk in front of a camera or they were out of a job. Studio musicians who normally provided mood music fell victims to progress. Finally, theaters all over the world that had made it their business to run silent films now had to be wired for sound or face closing their doors.

The Academy responded to the technical issues that accompanied the sound revolution. Their technical committee with Joseph Arthur Ball, Irving Thalberg, M.C. Levee and Fred Beetson took on three critical issues: camera noise, improved set materials, and stage construction, along with the buzzing of the arc lights.

Meetings were held exclusively to discuss the impacts of sound on the industry as the *L.A. Times* reported on September 23, 1928:

> The academy has been holding a series of conferences on the subject of talking pictures, which have been very actively and largely attended. . . .
>
> One report has already been published on the investigations into the subject of incandescent illumination, which occupied the attention of the body for four or five months. This deals extensively with the cost of this new form of lighting, the use of which in studios has been stimulated through the academy efforts. It also takes up the problems of photography, make-up and the like which have been induced by the change from the old form of arc lighting. Practically all studios

now use the incandescents in a majority of sets. They are virtually a necessity for sound pictures.

The impression is gleaned from all this that the academy is providing by degrees a clearinghouse for the exchange of ideas in the industry. And while a great many of the subjects dealt with have little of interest for the public at large, they are of enormous value to the industry, and it is surmised will lead to economies and other benefits in the making of pictures.

The Academy of Motion Pictures Arts and Sciences was off to a running start with forward-thinking founders and committed members who wanted to secure not just the industry, but also the art form for future generations to come. And those original men and women who got the ball rolling still had a lot more to offer.

Part Three

BABY, TAKE A BOW!

Chapter Eighteen

SCHOLARS, TOUGH GUYS AND BISHOPS

atinée idol Milton Sills valued education. A former college professor, now considered one of Hollywood's most steadfast leading men, Sills believed that the motion picture industry, in order to remain successful, must be passed on to a new generation of formally trained filmmakers. It's no wonder that he chaired the Academy's Committee on College Affairs. Sills assisted with the development of the groundbreaking curriculum at the University of Southern California (USC) where a new four-year program dedicated to the technical training of filmmakers began in the fall of 1927. Students would not only earn their degrees, but would also be given a chance to work in the studios. According to Dr. Karl T. Waugh, USC Dean of the College of Liberal Arts:

As is the case with all newly-evolved and rapidly growing enterprises, the motion-picture industry has been manned largely by those found readiest, who seemed to have some of the qualifications desired. It is now beyond the experimental stage, and has arrived at the point where success in the various lines of motion-picture work is to be achieved only by those who have made the most thorough and careful preparation for the work, and who have the best practical and cultural backgrounds for the tasks to be undertaken.

At work, Sills was in his third year under contract with First National Pictures where he continued to star in various dramatic roles that kept movie patrons returning to the theaters. His abundant fan mail flooded the studio's mailroom while his personal appearances created chaos. During a visit to Chicago, rowdy female admirers mobbed him just outside the Stevens Hotel. Security men came to the rescue and escorted the disheveled actor into the building where another crowd of ladies anxiously awaited their hero.

One of Sills' final pictures for First National was *His Captive Woman* (1929) adapted for the screen by scenarist Carey Wilson. The film was originally released in its silent form on February 3, 1929 and then again with sound a few months later—a common practice for studios at that time. Most theaters were not yet equipped to run talkies, and to ensure success at the box office, it was necessary to release two versions—one with sound and one without.

At home, Sills and his new wife had a son, Kenyon Clarence, born on May 6, 1927. The family lived in Brentwood Heights on an estate they called "El Sueño" (The Dream). His daughter, Dorothy, recalled that the newly built home was situated in the middle of a deserted area where wild coyotes gave chase to scampering rabbits. The house had a large library where the actor kept thousands of books, a private tennis court where he practiced a favorite sport and an elaborate garden for his carefully cultivated plants.

Sometime after filming *Love and The Devil* (1929) with Hungarian actress Maria Corda, Sills suffered what the press termed a "nervous breakdown." His wife took him to New York where he was admitted to a sanitarium in Westchester County. Kenyon, who declined to discuss the specifics of her husband's malady, blamed his illness on overwork. Once he was released from the hospital, a much thinner Sills spent most of his time golfing and relaxing with friends and family. One year later, a stronger Sills returned to moviemaking—this time with the Fox Film Corporation.

As sound transformed the movie industry, Sills had little to worry about. Unlike many of his contemporaries who couldn't progress into a talking world, his professionally trained stage voice came across well on-screen. His first film for Fox was a crime drama mixed with a little music—an innovative gimmick in those early days of sound. *Man Trouble* (1930) paired him up with former Ziegfeld girl Dorothy Mackaill. Sills was such a hit as the hard-hearted nightclub owner who falls for the pretty lass that Fox offered him a long-term contract. Now assured of his leading man status, his second picture for Fox was *The Sea Wolf* (1929) based on an adventure novel by author Jack London. Sills, in one of his finest roles, played no-nonsense sea captain Wolf Larsen. With his compelling performances and his equally strong voice, it wasn't sound that ended Sills' career—it was an unreliable heart.

Six days before his latest picture was scheduled for release, Sills was on his tennis court. The forty-eight-year-old star wasn't particularly well that day, but still felt up to lobbing the ball with his wife, daughter and her friend, Ted Lawton. Despite the pain he felt in his left shoulder, he continued with his game until he suddenly collapsed. Lawton and scenarist John Goodrich, a long-time friend who was also visiting that day, carried Sills into the house. Medical help was summoned but despite their best efforts, the emergency team could not revive Hollywood's pet highbrow.

Felled by a heart attack and the first founding member to lose his life, Sills' unexpected death on September 15, 1930 shocked Hollywood and left his fans stunned. Sills' final movie, *Sea Wolf*, debuted two days after his funeral. The well-received talking picture would have assured the silent matinée idol a solid future in the new world of sound.

Adjusting to sound was something most Hollywood heavyweights had to contend with regardless of their job descriptions. Title writers like Joseph Farnham found themselves on the verge of extinction. If they couldn't write dialogue, they were out of work. Still considered one of the best in his field, Farnham penned titles for eighteen movies in 1927 alone.

In addition to the Academy, Farnham was also a founding member of a new organization established exclusively for title writers—the Titular Bishops. It was an elite group with only nine members who earned anywhere from $50,000 to $150,000 each year. Made up mostly of former newspapermen, these individuals rose to the top of their ranks and were known for their extravagant lifestyles. One member, Malcolm Stuart Boylan, wrote about the group in an article for the *New York Times*:

> . . . The membership clings jealously to the original nine, and to break into the sacred membership is no more difficult than getting into the College of Cardinals. . . . but the screen is a fickle mistress and tomorrow a distressing phenomenon may take place. The enchanted nine may haul up at their several studios to find that nine other young upstarts, heretofore unknown, are seated on the inflated cushions. Then, perhaps, there will be a membership drive for the Titular Bishops and a refurbishing of Rolls-Royces to make them last another year.

In 1928, Farnham was still creating titles with thirteen films to his name. The next year, his multiple title writing credits were topped off with a scenario about university life, *So This is College* (1929) featuring actors Robert Montgomery and Elliott Nugent. The two men played college senior football players, Biff and Eddie, who were best friends, as well as roommates, until flapper Babs Baxter came between them. She not only jeopardized their friendship, but also the school's biggest football game.

That same year, the Academy honored Farnham with an Award of Merit for Best Writing (Title Cards) at their first annual award ceremony.

He took top honors for the titles he penned in *Fair Co-Ed* (1927), *Laugh Clown, Laugh* (1928), and *Telling the World* (1928). It was the one and only time that the Academy designated an award for this category as sound soon replaced silence and made title writing obsolete, which brings to mind another distinction Farnham holds. Still working for MGM, but now developing dialogue, the forty-seven-year-old writer also died from heart disease on June 3, 1931 at his Beverly Hills home, making him the first Award of Merit winner to die.

Producer Irving Thalberg also had a bad heart and one of his favorite girls, comedienne Constance Talmadge, broke it. The party girl wasn't interested in settling down with a film executive like her sister, Norma, so she ended their romance. Thalberg consoled himself by squiring several starlets around Hollywood, including a young actress from Montreal by the name of Norma Shearer. He thought Shearer had on-screen potential and put her under contract at MGM. Shearer referred to herself as "Irving's spare tire"—he only asked her out when no one else was available.

Shearer, however, was smitten and made up her mind to one day marry the boss. Eventually, Thalberg noticed. He especially admired her individualism—like the time she sported a shocking red dress at a ball where the ladies were specifically told to wear white. He liked her devotion to the movies. He was also impressed when the clever Shearer went out of her way to make friends with his mother, Henrietta, and sister Sylvia.

One afternoon, the practical Thalberg called Shearer into his office and presented her with a tray of diamond rings. She simply picked one out—a large blue marquis and the deed was done. They married shortly thereafter on September 29, 1927. Shearer's brother, Douglas, gave the bride away with Mayer acting as best man and Sylvia maid of honor. After a brief honeymoon on the Monterey Peninsula, Shearer moved into her husband's home where Henrietta ruled.

The newlyweds stayed in separate bedrooms as Mama Thalberg took care of her son, the way she always had. Despite her mother-in-law's shortcomings, Shearer liked being part of Hollywood's upper echelon and her status at the studio took a leap. Shearer often got the plum roles much to the dismay of other MGM actresses. Joan Crawford once moaned. "How can I compete with Norma when she sleeps with the boss?" Not on Henrietta's watch.

Shortly after the Thalberg-Shearer nuptials, *The Jazz Singer* (1927) debuted. Initially, Thalberg wasn't impressed, but he soon realized that talking pictures were not just a passing fad. If MGM wanted to remain on top, they had to make themselves heard. It was unfamiliar ground and Thalberg needed someone he could trust. His brother-in-law, Doug Shearer, had an engineering background so Thalberg put him in charge of a new sound department. MGM then officially began the multifaceted process of upgrading their silent film studio to a modern moviemaking facility.

Once Thalberg realized the benefits of sound, he took things further. Instead of just dialogue, he wanted ringing telephones and slamming doors. Then came the challenge of MGM's first all-talking picture, *Broadway Melody* (1929), a singing and dancing extravaganza. When Thalberg viewed the final cut, he wasn't happy with one of the musical numbers and ordered it reshot. Doug Shearer suggested that they use the original sound recording and sync it up with the new action—effectively cutting the cost of recalling an entire live orchestra. As a result, the first playback system was devised and Thalberg triumphed with an Academy Award for Best Picture.

That year, in addition to converting the studio to sound, Thalberg was responsible for the production of approximately fifty pictures. During pre-production, he met with directors and writers, meticulously going over each script. He approved the players, costumes and sets. He also took charge of publicity and advertising. During filming, he oversaw the budget and settled disputes. He also resolved production issues giving advice to his crew when they asked and sometimes when they didn't.

Once the movie was finished, he stepped in again. "Movies aren't made, they're remade," he acknowledged altering the old adage "writing is re-writing." Thalberg perfected the post-production previews, which ran in front of test audiences. Their reactions would then be carefully measured.

If people voiced dissatisfaction, scenes were reshot, even if the sets had to be rebuilt and the entire cast reassembled. In addition to his demanding day job, he also sat on the Academy's Producers-Technicians Joint Committee as well as the Committee on College Affairs.

At home, Shearer gave birth to a son, Irving Grant, Jr., on August 24, 1930 and the Thalbergs finally moved into a place of their own—away from Henrietta. Then fate smiled even more on Thalberg when he crossed paths with a young unknown, Clark Gable. He cast the unpolished actor as a gangster in *A Free Soul* (1931), opposite Shearer. This was a pivotal role for Gable. As Shearer's leading man, the script required him to shove her down. Surprisingly, audiences loved the rough stuff and a new kind of movie hero emerged.

Thalberg went on making box office history with *Grand Hotel* (1932) and its all-star cast. Up until then, it was considered a waste of talent to have more than two famous players in the same movie. For this film, however, Thalberg insisted that an MGM star portray each of the main characters. He cast John and Lionel Barrymore, along with Greta Garbo, Joan Crawford and Wallace Beery. The film cost over $700,000 but it not only made money for the studio, it claimed another Best Picture Award of Merit.

By 1932, MGM was financially sound, but due to the Great Depression, profits were down. With an annual salary of $500,000, Thalberg continued churning out successful pictures. His relationship with Mayer, however, was strained. Thalberg believed that Mayer and his New York boss, Nicholas Schenck, now top man at Loew's, Inc., were getting rich off of his accomplishments. As for Mayer, he felt threatened by Thalberg's growing power over the studio.

Thalberg's grueling schedule continued but physically, he was wearing down. On September 5, 1932, the untimely death of his friend and MGM colleague, producer Paul Bern, from a reportedly self-inflicted gunshot wound, devastated Thalberg who just three months earlier, had witnessed Bern's marriage to the glamorous Jean Harlow. The resulting rumors of Bern's impotency were even harder to deal with. Thalberg's taxing work responsibilities and his emotional overload took a toll. Often irritable and tired, he wanted nothing more than a relaxing trip to Europe. Besides, he knew that at age 32, he had already outlived his doctors' most optimistic predictions.

It wasn't long before fate intervened. On Christmas morning, 1932, Thalberg was struck at home by another heart attack. This time, his doctors chose not to admit him to the hospital. They just sent him to bed, feeling that rest would do more for him than anything a hospital could offer at the time. Shearer kept everyone away including Henrietta, Mayer and Schenck. By February, Thalberg was feeling well enough to take that long-awaited European cruise.

Before the Thalbergs' departure, Mayer, with Shearer's approval, paid her husband a visit. He explained that in order for MGM to continue running smoothly, Mayer had no choice but to replace him. Mayer chose his son-in-law, David O. Selznick, current head of RKO studios, for the job. Mayer even gave him a unique contract that included freedom from Thalberg's leadership. Unlike the other MGM producers, Selznick would report directly to Mayer and Schenck.

Thalberg was furious. As much as he respected Selznick, he knew he had been undermined. His MGM team agreed and Selznick's presence caused a major rift within the studio. The Thalberg camp supported their ailing leader while Camp Mayer stayed loyal to Louis B.

On June 13, 1933, Thalberg was still relaxing on the French Riviera when he received a telegram from Mayer. MGM had been reorganized. Thalberg's job as Head of Production was eliminated. Mayer's telegram didn't mention that he also offered each of Thalberg's crew their own individual production units. Unknown to Thalberg, the subordinates he left behind would now be his peers.

When Thalberg returned home via New York, he met with Schenck who strategically offered him a filmmaking unit of his own. Schenk also assured the former Head of Production that he would have sole control of his unit and could choose whatever projects he wanted. Loew's headman further explained that due to Thalberg's failing health, no one expected him to carry the same workload as he had before. Most importantly, Thalberg would not report to Mayer, but directly to Schenck.

The deposed Thalberg had his own agenda, however. He wanted to film the story of *Marie Antoinette* starring Shearer as well as produce a musical version of *The Merry Widow*. Once Schenck gave his blessings to both projects, Thalberg agreed to the new arrangements.

Upon his return to MGM in August 1933, Thalberg discovered the truth. Instead of being in charge of MGM productions, he must now compete with other studio producers including Selznick. Despite his loss of power, Thalberg remained successful producing such classics as *Mutiny on the Bounty* (1935), *The Barretts of Wimpole Street* (1936) and *Marie Antoinette* (1938).

Selznick had his own MGM triumphs including *Dinner at Eight* (1933), which curiously boasted an all-star cast, much like its predecessor, *Grand Hotel* (1932). Mayer's son-in-law knew, however, that he didn't receive the same warmth or loyalty from the staff that Thalberg did and was savvy enough to realize he never would. Against his father-in-law's wishes, he ultimately left MGM to start a production company of his own. Always an admirer of Selznick's high standards, Thalberg quietly invested money in the new venture.

At home, Shearer was once again expecting. When it was time for the baby to come, Shearer, always the protector, refused to disturb her busy husband at work. After their daughter, Katherine, arrived on June 13, 1935, she sent word to the new father that all was well.

Thalberg continued working long hours, often coming home exhausted. Shearer begged him to lessen his workload. His solution was to hold meetings and story conferences at home. Late in the summer of 1936, Thalberg was given a fifty-page summary of Margaret Mitchell's Civil War novel, *Gone With the Wind*. Thalberg liked it, but declined. "No more epics for me now. Just give me a little drawing-room drama. I'm tired. I'm just too tired."

And Thalberg was tired. Rundown, he caught a cold that Labor Day weekend while visiting the Monterey Peninsula. Back home, he was diagnosed with strep throat. Routine treatment failed and he quickly weakened. Shearer brought in a heart specialist from New York who assured everyone that Thalberg's heart was strong, but his health did not improve. Arrangements were made to fly him to the Mayo Clinic where doctors could try a new drug, but he wasn't strong enough to travel.

Within days, his condition grew grave as he coughed up blood and shook with chills. He asked for one of his secretaries and, attempting to humor him, Shearer sent for her. By the time the woman arrived, Thalberg had slipped into a coma. On September 15, 1936, his tired heart allowed one final beat. Always a fighter, he had outlived doctors' original prediction by almost a decade. News of his death hit Hollywood hard.

Two days later, MGM suspended the day's production while Irving Grant Thalberg was laid to rest. Throughout Hollywood, movie productions at other studios paused for a moment of silence. President Roosevelt sent his condolences. "The world of art is poorer with the passing of Irving Thalberg. His high ideals, insight and imagination went into the production of his masterpieces . . ."

During his lifetime, Thalberg refused to allow his name to appear in any of the films he produced. "Credit you give yourself isn't worth having," he explained. His final movie, *The Good Earth* (1937), released after his death, was the only one that carried his name. Mayer authorized a title card to be seen before the credits, which read:

To the Memory of Irving Grant Thalberg
We Dedicate this Picture, His Last Great Achievement.

In 1937, the Academy of Motion Picture Arts and Sciences embodied his memory in a statuette honoring "a creative producer who has been responsible for a consistently high quality of motion picture production." The much-coveted Irving G. Thalberg Memorial Award has been given

Paramount founder, Jesse L. Lasky (Jesse L. Laskey Photo File, The American Heritage Center, University of Wyoming)

Epic-Maker Cecil B. DeMille (Cecile B. DeMille Photo File, The American Heritage Center, University of Wyoming)

Matinée Idol Richard Barthelmess (Edward Levy
Collection, The American Heritage Center, University of
Wyoming)

Hollywood's pet highbrow, actor Milton Sills (Edward Levy Collection, The American Heritage Center, University of Wyoming)

Handsome Conrad Nagel (Edward Levy Collection, The
American Heritage Center, University of Wyoming)

The last founder standing, director Henry King (Henry King Photo File, The American Heritage Center, University of Wyoming)

The man in charge of Warner Bros., Harry M. Warner (L. Kenneth Wilson
Collection, The American Heritage Center, University of Wyoming)

The youngest of the four Warner Brothers, Jack L. Warner (L. Kenneth Wilson Collection, The American Heritage Center, University of Wyoming)

to such distinctive filmmakers as Cecil B. DeMille, Walt Disney, and George Lucas. Even though the award is presented at the Academy Awards ceremony, it's not given out every year—and it doesn't even look like an Oscar. It looks like Irving Thalberg.

While Thalberg was the youngest founding member of the Academy, Frank Woods was the oldest. In addition to being the Academy's first Secretary, he was actively involved in their arbitration process. Woods proudly told journalist Edwin Schallert that within the Academy's first year, approximately thirty disputes were resolved along with fifty informal complaints. He was also happy to report that many legal proceedings were averted due to the Academy's intervention.

Woods also continued his work with the Motion Picture Relief Fund. By mid-1929, many Hollywood employees, including once highly paid actors and directors, were financially strapped. He saw a fifty percent increase in requests for assistance because so many were out of work while studios made the transition to talking pictures. Film production slowed down while sound stages were built and theaters wired to accommodate the latest technology. Woods remained optimistic that once the adjustments were made, production would pick up again and more jobs would become available.

As for new writers, Woods had some very practical advice: Don't submit a manuscript directly to a studio—write a book or a Broadway play first. Studios were always interested in adapting successful works from other mediums for the silver screen. They were not so anxious to do business with unknown penmen. In 1931, Woods further explained the industry's position:

It is impossible now for anyone not an established writer to sell an original story to the studios unless he has some friend inside. The studios simply won't read originals unless they come from established writers. They do not even receive them, but return them unopened. That is because they have had to fight so many suits. Clever crooks . . . would send in stories in which a boy and a girl fell in love with each other and, after a few heartaches, married. They would have proof that they sent such a story to a certain studio on a certain date—knowing that within the next few years that studio was sure to use a story somewhat resembling theirs. The studios simply had to quit reading original stories for self-protection.

The following year, Woods' seventy-seven-year-old brother, Arthur, was still working as a researcher for Douglas Fairbanks when he came down with pneumonia. After three days of battling the virus, he died at home leaving his wife, writer Lotta Woods and a daughter. Five years later, Woods also lost his long-time wife, Ella.

Now alone, Woods lived another two years, but at the age of seventy-nine, died at home on May 1, 1939 after a brief illness. He was remembered by *L.A. Times* columnist Lee Shippey as ". . . always a credit to his much-maligned business, being just as pure of heart and sweet of soul as any minister of the gospel, and I've met plenty who weren't as clean of speech as he was."

A founder and active member of many professional groups including the Writer's Club, the Screen Writers Guild, and as the Academy of Motion Picture Arts and Sciences, Woods was one of Hollywood's most respected citizens. Considered the film industry's first serious film critic, as well as the first writer to pen a feature-length photoplay, *Birth of a Nation* (1915), Woods revolutionized filmmaking. From off-the-cuff ideas to carefully thought out photoplays, "Daddy" Woods not only witnessed the evolution of film, but helped shape those early flickers into an art form.

Compared to Frank Woods, Douglas Fairbanks was a latecomer. He entered the movies in 1916 at the urgings of D.W. Griffith after a successful stage career. Now an international celebrity and first President of the Academy, Fairbanks was married to "America's Sweetheart," Mary Pickford. The couple lived a sumptuous lifestyle at Pickfair—so named by the press.

The eighteen-acre estate was Fairbanks' wedding gift to his wife. As befitted the top box office stars of their time, their hilltop home was situated on Summit Drive in a little-known area to the west of Hollywood called Beverly Hills. Their residence had two large wings with a magnificent view of the Pacific Ocean. On the grounds, a private beach surrounded their oyster-shaped swimming pool. Before long, other film industry giants were building their own mansions nearby and Beverly Hills became a popular place for Hollywood's elite. Party or not, the dinner table was always ready for 15 guests since Fairbanks had a habit of inviting "funny people" to dinner, as Pickford once described her husband's acquaintances.

A golden couple by any standards, the Fairbanks lavished each other with gifts and were inseparable for the first eight years of their marriage. They never spent one night apart. Together, they met the world head-on leading parades, attending dedications and working on charity drives. In between pictures, they traveled around the world. As they partied with royalty and played with aristocrats, the Fairbanks enchanted them all.

Each, however, was driven by their own differences. Pickford felt compelled by the duty that came with her position in Hollywood while Fairbanks just went along for the fun. She enjoyed the movie capital, while he wanted the world. Pickford preferred being home, making films and tending to social functions. A victim of wanderlust, Fairbanks relished adventure, traveling to faroff and exotic places. Eventually, Pickford grew tired of life on the road and wanted to settle down. Bored within the confines of Hollywood, Fairbanks took to traveling alone.

At work, Fairbanks' newest release, *The Gaucho* (1927), had the misfortune of competing with Hollywood's first talking picture, *The Jazz Singer* (1927), which eclipsed most of its silver screen rivals by the sheer novelty of hearing Al Jolson sing while he moved about on-screen. To make matters worse, Fairbanks played an outlaw who had no redeeming qualities, which didn't endear audiences to the character. Of course, he changed for the better by the movie's end because the censors wouldn't have it any other way, but it didn't help at the box office.

His final swashbuckler and last silent film was *The Iron Mask* (1929) where he reprised his role as D'Artagnan. The two had much in common— both still affective, but aging. Their long and successful careers were fading. At the end of *The Iron Mask*, and only after our hero rescued his country and everyone in it, he looked up to see a wispy vision of his co-musketeers who preceded him to the great beyond. They beckoned D'Artagnan to join them. As his body dropped to the ground, his spirit leaped upward, happy to reunite with his brothers, and poignantly marked the end of an era.

By now, Fairbanks was forty-six years old and there was only so much leaping and lunging left in him. Talkies were quickly replacing silent movies, but it wasn't his voice that finished him. He sounded fine. The new medium just didn't suit that grandiose Fairbanks style. After an unusually long run with more successes than most of his peers, his star was simply dimming as was Pickford's who was just getting too old to play the coquettish young girls people wanted to see her as. The super couple filmed one talking picture together, *The Taming of the Shrew* (1929), but ticket sales were down. The Great Depression along with the audience's changing taste didn't help either. Four pictures later, in 1934, our hero stopped making movies altogether.

By now, Fairbanks usually traveled alone. During one such trip to Europe, he met Lady Sylvia Ashley—a title she gained through marriage. As Fairbanks dallied with the still-married Ashley, Pickford kept company with a much younger Buddy Rogers. Despite several half-hearted attempts to patch things up, Hollywood's golden couple remained on shaky ground. Then the Fairbanks-Ashley affair went public when her lordly husband sued for divorce citing Fairbanks as the reason why. A humiliated Pickford reached her breaking point and on December 8, 1933, she sued Fairbanks for divorce claiming mental anguish. Devastated, Fairbanks returned home begging her forgiveness. She refused. Two years later, their divorce was final. Hollywood's royal couple was no more, signaling an end of the era of silent film glory in more ways than one.

Looking for a diversion, Fairbanks traveled to New York with his son, now an actor in his own right. The two men talked of filming a movie together, but one morning when Doug, Jr. was supposed to meet his father for breakfast, the elder Fairbanks had vanished. He had impulsively booked passage for Europe the night before and was already at sea. Shortly after his departure, a telegram arrived for him, and in his absence, the desk clerk gave it to his son. The message was from Pickford. She wanted Fairbanks to come home.

Doug, Jr. frantically searched his father's room for the name of the ship he was sailing on. It took some time to place the call, but when he finally reached his father, Doug, Jr. read him the telegram. Fairbanks didn't believe him. He accused his son of lying and always taking Pickford's side before abruptly hanging up. He continued on to Europe and on March 7, 1936, married Lady Ashley in Paris. The following year, Pickford wed Buddy Rogers.

When the new Mr. and Mrs. Fairbanks returned from abroad, they settled into a quiet life at Fairbanks' Santa Monica beach house—mostly entertaining her friends. Gone were the lavish parties with Chaplin and Barrymore and the dedicated staff that surrounded the once-agile actor. He no longer had an executive suite at the studio, or a gymnasium or a Turkish bath. Now in his fifties, Fairbanks was no longer the top man in Hollywood—something he couldn't accept.

Several weeks after Britain's Prime Minister Neville Chamberlain officially declared war on Germany, 56-year-old Fairbanks suffered a heart attack. A gregarious sportsman who always worked out, he liked being physical and took great pride in his shipshape appearance, so when doctors ordered complete bed rest, Fairbanks found it unthinkable.

Just before midnight on December 11, 1939, he requested that his nurse dim the lights and open the window so he could hear the sounds of the ocean. When asked how he was feeling, he flashed that Fairbanks grin and said: "I've never felt better." Less than two hours later and totally out of character, he peacefully slipped away.

Before Fairbanks, moviegoers had never witnessed so much on-screen action. Whether he was leaping, fencing or cracking that whip, he set the standard for those who had enough nerve to follow. Without his vibrant presence and desire to dazzle, Hollywood's patina would never have shined quite so brightly.

Chapter Nineteen

THREE MEN AND A LADY

Frank Woods knew what he was talking about when he discussed the studios' problems with lawsuits and screenplays. Several months after *The King of Kings* (1927) debuted, former film actress Valeska Suratt brought charges against Cecil B. DeMille and Jeanie Macpherson for stealing her story. She claimed that Macpherson's script closely resembled her own, which DeMille had previously rejected. Suratt wanted one million dollars in damages. The director defended Macpherson, publicly stating that her work was based on well-known information from the bible—not on Suratt's script. The actress lost her case.

After *King of Kings* (1927), Macpherson used her pen to write the photoplay for yet another DeMille drama, *The Godless Girl* (1929). The film starred Lina Basquette and Marie Provost who played high school students who secretly attended atheistic gatherings and ended up in reform school. The school was built on a back lot and then burned down in a spectacular fire as the camera caught dozens of extras, dressed as students, fleeing the structure. Despite some precautions, like spraying the actors' clothes with asbestos, multiple injuries occurred. Basquette claimed her eyebrows were burned and never grew back quite the way they were. The final assault took place at the box office where the blazing film just plain flopped.

Without DeMille, Macpherson took a break from high drama as she worked for Hal Roach, penning *The Devil's Brother* (1933) featuring Stan Laurel and Oliver Hardy as eighteenth century Italian bandit brothers, Stanlio and Ollio. It was the funny men's first foray into comic opera. The movie was such a hit that they tried it again a few years later with *The Bohemian Girl* (1936)—this time without Macpherson who by now was back with her director of choice.

When DeMille began work on *Cleopatra* (1934), yet another of his historical epics, Macpherson left the writing to someone else. She took on the role of head researcher. DeMille put her in charge of 12 people responsible for period architecture, interior design, props, and costumes that would bring ancient Egypt to life. For months, Macpherson and her team read all they could about the Queen of the Nile and the time period she reigned. They visited museums studying everything from hairpins to chariots making sure that any items appearing in the movie would be authentic. Under Macpherson's direction, studio workers recreated every-thing Egyptian from battle gear to palatial rooms to ornate headpieces. If Cleopatra herself had visited the set, she would have felt right at home.

At the studio, Macpherson's unusual office was right next to DeMille's. The walls, lined with logs, gave a rustic impression of cabin life. She worked at an oversized desk, but also had an additional table with chairs and books, books, books. She once described her space as a blend between a workshop, a library and a den. Her typical workday began when she arrived at the studio between nine and ten in the morning. She spent her first hour taking care of correspondence along with routine matters that needed daily attention.

Once she had an idea, she ran it by DeMille. If he liked it, she drafted a solid story always centered on a specific theme. A stickler for details, she spent long hours researching information needed to ensure her manuscript's authenticity. When she was finally ready to compose the actual photoplay, Macpherson preferred to write it out on paper and then let her secretary type it. After a day of writing, she often conferred with DeMille in the evening, staying as long as it took to get the job done. Her drawn-out days and DeMille's impatience didn't leave much time for the inspirational muse, as she once explained:

> . . . While other authors gave themselves long vacations to woo inspiration, I sat and worked at my desk. I have found that if a director and a picture company are waiting for you to write a story for them, and you know that each day you delay means a wasting of their time and money, you're very apt to produce the goods. Wooing inspiration is a long and thankless pastime. For the more one woos her, the farther away she flies. So I sit at my desk and work. . . .

Remaining with DeMille, Macpherson worked on adventure films like *The Crusades* (1935), which told the story of Richard the Lionhearted and *The Buccaneer* (1938) starring Frederic March as the pirate Jean Lafitte. In the late thirties, Macpherson traveled to Rome to work with Italian producer Vittorio Mussolini, the son of "Il Duce," on one of his ill-fated film ventures.

In 1939, Macpherson and DeMille created a movie made up of a series of scenes from various other films depicting the history of the United States from pre-Revolutionary days through the current year. Some of the footage came from classics like *Billie the Kid* (1930) with Johnny Mack Brown, *San Francisco* (1936) with Clark Gable and *The Story of Alexander Graham Bell* (1939) with Don Ameche. *Land of Liberty* (1939) was produced by the MPPDA and made specifically for the New York's World's Fair with Macpherson doing some of the narration.

While filming *Unconquered* (1947), DeMille called upon Macpherson's services one last time. Her girlish good looks and days as the director's mistress may have been behind her, but he still valued her professional prowess. She made a valiant effort to assist him with the historical drama starring Gary Cooper and Paulette Goddard, but advanced cancer prevented her from finishing the job. DeMille, accompanied by his adopted son, Richard, visited Macpherson at the hospital a few days before she died. According to Richard: "[DeMille] held her hand and told her they would surely meet in the next world. She murmured that they would."

After more than thirty years of loving, working and flying with DeMille, Macpherson fell into a coma. She died on August 26, 1946 at the age of 58. Once, when commenting about the secret to DeMille's "bigness," she simply said: "He will take advice from anyone—if it's right. He won't take it from anyone if it's wrong."

Like Macpherson, Roy Pomeroy was another alumnus of Paramount whose "bigness" came from his ability to create on-screen magic. From complex special effects to sound, he was the man who Paramount relied on when they needed more than just a mere mortal. Thanks to Pomeroy, director William Wellman's war drama *Wings* (1927) had more than just thrilling aerial combat scenes. Audiences around the world heard buzzing planes, thunderous explosions and the staccato popping of machine-gun fire. Movies were changing and Pomeroy was at the forefront. He was even honored with an Award of Merit for his special effects in *Wings*. A member of the Academy's Committee on College Affairs, he was an advocate of formal technical training for the next generation of filmmakers.

With the popularity of *Wings* and the tremendous success of *The Jazz Singer* (1927), Paramount turned to their miracle man. Designating him Director of Sound Effects, they sent Pomeroy back east to investigate various methods of recording at Western Electric and RCA. When he returned to Hollywood, Lasky described Pomeroy as "something of a sacred oracle" and the only man in town who clearly understood this mysterious new process. Pomeroy was put in charge of a committee formed by several studios including MGM and First National to study sound.

He was also assigned the task of testing the voices of all Paramount stars. The players were petrified that this powerful potentate might cast them off the mountain if he felt that their voices didn't measure up. Pomeroy declared that Mary Pickford sounded best and approved the terrified Clara Bow, who stuttered. He also advised the studio to let others, like top Paramount player Bebe Daniels, go. Evidently, he didn't know everything because Daniels moved on to another studio where her voice worked out just fine.

When the writer's branch of the Academy came together to discuss sound, Pomeroy did most of the talking. He assured the members that a sound film would take one year to complete and required a very expensive budget. He further explained that strategically placed microphones must be hidden around the sets and the players' movements limited, ensuring that they stayed within range. He also believed that there should be a significant lapse in time between speakers so befuddled spectators could adjust from one character to another. In addition, he advised that when characters speak, they should never be photographed from behind because the audience wouldn't understand who was talking. By the end of 1928, Pomeroy had designed and was in charge of the construction of four more sound stages at Paramount, each measuring 70 feet wide by 100 feet long.

In order to remain competitive, Paramount also needed a talking picture. Pomeroy assured Lasky and Zukor that he, and only he, could deliver the goods. He convinced them that no one else at the studio was qualified to direct a talkie because of the complex process involved. Pomeroy then demanded and got a raise from $250 to $2500 a week. Lasky later recalled in his autobiography:

> So our first talkie was directed by a special-effects man who became a sound engineer by virtue of a trip through the laboratories of Western Electric and RCA. We couldn't have treated him with more awe and homage if he had been Edison himself.

The film, *Interference* (1929), was shot on a small sound stage where Pomeroy, sometimes called "the Marconi of the movies," ruled over the production from a chair. At his signal, large stage doors swung shut and after one final look over the scene, someone yelled "Interlock!," which meant that the cameras and recorders were now in sync and ready to roll. The traditional shout of "Camera!" just didn't work in Pomeroy's new world. A bell would then ring ordering silence on the set followed by a flashing red light. Finally, the scene would begin. Once it was over, the doors would reopen and studio workers could continue on with their business of the day.

To help contain background noise, floors were carpeted and the actors' shoes soundproofed with special material that cut down on unwanted squeaks and thudding footsteps. Swishing clothes and jingling jewelry also had to be dealt with. A scene in Paramount's film *Varsity* (1928) required the rustling of a newspaper. Once replayed, however, it sounded more like a machine-gun spewing bullets at the bad guys. Pomeroy's solution was to wet the pages before the paper was handled. Likewise the shrill tone of a police whistle was ear-shattering on film so Pomeroy had the whistle blower stand behind a thick curtain effectively muffling the sound.

No one was allowed inside Pomeroy's domain except the cast and crew. The entire production was shrouded in secrecy. The miracle-man was at work and his mystical magic was not something he wanted to share. When director Victor Fleming tried to enter along with his assistant, Henry Hathaway, a policeman guarding the locked doors refused to let them in. Pomeroy had given the officer strict orders to keep everyone out. An irate Fleming stormed off to the production head's office and protested: "Look, this guy's got locks on his doors! Jesus Christ, are you only going to have one director for sound? . . . We're all going to have to know about it. This son of a bitch, he can't direct all the pictures." The doors were promptly unlocked and stayed that way.

Even other studios had to deal with Pomeroy. His sound stage was one of just a few in Hollywood at that time. Other companies were forced to ask permission to use it when filming talkies of their own. If Pomeroy gave the okay, outsiders filmed only at night when he wasn't working.

Lasky shrewdly assigned William DeMille to "assist" Pomeroy. He was quite pleased to have someone as important as a DeMille reporting to him. DeMille, however, had his own agenda and learned how to work with sound. Soon Pomeroy wasn't the only kid in town who could handle a microphone.

Then Lasky's oracle had a fateful run-in with David O. Selznick. When the producer mentioned that a particular actor had been cast in Paramount's next talkie, Pomeroy was livid. He let Selznick know that no one could cast a talking picture without his approval. Finally, Paramount executives realized that other studios were producing successful talkies without Roy Pomeroy. Zukor and Lasky contacted Western Electric who sent out their own technicians to work at the studio. After sharing their knowledge, Pomeroy was no longer a mystic, but a man who could be dispensed with.

When Pomeroy demanded yet another pay hike—this time he wanted $3500 a week—his request didn't fly with the Paramount brass. Instead, they fired him. Picked up by RKO, he directed and produced *Inside the Lines* (1930), a World War I spy drama.

The following year, Pomeroy tried something new. He entered the mining business. Along with a group of filmmakers, he purchased several Bullfrog district mines, which were located in southern Nevada's Bullfrog Hills where gold had once been discovered. The group incorporated their business as the Rhyolite Consolidated Mining Company with Pomeroy as president, but he soon sold out of the unsuccessful venture.

By 1932, Pomeroy was in the midst of establishing a motion-picture technical institute and bureau of research that would work with every studio in Hollywood by assisting with their individual technical and/or special effects problems. The institute would have a complete machine shop, laboratory and storage space for specialized "mechanical miniatures."

Pomeroy was also instrumental in fine-tuning the Dunning-Pomeroy Self-Matting Process where background scenes were filmed in one location and brought to the studio. Actors would then appear in front of a screen where the background film would run making it look as if they were in any number of exotic places when in fact they never left the soundstage.

The last movie he directed (and wrote) was another World War I drama, *Shock* (1934) for W.T. Lackey Productions. He spent the remaining years of his life more or less in obscurity and died in Los Angeles on September 3, 1947 survived only by his wife, Sylvia. His power trip in Hollywood didn't last long as he rode the sound waves that revolutionized the motion picture industry, but for a few great years in Hollywood, when Roy J. Pomeroy spoke—everybody listened.

MGM director Fred Niblo had no problem getting people to listen to him. Still sought after as one of filmdom's favorite hosts, he was the first Vice President of the Academy of Motion Picture Arts and Sciences. Niblo also continued working in a silent world with top stars such as Lillian Gish in *The Enemy* (1927), and Greta Garbo in *The Mysterious Lady* (1928).

Still loving life on the road, Niblo visited several movie theaters now wired for sound while vacationing in 1929. Disappointment marred his experiences as a spectator. It seems in the big cities such as New York or Chicago, sound quality was top notch, but in the smaller towns, not so much. Niblo explained:

> I enjoyed an all-talking picture in Hollywood, then attended it again in Salt Lake City. Although familiar with the story, I could not understand a word because the dialogue was so blurred due to faulty projection. . . . Distort the sound a bit, and the result is laughable or irritating in the extreme.

Nonetheless, his first talking picture was released the following year. He helmed the drama *Redemption* (1930), which featured silent superstar John Gilbert in one of his first speaking roles.

At home, the fifty-four-year-old Niblo and his wife, Australian actress Enid Bennett, had four children—Fred, Jr., whose mother was Niblo's first wife Josephine Cohan, along with Loris, Peter and Judith. The Niblos built a semi-circular Spanish-style house topped by a red tile roof on their estate, Misty Mountain, in Beverly Hills. The twenty-two-room home, with its oversized veranda and private movie theater, was more than 8,000 square feet and perched at an elevation of 1,000 feet overlooking Catalina and the Channel Islands. The grounds included a children's play area, a large swimming pool and a specially designed croquet lawn. His son Peter, recalled:

> At home, Dad was strict. . . . when I got carried away, one look from my Dad ended it all. . . . He was tough, but very much on the right track. He loved classical music and gave me a look when I cranked up the phonograph to play Dixieland.

Niblo was tapped for his hosting talent to emcee a premiere of the award-winning western *Cimmaron* (1931). As he introduced the cast at the Los Angeles Orpheum Theater on February 6, 1931, the building was rocked by a sudden explosion. Just outside, a large piece of pavement catapulted into the air taking a taxi with it and tossing several people into the street. As panic overcame the crowd inside the theater, the quick-thinking Niblo assured patrons there was nothing to fear—or he would have been the first to run outside. Momentarily pacified, the crowd calmed down. Then they heard sirens outside and bolted through the doors. It was ultimately determined that natural gas had exploded directly in front of the theater injuring 31 people—some had been inside the lobby while others were outside just waiting to catch a glimpse of their favorite stars.

In 1932, Niblo put down his director's megaphone and eventually turned to acting. He continued working in front of the camera for several more years. His last film appearance was in an uncredited role in the musical comedy *Crazy House* (1943), where he played a studio executive.

Niblo soon retired from filmmaking altogether and spent most of his later years on his Lake County ranch. In need of money, he had been forced to sell Misty Mountain in 1940 for just $35,000.

In the fall of 1948, Niblo and his wife were enjoying a cruise to celebrate their thirtieth wedding anniversary when he fell ill with pneumonia. The couple disembarked in New Orleans where the seventy-four-year-old director was admitted to a local hospital. Two weeks later, he passed away on November 11, 1948.

Always a fan of life on the road, Fred Niblo started out in vaudeville before traveling the world. Once he landed in Hollywood, Niblo stayed to direct many of the silent greats like Douglas Fairbanks, Rudolph Valentino and John Gilbert. Whether it was a live audience made up of his peers or a crowd of spectators inside a darkened theater, Fred Niblo loved to entertain. All it took was a clever line, a striking visual and a little zigzag.

Another former vaudevillian, producer Harry Rapf, remained part of the MGM triumvirate up through the advent of the Second World War. While Irving Thalberg emerged as the man in charge of the studio's high-profile productions, Rapf worked hard producing more light-hearted fare. True to his theatrical background, he preferred treating his audiences to singing, dancing and a bevy of beautiful girls leaving toe-tapping spectators with a smile. He also liked to make 'em laugh and realized the value of a good screen team.

Harkening back to his vaudeville days, he remembered many of the greatest duos in entertainment such as the comic team of Weber and Fields. Wanting to resurrect some of that lively to-and-fro, he often created odd screen couples. Pairing up actress Marie Dressler with ruffian Wallace Beery for the film *Min and Bill* (1930) resulted in one of the silver screen's most dynamic teams.

Top screenwriter Frances Marion came to Rapf about a novel called *The Dark Star* written by her friend author Lorna Moon. He bought the rights even though he wasn't quite sold on the idea. Rapf knew that Marion's writer friend was ill with tuberculosis and needed money to enter a New

Mexico sanitarium for treatment. Rapf, who had lost his own father from the dreaded lung disease, could not find it in his heart to refuse. Marion's final script did not resemble the book, but the money allowed Moon admittance to the facility prior to her death on May 1, 1930. *Min and Bill*, released later that year, was one of MGM's biggest hits with a Best Actress Academy Award going to Dressler.

Rapf also liked sentiment. He persuaded Louis B. Mayer to take a gamble on *The Champ* (1931), pairing up the ill-tempered Wallace Beery with child actor Jackie Cooper. The film depicting a has-been boxing champion who is cared for by his young son was nominated for Best Picture with top honors going to Beery as Best Actor and King Vidor as Best Director.

Rapf was also in charge of the "B" pictures and "shorts," which were the least costly films and used in conjunction with major features to round out theatrical bills. These low-budget features were also a testing ground for new talent both human and non-human—something that was right up Rapf's alley. With Rin Tin Tin still making features at Warner Bros., Rapf went looking for MGM's own canine star. He found Flash the Wonder Dog, a Chicago-born German Shepherd with his own radio show. After bringing the three-year-old pooch to Hollywood for a screen test, Rapf put him under contact and starred him in *Shadow of the Night* (1928). With Rinty still leading the pack, however, Flash didn't quite measure up.

In addition to his movie-making duties, Rapf sponsored the MGM Lions—a football team comprised of juvenile players headed up by Mickey Rooney. He often talked MGM stars like Clark Gable into refereeing the games. He also found work for family members. His eldest son, Maurice, delivered mail to the stars and also gave tours of the studio to interested visitors. As Rapf's son, he gained entrance to many of the otherwise closed movie sets.

With such a dizzying pace and so many pictures to keep up with, Rapf, like Thalberg, suffered a heart attack in 1932, which began a subtle shift in power at MGM. In 1933, Mayer gave David O. Selznick a two-year contract and his own production company while an ailing Thalberg recuperated in Europe. Mayer took on the responsibilities of production and named Rapf, along with several others, as his executive assistants, effectively weakening both Rapf's and Thalberg's power at the studio.

When he wasn't working, Rapf enjoyed fishing. After building a second home on the beach in Malibu, he was either casting a line from the pier or from a chartered boat almost every summer Saturday. One of his fishing expeditions turned deadly when a violent storm with 65-mile-per-hour winds suddenly materialized off the coastline, north of Los Angeles. Dozens of boats were destroyed or missing as the U.S. Navy was brought in to search the waters for more than forty men, women and children. Rapf watched in horror as one vessel, carrying twenty-six people, capsized when a thirty-foot wave broadsided her. Only one man and one woman survived. Rapf fared better that deadly afternoon when his fishing boat safely reached shore.

As if he didn't have enough to worry about, his Malibu home caught fire in 1934. No one was inside at the time, but the damages were substantial. Part of the roof was destroyed and much of the home ruined by water for a total loss estimated at $3,000 to $5,000.

At MGM, Mayer remained in charge and wanted to stay that way. He formed an executive staff made up of several vice presidents—Rapf included. Eventually, a nine-man committee supervised the actual productions while Mayer supervised them. Rapf still ran the "shorts" department that now replaced the phased-out "B" pictures. Mayer teamed him up with a former MGM writer who was now promoted to producer, Dore Schary. The Rapf-Schary unit was formed in 1941. Their first two projects were *Mr. and Mrs. North* (1942) starring funny girl Gracie Allen and the thriller *Joe Smith, American* (1942) based on a story by author Paul Gallico.

Despite their successes, Rapf and Schary did not get along and were often at odds with each other over creative differences—mostly who was in charge of them. Their constant quarreling led Mayer to fire his long-time associate, Rapf, on April 21, 1942 for hindering production.

When Rapf assembled his producers to say good-bye, they were outraged. According to Sam Marx, who worked for Rapf, these loyal men ganged up on Schary insisting he go back to Mayer and have him rehire Rapf. The next day, Rapf penned this note to Marx:

> Dear Sam—It is only in time of trouble that the true strength of friendship can be found. Your sincerity and loyalty to me yesterday was something I will never forget.

The following year, Rapf, still looking for his next canine celebrity, cast a dog named Pal in the movies. The picture-perfect collie played the brave and beautiful Lassie in the drama *Lassie Come Home* (1943). It was another case of cross-dressing, however, since Pal was a boy and Lassie a girl. In the sequel, *Son of Lassie* (1945), Pal played the title role of Laddie and another collie named Lassie played his mother.

While Schary left the studio only to return with a vengeance several years later, Rapf remained with MGM until his death from another heart attack on February 6, 1949. His final production, the drama *Scene of the Crime* (1949) starred Van Johnson and Arlene Dahl. It was released almost six months after Rapf's death. Of all his accomplishments, he was proudest of those whom he helped reach the top:

> . . . not just the little fellows who have jobs and are making living wages for their families, but 125 very successful men and women in the business, each one of whom had his first picture job from me. That means more to me than anything I can think of.

Chapter Twenty

MAD HATTERS, MACHO MEN AND MEXICAN DIVORCES

R ecently widowed, director John Stahl left MGM to start up his own company in conjunction with Tiffany Pictures, which was run by producer Phil Goldstone and best known for several features starring popular actress Mae Murray. As vice president in charge of production for Tiffany-Stahl Productions, Stahl went right to work as a producer. Between 1927 and 1929, he produced over forty films—none of which were particularly memorable, but profitable enough to keep his career in a holding pattern. Stahl left the company in November 1929, selling his interest to controlling stockholders. He then moved on to Universal where he once again picked up the megaphone.

Stahl also married former silent screen actress Roxana McGowan. Born in Chicago, McGowan once worked for Mack Sennett, but her movie career ended in 1919. By the time she married Stahl in 1931, McGowan had two children, Albert, 9, and Roxana, 6, from her first marriage to director Albert Ray, which ended in divorce. Besides gaining a wife, Stahl adopted her children and found himself with a ready-made family.

Later that year, Stahl made his second film for Universal, *Strictly Dishonorable* (1931). The movie was based on a play by writer Preston Sturges featuring lots of romance, comedy and opera. A box office success, it brought Stahl back into good-standing director status. His next film, however, established his position as the master of melodrama. *Back Street* (1932), starring actress Irene Dunne with her leading man, the dapper John Boles, is the story of a successful businesswoman who has the misfortune of falling in love with a married man. Scandalous, titillating yet moving, the film focuses on the long-suffering Dunne and her loyalty to her unattainable lover. Then came two more classics, *Imitation of Life* (1934) followed by *Magnificent Obsession* (1935), putting Stahl on top of the melodrama madness.

When asked about his movies' popularity, the silver-haired Stahl admitted that he played to the female part of the audience:

> It's my commercial instinct, as much as anything. Matinees are made up of women patrons, and at night the women drag in the men. In directing, I simply remember to use the feminine approach.

He focused on the human aspect of his characters bringing out their emotions and feelings. Personally, he rarely watched his own movies. He just couldn't sit through them without being critical. He much preferred a good laugh that came from the funny papers or a slapstick comedy, something he didn't specialize in professionally. Journalist Margaret Reid once reported that Stahl's personal creed was: "God, my mother and Charlie Chaplin."

Stahl returned to MGM to direct Clark Gable in *Parnell* (1937), which detailed the life of Irishman Charles Stewart Parnell and his struggle to gain Ireland's independence from England. The film was Gable's biggest box office flop. It was so bad that Gable swore off period pictures from that point on. Only with great reluctance did he agree to play Rhett Butler two years later, the role that would make him the undisputed King of Hollywood.

For Stahl, it was back to Universal where he filmed *Letter of Introduction* (1938), which featured ventriloquist Edgar Bergen and his wooden chum, Charlie McCarthy. While Bergen worked hard and did his best to follow direction, McCarthy threw fits on the set making everyone aware of his complete distaste for filmmaking. Whenever Stahl ordered retakes, Bergen just smiled while McCarthy spewed words that would make a sailor blush. No one, not even the normally in-control Stahl, was quite sure how to handle the incorrigible little stiff.

Stahl stayed with Universal for five years before making one picture for Columbia, a comedy, *Our Wife* (1941) starring the much-acclaimed Melvyn Douglas. The director then signed a contract with Fox where he made more classics like *Keys of the Kingdom* (1944) featuring a young Gregory Peck in his first major role and *Leave Her to Heaven* (1945) with Gene Tierney. His final movie was also his only musical, *Oh You Beautiful Doll* (1949)—a not-so-memorable film starring actress June Haver.

In August 1949, the Stahls hosted their daughter's wedding reception at their Beverly Hills home when she married Daniel Steen Fletcher, Jr. That night, their son, Ray, announced his engagement to Texas-born actress Martha Hyer. Unfortunately, Stahl did not live long enough to attend their wedding. After suffering a heart attack on New Year's Day, he died from complications of pneumonia on January 12, 1950.

John Stahl may not have been the only director who specialized in melodrama, but he certainly perfected the genre, creating his own mark in Hollywood history. Love. Hate. Tragedy. Triumph. Stahl's stories were interwoven with the human spirit. His characters evoked emotion, from unbridled happiness to bottomless grief. Perhaps his career was best summed up in his own words:

> . . . everything depends on character. This is not a new thing. In fact,
> it has always been the prevailing factor in drama. What Shakespeare
> play, for instance, that does not live in the characters? Only by making

your situations and your plot grow out of your people can you really succeed in making your drama real.

Hollywood was filled with characters, but none more loved than Sidney Patrick Grauman. After opening the Million Dollar Theater, the New Rialto, the Metropolitan and the Egyptian, Grauman envisioned one more—the most memorable of all. In keeping with his knack for publicity, he invited actress Norma Talmadge to dig up the first spade full of dirt with a gold-plated shovel at the April 10, 1926 groundbreaking ceremony on Hollywood Boulevard and Orange Drive.

More than one year and two million dollars later, Grauman's Chinese Theater lavishly opened on May 18, 1927 with the flashy premiere of Cecil B. DeMille's *King of Kings* (1927). Preceding the movie was one of Grauman's famous prologues—a live musical called *Glories of Scripture*, accompanied by a 65-piece orchestra. Two dozen searchlights lit up the area while oriental girls from San Francisco's Chinatown acted as usherettes. It was by invitation only that the 2,200 Hollywood elite were asked to attend, but the crowd of fans who gathered to cheer for their favorite movie stars was 50,000 strong.

With its Chinese-style architecture that prominently featured a pagoda and dragon, the opulent theater made history—but not because of the building. It was the theater's forecourt that garnered the most attention. In an idea dreamed up by Grauman, Mary Pickford and Douglas Fairbanks regally placed their hands and feet in a block of wet cement preserving them forever in front of the theater. They started a tradition that has lasted over eighty years and has evolved into one of Hollywood's highest honors and singular trademarks.

Grauman envisioned the forecourt filled with famous handprints, footprints and signatures. To accomplish this, he hired Jean W. Klossner, a French mason, who had a secret formula for mixing concrete. Klossner started three days before each ceremony preparing the mysterious "ingredients" that he would combine with the wet cement. This mixture was slow to dry but maintained detail. If something went wrong—no problem. The wet slab could easily be smoothed over for another try. Once it dried, however, Klossner's concrete was made to last. Not one of the specially made blocks that he personally laid has ever cracked. That's no small achievement considering the millions of visitors who have stood in those famous footprints. How did he do it? No one knows for sure. Klossner died in 1965 taking his secret recipe with him.

Some stars left more than prints of their hands and feet. Harold Lloyd left an impression of his famous glasses; William S. Hart, his six-shooters; Betty Grable, her million dollar legs; Jimmy Durante, his celebrated "schnozola." John Barrymore left his legendary profile. Photographs taken right after the ceremony show him irritably digging wet cement from his left ear. He was also heard to quip: "I feel like the face on the barroom floor!"

Sid Grauman didn't actually own the theater that carried his name. He had a one-third interest in it along with several partners that included Mary Pickford and her husband, Douglas Fairbanks. That all changed in 1929 when Grauman took a huge financial hit due to the stock market crash. Paramount chief Adolph Zukor came to the rescue when he purchased Grauman's share of the Chinese Theater and kept him on to run the place.

Studio heads, stars and directors actively sought Grauman's favor. Everyone wanted their movies showcased in one of his fabulous cinemas. Even better, they genuinely liked him. In a town where many have hidden agendas, Grauman never did. He always went out of his way for his many friends, never expecting anything in return. He was also popular with the public, as his prologues proved. Before each movie was shown, Grauman's theaters would hold an exhilarating live show intended to stir up the audience. Douglas Fairbanks, Jr. once described these prologues as ". . . essentially half the evening's entertainment— the film the second half. The prologue took almost as much time as the film. He used them to set the atmosphere for the feature, and they were too lavish to be believed." Sometimes, Grauman even took the stage himself. A slightly built man with a thick head of curly hair, writer

Anita Loos once commented that Grauman reminded her of Alice in Wonderland's Mad Hatter.

When Grauman wasn't entertaining, he was setting up his friends. He once conned Marcus Loew into a speaking engagement for theater owners at the Ambassador Hotel. With the lights dimmed, Loew began his motivational talk and got no reaction from the crowd. He had no idea that he was speaking to a bunch of dummies—literally. Grauman had borrowed them from a local wax museum. During another of his escapades, a distressed Grauman telephoned Charlie Chaplin for help. When Chaplin rushed over to Grauman's room at the Ambassador Hotel, he saw his friend hovering over a bloodstained body in his bed. Shaken, Chaplin wanted to call the police, but Grauman refused, claiming he couldn't handle the scandal. When Chaplin finally got a closer look, he discovered a catsup-covered wax figure!

A confirmed bachelor and a long-time resident of the Ambassador Hotel, he wasn't a morning person. He much preferred sleeping in and staying up late to gamble. His game of choice? Gin rummy. It's said that he once lost the Chinese Theater in a card game and then forced the players to keep dealing until he won it back. He didn't drink, but he puffed his way through four packs of cigarettes every day.

When he wasn't playing cards or pulling pranks, Grauman most enjoyed the unique role he played in Hollywood as the resident "theater man." His ingenious ideas, along with his elaborate prologues, were legendary. He was the first to use souvenir programs and sell advance tickets to moviegoers. It was Grauman who thought to use searchlights for attracting attention. He even dreamed up that majestic red carpet. In recognition of Grauman's contributions to film, the Academy gave him an honorary Oscar in 1948, more than twenty years after its formation, for being a "master showman who raised the standard of exhibition of motion pictures."

A few days after John Wayne left his mark in front of the Chinese Theater, Grauman died of heart failure on March 5, 1950, just shy of his seventy-first birthday. His obituary stated that: "Among his intimate friends, he was known as a great gagger." Sid Grauman was also a great dreamer who shaped the way movies were shown. Proud of his lifelong association with the film industry and the many filmmakers he counted as friends, Grauman remained a humble man who often credited his success to "The Big Boss Upstairs."

While Grauman was busy cementing famous footsteps, actor Jack Holt was building his screen credits much to his fans' delight. In 1927, he followed up Zane Grey's *The Mysterious Rider* with two dramas. He played an Englishman in *The Tigress* and a spy in *The Warning*. His next film, *The Smart Set* (1928), was a comedy in which he fittingly played a polo team captain—a sport he understood first-hand. That same year he also joined the General Society of Colonial Wars in the State of California. Proud of his heritage, Holt was eligible for membership due to his great-great-grandfather, Revolutionary War Captain and fourth Chief Justice of the Supreme Court John Curtis Marshall.

The actor who specialized in tough guys had no trouble transitioning to sound. After leaving Paramount for Columbia, he filmed his first talking picture, *The Donovan Affair* (1929), a drama directed by Frank Capra. He successfully played policemen, soldiers, gangsters, detectives, secret service agents, a deep-sea diver, seal hunter, lawyer, and football coach, clearly making the transition into sound with aplomb. He even took on a supporting role in Shirley Temple's Civil War classic *The Littlest Rebel* (1935). In between pictures, he continued playing polo.

Relations at home, however, were not so copasetic. The Holts were separated. In 1933, Margaret Woods Holt filed for and obtained a divorce through the courts in Chihuahua, Mexico charging that she and her husband were no longer compatible. Holt, required to give his ex-wife both money and property, took a financial hit worth approximately $100,000. All matters were handled through their attorneys with neither party making an actual appearance in court. Fifteen-year-old Charles, Jr. remained with his father in California, while Elizabeth, now twelve, traveled to South America with her mother.

Later that same year, the Mexican Supreme Court overruled their individual states' legal decisions declaring that a divorce could not be granted without a hearing where both parties were present. American lawyers countered this claim by asserting that couples did partake in these hearings through their attorneys.

In 1939, the Holts were back in court—this time in California. Holt claimed that because his wife obtained the divorce in Chihuahua, Mexico, it was not valid. In his mind, if the divorce wasn't valid neither was the property settlement. Mrs. Holt countered that the Mexican divorce was lawful and that she was entitled to half of his income. She also asserted that she only received about $500 each month, which was hardly enough. The California courts declared the divorce invalid since it was more or less obtained through the mails. Although the Holts never officially divorced, they remained separated for the rest of their lives.

When World War II began, the fifty-four-year-old actor put his long career on hold to join the U.S. Army at the personal request of General George C. Marshall. Due to his expert horsemanship, he was trained at Fort Warren in Wyoming and assigned to the Army Quartermaster Corps. He held the rank of Captain and acted as a military horse-buyer. By the time he was honorably discharged, Holt had reached the rank of Major.

After a three-year military absence, he returned to Hollywood, where he continued working as if he had never left. Now employed by MGM, his first feature was a World War II drama, *They Were Expendable* (1946), starring John Wayne and directed by John Ford. By now, his children, Charles, Jr. and Elizabeth, were known as Tim and Jennifer Holt—both successful actors, mostly in westerns, following in Daddy's footsteps.

In 1949, Holt tried something new. Inspired by his grandson, Lance, he teamed up with writer Carolyn Coggins and wrote a children's book titled *Lance and His First Horse* with illustrations by Wesley Dennis, which was quite successful. He followed-up with a second book called *Lance and Cowboy Billy*, but Holt's writing career was cut short. After suffering several heart attacks, he died on January 18, 1951 in a Los Angeles veterans' hospital. The 62-year-old actor worked right up until the end despite his illness. His final movie, a western with Clark Gable, *Across the Wide Missouri* (1951), was released ten months later.

Following a full military funeral, the *L.A. Times* reported that two days before he died, Jack Holt amended his will, angry about the "divorce" to the last. "To my wife, Margaret W. Holt who has been amply provided for in the past and for whom full provision was made in a property settlement, I bequeath $1 and no more."

Unlike Jack Holt, Joseph Arthur Ball never worked in front of the camera. He concentrated on the color behind it as one of Technicolor's top team members. For Ball, 1927 was an eventful year. In addition to founding the Academy, he became a new father. His only child, David Jeremy Ball, was born on February 16, 1927. Just three months later, however, tragedy struck the family when Ball's brother-in-law, Norman Osann, also a respected employee of Technicolor, shot himself on May 4, 1927.

Osann had recently worked with Cecil B. DeMille as a technical advisor on *King of Kings* (1927). Authorities believed that the thirty-seven-year-old might have been despondent over some health issues. The previous day, Osann had asked coworker Robert Monroe if he could borrow a gun to use on a trip to the mountains. That evening, after Monroe dropped off the gun, Osann pulled the trigger firing that fatal shot. He left behind a message apologizing for his suicide, as well as a promissory note for $750 made payable to his brother-in-law, Joseph Arthur Ball.

By the end of 1927, Technicolor Corporation released a short, *The Flag: A Story Inspired by the Tradition of Betsy Ross* starring Francis X. Bushman as the first president and Enid Bennett as the famous seamstress. The film's high point came at the end when Bushman boldly unfurled the American Flag in a colorful wave. A hit with the audience, Technicolor continued manufacturing their color shorts to be shown along with black and white feature-length films in theaters across the country. With so much success and audience approval, the company then attempted their first color feature, *The Viking* (1928), starring English actor Donald Crisp, sporting a full Viking beard.

That same year, Ball was appointed head of the Academy's Technical Bureau. The *L.A. Times* reported:

> . . . The motion-picture is peculiarly a combination of art and industry, and it has been frequently the rule that the artistic development is proportionate to the industrial. The scientific side of picture making has never perhaps received such well-directed attention and interest as it has since the academy has come into existence and this gives every promise of being one of its largest contributions. . . .

In addition, Ball joined two more committees sponsored by the Academy. He was a member of the Producers-Technicians Joint Committee focusing on issues that had an immediate impact on the film industry. During their very first meeting, they took on the challenges presented by sound. As a member of the Committee on College Affairs, he also worked on university curriculum and even lectured. The Academy also spawned the idea of a research laboratory. This facility would be established by the MPPDA with Ball supervising their work.

With The Great Depression hurting the studios, most of them cut back on color film production. The Technicolor team, however, continued working to enhance their product. By 1931, many improvements to their process were evident. They cleaned up the grainy picture removing what looked like bugs crawling on-screen. They also brought the price of color film down from 8.75 to 7 cents per foot. Ball described his team's accomplishments: ". . . improved sharpness, improved brilliance and a generally increased clarity and smoothness." But it was still a two-color world with Technicolor supplying the film, the cameras and the approved cameramen. They also developed and distributed the prints.

By 1932, the cost of color film dropped another two cents per foot while Ball and his team of researchers finally made a breakthrough. They discovered a method of capturing that elusive color "blue" with a 3-strip camera. This camera exposed three negatives at the same time through a single lens that sat in front of a prism. It took so long to change the film, however, that it was necessary to have a second camera on deck to avoid a break in the action.

The first theatrical release using this new method was a Disney cartoon called *Flowers and Trees* (1932), which was part of the Silly Symphonies series. The singing and dancing fauna with their colorful leaves and petals resonated with spectators and even won an Academy Award. In deference to Ball's hard work, Uncle Walt himself drew a picture depicting three of his most famous characters and wrote:

> To Arthur Ball in appreciation of the color that has given us new life!
> Sincerely, Walt Disney and the Three Little Pigs.

As Disney experienced continued success with color cartoons, Mickey Mouse himself, always a pioneer, first with sound in the short *Steamboat Willie* (1928), soon converted from black and white. Other studios followed suit, filming shorts entirely in color. For features, however, the new technology was limited to specific scenes. The first Technicolor feature filmed entirely in the three-strip process was *Becky Sharp* (1935) with southern belle Miriam Hopkins in the starring role. All scenes were filmed indoors and it wasn't until the following year that Technicolor was tried outside the studio in *The Trail of the Lonesome Pines* (1936). Disney's classic *Snow White and the Seven Dwarves* (1937), a full-length, color, animated feature, soon followed.

In 1939, Ball was given a special award by the Academy "for his outstanding contributions to the advancement of color in Motion Picture Photography." He also held many patents relating to color photography. In his later years, he acted as a consultant with Springdale Laboratories of Time, Inc. located in Stamford, Connecticut, as well as Walt Disney Productions. He also worked for the E.I. du Pont de Nemours & Co. where he helped develop du Pont's motion picture color positive film and related products. Ball split his time between Los Angeles and New York where he was a member of the New York Athletic Club. He died on August 27, 1951 of carbon monoxide poisoning by his own hand. Like so many tragic suicides of the time, little is known about the reasons why.

Like Joseph Arthur Ball, Milton Hoffman also worked out of camera range. By 1927, Hoffman was considered one of Hollywood's most experienced film executives. Back at Paramount after a brief stint with Metro Pictures, he now reported directly to production head B.P. Schulberg. Instead of overseeing studio business, however, he was now involved in actual filmmaking. This was in addition to his new position as President of the Central Motion Picture District, Inc.

This organization was patterned after the Chicago Central Manufacturing District and tasked with bringing the motion-picture studios into a single district. Their $20,000,000 project was called Studio City. Their ambitious plans included the construction of new studios, widening existing roads, as well as building new ones, installing sidewalks and private housing. Located at Ventura Boulevard and Pacolma Avenue in North Hollywood, Mack Sennett was tapped to build an $800,000 production facility while MGM leased property for their outdoor sets. Utilities including electricity and telephones would also be made available by extending current lines into the area. A ten-mile-stretch of Ventura Boulevard was one of the first roads to be widened between Hollywood and Sepulveda.

One year later, Hoffman provided some of the group's outstanding accomplishments:

- 4,423,000 out of 8,747,00 cubic feet of dirt had been moved.
- 885,0000 out of 3,164,000 square feet of pavement laid.
- 203,000 out of 695,000 square feet of sidewalks were completed with seven out of 30 miles of curbing finished.
- Four miles of water mains were laid with eight more to go.

- Three and a half miles of electric wiring was strung with another seven and a half needed to finish the job.
- One bridge over the Los Angeles River was completed and open to traffic while a second was under construction.

Hoffman also announced even more ambitious plans for the following year. Studio City's production facilities would spend almost $15,000,000 in construction costs between 1928 and 1929 to accommodate talking pictures. In addition, the studios, which now included Warner Bros., Universal and Paramount, budgeted a total of $29,900,000 for movies during that same time period. Land was also set aside for an airfield that would be home to airplane repair shops, hangars, and light airplane manufacturing plants. Hoffman told the press:

> North Hollywood is destined to become the premiere manufacturing for airplanes, airplane motors, and other aviation accessories and sup-plies in California. . . . With the best facilities and accommodations for such an industry to be found in the nation, the San Fernando Valley will become a leading aviation center.

By the middle of 1929, Hoffman estimated that $30,000,000 worth of investments between the motion picture and aviation industries had been made in Studio City. Between 1929 and 1930, film companies associated with Studio City, with a budget of approximately $68,000,000, scheduled 687 motion pictures for production. In addition, Studio City was home to five tile factories and a flashlight manufacturer. The Apache Engine Company produced airplane motors while Bach Aircraft Corporation made passenger planes. Due to all of this impressive business activity, Hoffman was a very proud man who made the following observations after returning home from a motor trip:

Los Angeles is the best advertised city in the world. . . . I stopped overnight in a little town in Manitoba. Dropping into the hamlet's only motion-picture theater, the first thing that caught my eye were the words, "Made in Studio City" flashed on the screen. . . . A few days later I passed through a hamlet in North Dakota and there the local theater flashed the same words. . . . The process is an endless chain of advertising. . . . A conservative estimate of the number of theater patrons who have seen the slogan flashed on the screen would be around 100,000,000. . . . That's why Los Angeles will forever carry on.

In addition to his duties as president of the Central Motion Picture District, Inc. and his involvement with the building of Studio City, Hoffman remained with Paramount until 1941. He then worked for several other studios including RKO. Studio City, now home to more than 25,000 residents, may have carried on, but Hoffman died on July 21, 1952 at the Motion Picture Country House after a lengthy illness.

Chapter Twenty-One

BUSINESSMEN, ARTISTS AND MEDIATORS

W hile Fred Beetson was in charge of the Casting Bureau and a leading figure in the MPPDA, he also worked closely with movie czar Will Hays compiling a list of what came to be called "The Formula" or "The Don'ts and Be Carefuls." Hays hoped that these guidelines would placate local censors while giving filmmakers a solid sense of what was acceptable on-screen and what wasn't. The following laundry list was published in October 1927:

> *Resolved,* That those things which are included in the following list shall not appear in pictures produced by the members of this Association, irrespective of the manner in which they are treated:

> 1. Pointed profanity—by either title or lip—this includes the words "God," "Lord," "Jesus," "Christ" (unless they be used reverently in connection with proper religious ceremonies), "hell,"

"damn," "Gawd," and every other profane and vulgar expression however it may be spelled;

2. Any licentious or suggestive nudity—in fact or in silhouette; and any lecherous or licentious notice thereof by other characters in the picture;
3. The illegal traffic in drugs;
4. Any inference of sex perversion;
5. White slavery;
6. Miscegenation (sex relationship between the white and black races);
7. Sex hygiene and venereal diseases;
8. Scenes of actual childbirth—in fact or in silhouette;
9. Children's sex organs;
10. Ridicule of the clergy;
11. Willful offence to any nation, race or creed;

And it be further *resolved*, That special care be exercised in the manner in which the following subjects are treated, to the end that vulgarity and suggestiveness may be eliminated and that good taste may be emphasized:

1. The use of the flag;
2. International relations (avoiding picturizing in an unfavorable light another country's religion, history, institutions, prominent people and citizenry);
3. Arson;
4. The use of firearms;
5. Theft, robbery, safe-cracking, and dynamiting of trains, mines, buildings, etc. (having in mind the effect which a too-detailed description of these may have upon the moron);
6. Brutality and possible gruesomeness;
7. Technique of committing murder by whatever method;

8. Methods of smuggling;

9. Third-degree methods.

10. Actual hangings or electrocutions as legal punishment for crime;

11. Sympathy for criminals;

12. Attitude toward public characters and institutions;

13. Sedition;

14. Apparent cruelty to children and animals;

15. Branding of people or animals;

16. The sale of women, or of a woman selling her virtue;

17. Rape or attempted rape;

18. First-night scenes;

19. Man and woman in bed together;

20. Deliberate seduction of girls;

21. The institution of marriage;

22. Surgical operations;

23. The use of drugs;

24. Titles or scenes having to do with law enforcement or law-enforcing officers;

25. Excessive or lustful kissing, particularly when one character or the other is a "heavy."

To prove their sincerity, Hays and Beetson continued meeting with various groups around the nation to discuss their mission—keeping Hollywood sin-free. Beetson assured a group of women at a New York film conference, where twenty-one states were represented, that filmmakers were fully committed to working with them to ensure that future movies would not be offensive, but acceptable to all. Of course, that was well before the Catholic Church declared that watching an immoral film was sinful.

Continuing on his path of protection, Beetson advised the Vocational Guidance Association at one of their luncheons that child actors were carefully monitored and only worked under the strictest of conditions. While at the studio, minors had to be accompanied by a parent or guardian at all times. During a normal eight-hour day, children worked just four and, for the remainder, were either tutored by professional teachers or closely supervised at play. He even solicited suggestions for improving child working conditions promising the group that each and every idea they offered would be seriously considered.

By 1930, The Motion Picture Production Code had replaced "The Don'ts and Be Carefuls." This new code was based on three general principles:

1.   No picture shall be produced that will lower the moral standards of those who see it. Hence the sympathy of the audience should never be thrown to the side of crime, wrongdoing, evil or sin.

2.   Correct standards of life, subject only to the requirements of drama and entertainment, shall be presented.

3.   Law, natural or human, shall not be ridiculed, nor shall sympathy be created for its violation.

Various restrictions were also spelled out including no nudity or suggestive dancing. Reference to venereal disease and scenes depicting childbirth were forbidden. The sacred institution of marriage, along with the American flag, had to be treated respectfully. And since Prohibition was still part of the country's climate, alcohol remained taboo. The list went on and on and on . . .

The studios, however, didn't always adhere to Hays' guidelines, which sometimes got them in trouble with local censorship boards. For example, Universal had an unexpected tangle with the judgmental ladies of Kansas. The wary women approved both *Dracula* (1931) and *The Mummy* (1932), but refused to allow the showing of *Frankenstein* (1931). They felt the latter was too gruesome and wanted several scenes, as well as all close-ups of the monster, cut. Warner Bros. also took some heat when Beetson personally contacted them about their taut drama, *The Hatchet Man* (1932) starring Edward G. Robinson as Chinese hit man Wong Low Get. Beetson strongly warned them against referencing "racketeering," "gangs" and "gang rule" in their crime film. Unlike their real-life counterparts, movie gangsters were expected to tiptoe through their felonious acts.

Aside from keeping movies on the up-and-up, Beetson had his own personal problems to deal with. His wife Minnie filed for a divorce in 1931. She claimed that her husband often came home from work, ate dinner and then went straight to bed neglecting to "entertain" her. Minnie also accused him of being too busy, or too tired, to take her out. After all, a man in his position surely had tickets to all of the current movies and, as a Hollywood housewife, she certainly had a right to some amusement.

By the end of 1932, Beetson was recovering from his divorce with a new wife, Mabel Johnson, who formerly worked for the MPPDA. Hollywood was also getting back on its feet despite the Great Depression and the shift to sound. Beetson reported to the *L.A. Times*:

> Activity in the motion-picture industry continues on an upward trend. Studios are steadily increasing production schedules. . . . There is a decidedly gratifying improvement in this industry which indicates a steady return to normalcy.

Normalcy was one thing, but Hays' rules were another matter entirely. Studios were haphazardly picking and choosing their way down the list. Finally, in 1934, the Production Code became mandatory—not coincidentally, the same year that the Catholic Church formed their Legion of Decency. With millions of Catholics pulling together to save themselves and their children by boycotting movies and taking the heartfelt Legion of Decency pledge, Hollywood had no choice but to pay attention. Even the Pope chimed in, advising his flock that they had a moral obligation to clean up the cinema. With many theaters experiencing a 40% decrease in ticket sales, everyone's bottom line was affected—not to mention the bad publicity. The Production Code seemed more important than ever until unsettling world events and a war directed everyone's attention elsewhere.

As World War II unfolded, Hollywood stepped up and so did the civic-minded Fred Beetson. He joined both the Hollywood Victory and the War Activities Committees. The Victory Committee gave celebrities and other filmmakers who were not on active war duty a chance to entertain the troops and participate in bond drives. The War Activities Committee was responsible for assistance with, and distribution of, government films throughout the nation. Hollywood suddenly became a place of heroes.

Before the war ended, however, the sixty-something Beetson experienced health problems, causing him to relinquish many of his duties including his position as president of the Central Casting Corporation. He continued working on an advisory basis for the MPPDA until his death on March 31, 1953. Looking back on his many accomplishments, Beetson's sharp leadership skills, along with his high ideals, brought many long-term improvements to the fragile business of filmmaking. While he protected America, he also looked out for the players, the extras, the children, the animals and many others who needed a guardian to ease their way.

Along with Fred Beetson, big-time producer Charles H. Christie was also an executive of the MPPDA—at one time he even held the organization's presidency. All the while, he and his brother, Al, continued churning out successful comedies and prize-winning pooches. They also purchased thirty acres in Studio City joining several other major studios like Paramount and Universal who were building updated facilities in the area. For the time being, the brothers agreed to use the property for exterior work only. All interior shots would continue to be filmed at their Sunset Boulevard and Gower Street location. Charles Christie announced their plans in late 1927:

> Our present property in the thickly built up parts of Hollywood is cramped for motion-picture work. We feel that it is only a matter of a short time when we will find it necessary to move entirely from our present location on Sunset Boulevard. Our old studio site is more suitable for the building of close-in apartment-houses and the business enterprises which must serve a thickly populated residence district.

The following year, Christie was hit with a lawsuit. Actress Alys Murrell charged him with "breach of promise to wed, seduction and breach of contract." She wanted $1,847,500 for damages suffered. Christie's attorney, Warren Williams, described the charges as "just plain blackmail." He further claimed that Murrell, also known as Alys B. Mims, had been trying for some time to extort money from Christie. One month later, the charges were dropped and the case settled out of court. Although the exact sum was not made public, the settlement reached was based solely on the breach of contract—seduction and the promise of wedding bells were nixed.

The Christies met the challenge of sound head-on promising that their comedies for the 1928-1929 season would be synchronized with music, sound effects and dialogue. Five hundred thousand dollars was budgeted for sound stages. The brothers also hired African American Spencer Williams, Jr. as a sound technician after hearing some of his work for a New York recording company. Before long, they noticed his talent for writing and soon paid him to pen stories. The Christies were also among the first filmmakers to produce talking pictures for African American audiences. Working with Harlem's Lafayette Players Stock Company, they produced various musical comedy shorts based on a series of *Darktown Birmingham* stories authored by Jewish writer Octavus Ray Cohen and published in the *Saturday Evening Post*. Williams appeared in many of these shorts and eventually went on to television where he portrayed Andy Brown in the 1950's series *Amos 'n' Andy*.

When the stock market crashed in 1929, it devastated the Christies. The following year, the brothers merged with the Metropolitan Sound Studios, Inc. with plans to make feature-length talking pictures. The *L.A. Times* reported on September 30, 1930 that the company, now known as the Metropolitan Christie Picture Corporation, was organized under the laws of the State of Delaware as a $10,000,000 corporation with all common stock. Charles H. Christie was named President. "All agreements connected with the deal have been signed. These including the purchase of the Metropolitan Sound Studios and the Christie property at Studio City on Ventura Boulevard, which will be held for future development and the purchase of certain stock interests in the Christie Film, Company." The Christie property at Sunset and Gower was not part of the deal—neither was the Great Depression.

Despite their merger and their grand plans, the brothers filed for bankruptcy in 1932. Their companies, the Christie Film Company, the Metropolitan Sound Studios, Inc., and the Christie Realty Corporation, Ltd., all went into receivership. After more than two decades of enormous success in the film industry, the Christies were forced to liquidate and never recovered from their losses. While brother Al continued making movies for other film companies, Charles turned his interests toward real estate. Neither of the men ever reached that same level of financial success the movies had brought them in those early days.

Al Christie retired from filmmaking in 1942 and joined the Douglas Aircraft Corporation. He remained an employee there until he died of a heart attack on April 14, 1951 in his Beverly Hills home where he still lived with his brother and sister. His estate was valued at just $2,597—$1,697 in cash along with $900 in personal property. After two decades in the real estate business, Charles also died in the same house on October 1, 1955 after a long illness.

By 1928, photoplaywright Benjamin Floyer Glazer was also a producer. He gained the prestigious title with the Paramount drama *Street of Sin* (1928) starring Swiss-born actor Emil Jannings and Fay Wray in her pre-King Kong days. Still a successful writer, he also won an Award of Merit for penning the highly acclaimed *7th Heaven* (1927).

Just as his contract for Paramount was ending, Glazer experienced a minor flirtation with Irish-Catholic businessman Joseph P. Kennedy and his Hollywood connections. Kennedy needed experienced men to run his newly acquired studio. He convinced Glazer and MGM producer Paul Bern to come and work for him. He promised them that once his empire was fashioned they would be working for Hollywood's greatest studio and would have full reign over film production. As they waited for the Irishman's grand plans to unfurl, Kennedy put Glazer in charge of sound productions at Pathé and FBO Pictures Corporation, both companies now part of his organization. He also named Bern chief of production at Pathé.

Due to his prior experience with director Erich von Stroheim, Kennedy assigned Glazer to manage von Stroheim's production of *Queen Kelly* (1929) starring Gloria Swanson. The strong-willed filmmaker hadn't changed. He shot the film in sequence working long hours and demanding multiple retakes with no regard for cast, crew or budget. Producer and director clashed over the script. Glazer felt it was too long, but von Stroheim wouldn't budge. Bern also encouraged cutting scenes, but to no avail. When Swanson complained to Kennedy about some of the director's unorthodox ideas, such as another player drooling tobacco juice all over her hand, Kennedy fired von Stroheim. Glazer was then tasked with cutting sixteen boxes of film down to a more realistic viewing time, but *Queen Kelly* was not completed. Three years later, the film was pieced together and released, but only in Paris, France. Decades later in 1985, a restored version was shown in the U.S.

In addition to his *Queen Kelly* duties, Glazer overlooked sound production at Pathé and FBO. He shared some insight on that phenomenon:

> I can give you a close-up of a sound, just as I can give you a close-up of a person. It is within my power to exclude any sound without offending your sense of reality. For as I show you only what action I want you to see, likewise, I let you listen only to what sounds I want you to hear. . . .

He also believed that many stage actors who learned to project their voices inside of a theater were not as effective on a movie set where sensitive microphones captured and exaggerated the slightest of sounds. A "natural" voice came across as more realistic on-screen. Instead of a long-winded speech or a never-ending oratory, simple conversation worked best. Dialogue was a challenge for all filmmakers from writers to producers to directors to actors. Learning what worked and understanding what didn't in the changing medium took time and a lot of frustrating experimentation.

In between films, Glazer witnessed weddings. He played best man for his good friend silent screen star John Gilbert when he wed actress Ina Claire on May 10, 1929. Glazer also stood up for MGM art director Cedric Gibbons when he married actress Dolores del Rio on August 6, 1930.

Glazer's own marriage unraveled in 1931 when he and Alice divorced based on her charges of neglect. The next year, Glazer married Paramount actress Sharon Lynn in Yuma, Arizona. Glazer pal Cedric Gibbons along with his wife, Dolores del Rio, witnessed the nuptials. Born in Weatherford, Texas, Lynn's career got started when she entered a beauty contest and won a screen test. The couple eventually had two daughters, Charlene Frances and Barbara Helen.

At work, Glazer produced several films for Pathé including *Strange Cargo* (1929), which he also wrote and directed. Moving on to Paramount, he produced Ernest Hemingway's *A Farewell to Arms* (1932) and *Alice in Wonderland* (1933) featuring newcomer Cary Grant as the Mock Turtle and the more experienced Gary Cooper as the White Knight. In addition to his movie work, Glazer also took punches.

While on the set of *Bolero* (1934), tough guy George Raft had words with Glazer about a line in the movie. When the producer refused to alter the problematic words, Raft hauled off and slugged him right in front of the cast and crew—although Glazer later described it as more of a "push." Their dispute was settled in the executive offices with Raft apologizing and Glazer accepting. It was back to work for everyone.

Glazer received his second Academy Award for Best Writing with *Arise My Love* (1940), billed as "a romance that could only happen in 1940" featuring Claudette Colbert. That same year, he returned to Broadway— this time with a partner, Ernest "Papa" Hemingway. "Papa" penned his play, *The Fifth Column*, while staying at a Madrid hotel during the volatile Spanish Civil War. The story tells of the perilous situation faced by hotel inhabitants comprised of journalists, spies and members of General Franco's "fifth column" also considered rebel spies.

After several failed attempts to stage the play, Glazer caught wind of it. He persuaded Hemingway to let him have a go at it. The Hollywood producer had already successfully brought Hemingway's *Farewell to Arms* (1932) to the silver screen, and so "Papa" agreed. Under the terms of their contract, if "Papa" approved of Glazer's ideas, "Papa" would revise the play under his own name and the two writers would split any profits. If "Papa" didn't like Glazer's offerings, Glazer could go ahead with the play anyway, but it would only be billed as an adaptation of Hemingway's original play. In the end, "Papa" hated Glazer's version and tried to back out of their agreement with no luck. *The Fifth Column* debuted on Broadway in the spring of 1940—after the Spanish Loyalists faced defeat.

Directed by the legendary Lee Strasberg, the play starred actors Franchot Tone and Lee J. Cobb. With mixed reviews—some praised the acting while others knocked the writing—the play closed after fewer than 90 performances. Hemingway never saw one.

In 1946, Glazer and partner Nat W. Finston founded Symphony Films. The independent company completed one production, which Glazer wrote and directed, *Song of My Heart* (1948), a fictional telling of the life of the composer Tchaikovsky. Sixty-year old Glazer then left Hollywood.

On February 16, 1956, yet another adaptation of Glazer's beloved *Liliom* made it to the big screen. This time it was an Oscar and Hammerstein song-laden film, directed by Henry King. *Carousel* (1956) starred Gordon MacRae with his booming voice as the deceased Billy Bigelow and joined the ranks of the many popular musical films that began with MGM's *The Broadway Melody* back in 1929.

One month later, the 68-year-old Glazer died of circulatory failure at Cedars of Lebanon Hospital in Los Angeles. The rabbi who officiated at Glazer's service spoke eloquently when he said: "Some of us walk the earth treading the pavement, while others with sensitive souls are given the ability to see the beauty of things. They climb ladders—Jacob's ladders—high above the sky while others walk the earth."

Chapter Twenty-Two

MOGUL TO MOGUL

As Louis B. Mayer got the Academy rolling, MGM was flourishing. By the middle of 1927, the studio had more than 70 movies under development with several more ready for release. Of the original triumvirate, Thalberg was responsible for major productions, with Harry Rapf bringing up the rear. Mayer remained in charge of all studio business and reported directly to Marcus Loew of Loew, Inc., MGM's parent company. Mayer delivered topnotch entertainment and Loew was pleased with the fine films running in his theaters across the country. Loew and Mayer were businessmen who understood each other.

Their status quo came to an abrupt end on September 5, 1927 when fifty-seven-year-old Loew succumbed to heart disease and Mayer lost his greatest ally. Loew's estate was worth approximately $30,000,000. In addition, his widow and twin sons inherited his controlling shares of the company. Nicholas Schenck, Loew's right-hand man, inherited Loew's job—a move that concerned Mayer. Nick Schenck was hard to get along with—even his brother, Joe, knew that. Running his business decisions by Schenck rankled Mayer. At the same time, Schenck resented Mayer's control over MGM. Despite their differences, the two men continued working together, but their mutual aversion drove a deeper wedge in an already rocky relationship.

1927 also brought with it *The Jazz Singer* (1927). Like it or not, sound was now officially part of filmmaking, but MGM wasn't equipped to make talking pictures. Instead, Mayer had to cut a deal with Paramount chief Adolph Zukor allowing MGM's talking scenes to be filmed after hours on Roy Pomeroy's soundstage. By 1928, Mayer also had to find the perfect roar, as MGM's silent symbol now needed a voice. The Bronx Zoo recorded one of their noisier felines and that sound was synced up with the original Selig lion clip. The roaring lion was first heard as *White Shadows in the South Seas* (1928) began to roll.

In late January 1929, new U.S. President Herbert Hoover, whose campaign Mayer had vigorously supported, offered the studio head a diplomatic position—Ambassador to Turkey. Mayer turned him down, claiming he was just too busy with MGM. It was the truth. Mayer had his hands full.

The studio was catching up to the new technology as more than twenty sound stages were being built. Mayer was also actively involved with the first annual Academy Awards. As supervisor of the voting, he worked with the Central Board of Judges to identify the winners in each category. In addition, he dealt with difficult stars like Greta Garbo who had recently ticked off the Swedish royals due to her affair with their prince, which caused her to return to the States in a nasty mood. To top it all off, William Fox, head of Fox Film Corporation, bought controlling shares of stock in Loew's, Inc. from the Widow Loew and her children behind Mayer's back. Fox also bought Nick Schenck's shares. Feeling that Schenck sold him out, the MGM chief realized that if all went according to Fox's plan, there would be a corporate merger, leaving Mayer without a job.

Turkey might have been the better option if Fox hadn't had a serious car accident that put him out of action followed by the stock market crash. Both unfortunate events proved lucky for Mayer. Fox lost pretty much everything including his control over Loew's Inc. Mayer remained in charge of MGM and Schenck gained a nickname. Mayer took to calling his boss Nick "Skunk."

At the beginning of the new decade, both Mayer and Thalberg had new contracts assuring them positions at MGM for the next five years. Despite the Depression, the scandals and the temperamental stars, MGM, now completely converted to talking pictures, pulled in $12,000,000 worth of profits for 1931. Mayer once wrote in a telegram: "Spare nothing, neither expense, time, nor effort. Results only are what I am after."

He believed in showcasing great stars in great films and liked to brag that MGM had "more stars than there are in heaven." But keeping those stars shining bright was often a challenge. When faced with real or imaginary opposition, Mayer cajoled. He berated. He begged. He threatened. When that didn't work, he'd fall to his knees, hands clasped, as crocodile tears leaked from behind his glasses. His assorted tactics almost always worked. He got exactly what he wanted as many a bewildered celebrity bolted from his office wondering what had just happened.

He ran his studio like a grand old patriarch ran his family. He believed in motherhood, America and happy endings—a little beauty, glamour and optimism never hurt either. Mayer wanted to give the American people films they could be proud to bring their families to see. In that sense, he defined MGM and in turn MGM represented the best Hollywood had to offer. It all came down to that class and respectability he still craved.

If only it were so easy at home. Mayer had two headstrong daughters, now young adults and interested in men. As their father and head of the family, he had to sanction any would-be suitors. When daughter Edie announced she was seeing film executive William Goetz, Mayer approved, but ordered her to only go out with him every other night. After their engagement, he insisted on throwing a lavish wedding at the Biltmore Hotel befitting a man of his position, and most likely pleased his daughter and her intended.

Irene's choice of the wordy David O. Selznick aggravated Mayer. He took a dim view of their engagement despite the young producer's success at Paramount, and so in contrast to Edie's elaborate bash, Irene married Selznick at the family's beach house in Santa Monica. Mayer reluctantly gave the bride away using his father's recent death as an excuse for the low-key affair. He did, however, experience a change of heart toward his talented son-in-law two years later. When Thalberg had his heart attack, Mayer brought Selznick into MGM.

Without Thalberg to temper him, Mayer ran his studio with a firm hand. The individual production units he established eventually found their footing. Weekly board meetings were held by studio executives to discuss current business. Mayer, however, made all final decisions. Headman, father figure and secret-keeper, he guarded his studio like a king protected his realm. He gave praise, doled out punishment and dictated orders expecting loyalty and respect in return.

Mayer's choices in film took precedence and his participation in the production end of the business increased after Thalberg's death. With romantic dramas such as *Test Pilot* (1938) and classics like *Boys Town* (1938), Mayer pleased Depression-era spectators with just the right amount of adventure and sentiment. He cast the popular Mickey Rooney in the familial *Andy Hardy* series, and used Judy Garland to full advantage in *The Wizard of Oz* (1939)—only after being told that Shirley Temple wasn't available. And when his son-in-law David O. Selznick decided that only Clark Gable could play Rhett Butler in Selznick's production of *Gone With the Wind* (1939), Mayer and MGM garnered the distribution rights to the blockbuster film in exchange for their top star.

World events and Nazi Germany soon impacted Hollywood. As Hitler invaded country after country, Loew's, Inc. lost their European theaters as well as their control over the continent's MGM film distribution. In response, MGM churned out films like *Comrade X* (1940) concerning an American reporter in communist Russia, *Escape* (1940) about a young man searching for his mother in Nazi Germany and *Waterloo Bridge* (1940), the story of a British officer at the onset of World War II.

Once the United States entered the war, many top stars including MGM's recently widowed Clark Gable traded their studio costumes for military uniforms. Those who stayed behind volunteered their services at the Hollywood and Stage Door Canteens. Some worked on the Hollywood Victory and War Activities Committees. Being a genuine patriot and proud of his American citizenship, Mayer encouraged his employees to join the war effort—even if it affected MGM's bottom line, or business relationships. When actor Lew Ayres declared he was a pacifist and refused to enlist, Mayer released him from his contract.

When Mayer wasn't at MGM, he bred racehorses at his 500-acre ranch in Perris, California—about 70 miles north of Los Angeles. While riding there during the summer of 1944, he took a nasty fall and broke his pelvis. Rushed to the hospital, he underwent surgery to repair the damage. Undaunted, Mayer continued running MGM from his hospital bed. Rumors of his retirement surfaced. Mayer, however, would have none of it and by year end, he was back in the saddle as well as his office.

As the war finally reached its conclusion, things were looking up. One by one, the stars returned to work. Fan favorites like Clark Gable came back from the Army and Robert Taylor from the Navy. Even Mayer's horses were doing well at the tracks. He quietly shared his good fortune with several employees who were down on their luck. He gave money to his driver to help feed the man's family and a check for $7,500 to his caterer so she could buy a house for her mother. Always softhearted when it came to mothers, Mayer even gave the grateful woman an extra grand to take her mother shopping for new clothes.

While Mayer kept his studio humming, his marriage fell apart. Over the years, Margaret, a cancer survivor, had been in and out of mental institutions while Mayer, for the most part, kept his many dalliances discreet. After a long separation, the couple officially ended their 43-year union. The divorce cost him dearly. He had to give Margaret $1,500,000 up front and another $2,000,000 paid in installments over the next few years. She also got the beach house in Santa Monica. Mayer walked away with his freedom and soon became involved with a former Busby Berkeley dancer, Lorena Danker—a widow with a young daughter.

At 61 years old, however, Mayer was getting tired. He no longer had the energy to keep up with the studio and his Perris ranch. With over 200 fine horses, Mayer was often credited with raising the level of California racing. At a black-tie auction on February 27, 1947, he sold his beloved horses at what was then the largest horse sale the state had ever seen. Mayer brought in over $1,500,000 including the $200,000 paid by Harry Warner for the prize horse, Stepfather.

After cancer claimed Mayer's brother, Jerry, in the fall of 1947, he worried about his own health. The stress and strain of running the studio, along with the divorce and horse sale, was taking its toll, but the worst was yet to come. The following summer Dore Schary resigned from his position at RKO and Nick Schenck offered him the job of associate vice president in charge of production at MGM. Schary returned to MGM on July 1, 1948. Mayer saw it as a personal attack, and theirs was a power struggle from the start.

Later that year, Mayer made Lorena Danker his wife. The couple eloped to Yuma, Arizona and married on December 4, 1948. After a three-day honeymoon in Palm Springs, it was back to reality. Mayer still brooded over his health and worried that his control at MGM was waning. He also fretted over daughter Irene's divorce from Selznick who had left her for actress Jennifer Jones, perhaps reaffirming his original reservations about Selznick. Mayer and his stepdaughter whom he eventually adopted did not get along. She resented his old-fashioned ideas about children being seen and not heard. The tide was changing and MGM profits were at an all-time low. The public was no longer interested in the types of movies Mayer liked to make. Happily ever after and sainted mothers were out. Realism was in.

Nonetheless, Mayer continued championing upbeat films like *Annie Get Your Gun* (1950) and *Show Boat* (1951) while Schary put out hard-edged movies such as the violent *Border Incident* (1949) about illegal Mexican immigrants and *Intruder in the Dust* (1949) with its controversial depiction of racism—topics uncomfortable for Mayer. The "class factor" that Mayer had always clung to was going by the wayside. The studio he built and nurtured for over 25 years was turning into a stranger. Loyalties were divided. Some were firmly entrenched in Schary's new way of thinking while others remained in Mayer's camp. Television was also lurking. Like many filmmakers, Mayer detested the little box, feeling it was only a fleeting fad, but a competitor nonetheless to the films he made. Schary, on the other hand, saw possibilities on the small screen.

Things came to a head after Mayer received a special Oscar on March 29, 1951 for "distinguished service to the motion picture industry." Mayer accused Schary of going behind his back after signing a new contract with MGM. He may have felt that the brass thought he should retire, or worse yet, believed his ideas had become passé. He also accused Schenck of being arrogant and stupid. His outbursts came more often as his insecurities mounted. Reportedly, Mayer gave Schenck an ultimatum—choose between him or Schary. Schenck chose Schary. Finally, in the spring of 1951, Mayer resigned and simply left his office in a huff, never to return.

No longer associated with the studio that bore his name, Mayer simply told the press that he was "going to be more active than I have at any time during the past fifteen years at a studio and under conditions where I shall have the right to make the right kind of pictures—decent, wholesome pictures for Americans and for people throughout the world who want and need this type of entertainment."

Filled with bitterness and trying to find ways to get back into the motion picture industry, Mayer's health finally failed. He came down with pneumonia. After several tests, the deadly diagnosis came back— leukemia. Mayer, however, was simply told he had a bad case of anemia. Now battling a serious disease that he was unaware of, Mayer's physical condition deteriorated. After several weeks in the hospital and many transfusions, he was in severe pain and taking morphine. He often hallucinated and fought with the hospital staff. Eventually, he went into a coma and died on October 29, 1957 with Lorena at his side. *The Hollywood Reporter* declared: "Mr. Motion Picture is Gone."

The man who brought class and respectability to Hollywood was also the first U.S. executive to earn an annual paycheck of $1,000,000. The money was nice, but the prestige of running a major studio that stood apart from the rest was even better. Both Hollywood kings, Louis B. Mayer and his roaring-lion trademark, had a lot in common.

Instead of a lion at the helm, Paramount had Jesse L. Lasky and as Vice President in Charge of Production, he viewed *The Jazz Singer* (1927) with some skepticism. Lasky had been in the film business long enough to know that the concept of talking pictures had come and gone on several occasions. Believing that this new attempt at sound was no more than a passing fancy, he spoke to a group of salesmen in Atlantic City at their 1928 convention. He frankly told the group that Paramount had no sound pictures scheduled for production although he admitted that sound effects and occasional dialogue might be added to some of their films.

With the unexpected success of *Wings* (1927) and its loud, buzzing fighter planes, Lasky and Zukor re-evaluated their plan. They soon took some of their completed silent films like the baseball tale *Warming Up* (1928) and added noise—the quick, cracking sound of a bat as it met the baseball head-on along with the thunderous roar of the crowd as they shouted their approval. This last-minute fix was known around the film colony as "the goat gland process." It gave otherwise ill-fated silent movies a shot in the arm.

Once Paramount's first complete talking picture, *Interference* (1928), was released, there was no looking back. Just three months after Lasky told the Atlantic City salesmen that talking pictures were not part of Paramount's program, he changed his mind. Paramount would finish the silent movies that were already in production, but only talking pictures would follow. As a result, new sound stages had to be built, but just as the first one was finished, fire destroyed it before a single scene had ever been filmed. It took months for Paramount to replace their loss. Lasky later recalled in his autobiography:

> Within a year things were running smoothly again, but with many more craftsmen and auxiliary mechanical devices, less teamwork, more complex organization, less pioneering spirit, more expense, less inspiration, more talent, less glamour, more predatory competition, less hospitality, more doing, less joy in the doing.

Lasky had come a long way from his horn-blowing days at Alaska's Sourdough Saloon. His total worth was now estimated at $20,000,000. Aside from their estate in California, the Laskys rented a twenty-room apartment in New York that Bessie filled with European antiques. Lasky also renovated their Santa Monica beach house to include ten baths, a gymnasium, two swimming pools and a convertible solarium theater. Louis B. Mayer and Sam Goldwyn lived on either side. Unfortunately, Lasky never thought that his high-dollar income would one day dry up.

Paramount stocks took a dive after the stock market crashed in 1929. With Lasky investing heavily in his studio, his large living was suddenly jeopardized. The Paramount stocks he bought for $1,550,000 sold for a mere $37,500. He closed his New York apartment and moved his family into the Santa Monica beach house. Then, as if things couldn't get any worse, his beloved sister, Blanche, died on March 12, 1932 after a week-long battle with pneumonia.

New executives with an influx of cash were brought into Paramount. Lasky was told to take a leave of absence and on April 30, 1932, he left his Paramount office for the last time. Lasky described that fateful moment:

> . . . at long last I knew how Sam Goldwyn and Cecil DeMille must have felt when they had been eased out of the company the three of us had helped to launch. The wheel had come around full circle. Sam and Cecil had both gone forward to even greater glories in the business.

Would I do the same, I wondered—or did my best work lay behind me? My mind was filled with apprehension.

The following year, Lasky was back to work. He signed a three-year contract with Fox as an independent producer. Beginning with *Zoo in Budapest* (1933) starring the dark-haired Loretta Young, Lasky spearheaded a total of eighteen pictures. Among his more popular Fox features were the period picture *Berkeley Square* (1933) with British actor Leslie Howard and *The Power and The Glory* (1933), a film written by Preston Sturges featuring relative newcomer Spencer Tracy.

After meeting his contractual obligations with Fox, Lasky briefly teamed up with Mary Pickford to form Pickford-Lasky Productions, Inc. Two pictures later, Lasky turned to radio. His show *Gateway to Hollywood* was an early type of *American Idol*. Every Sunday night, the program brought young hopefuls from around the country to Hollywood. During the live broadcasts, a performer would team up with a movie star such as Joan Crawford or Cary Grant and read specially written radio plays for a set of professional filmmakers acting as judges. The victors received contracts and guaranteed screen roles at major studios. Winners like Rhonda Fleming got their start on the show and non-winners like Linda Darnell got noticed.

By 1941, *Gateways to Hollywood* was over and Lasky was looking for his next picture. He became obsessed with the story of World War I hero Sergeant Alvin C. York. After being turned down at many of the major studios, including Paramount, Harry Warner agreed to let Lasky make his film at Warner Bros. Lasky then bartered with his former brother-in-law and business partner, Sam Goldfish (now Goldwyn and running the Samuel Goldwyn Company), to borrow one of his top players, Gary Cooper. According to Lasky, when he told this bit of news to Jack Warner, he was delighted—until he learned that part of the deal was lending Warner Bros.' star Bette Davis to Goldwyn for his film classic *The Little Foxes* (1941). It all worked out, however, when Cooper won an Oscar for his performance as York and Davis got a nomination for her portrayal of Regina Giddens.

Lasky went on to produce only five more films—none, however, equaled the great success of *Sergeant York* (1941). He completed his autobiography, *I Blow My Own Horn*, which was published in 1957. Shortly after, he was the guest of honor on the television show *This is Your Life*, lured to the studio on the pretext that he would be talking about his book.

Lasky, who never recovered financially from his Depression-era losses, was still thinking about movies. He often said "You're never broke if you have an idea." He wanted to make a film about high school marching bands and was working on this project when he was struck by a heart attack at the Beverly Hilton Hotel on January 13, 1958.

Of his many outstanding moments, he still took pride in meeting his boyhood idol, bandleader John Philip Sousa. After the band's performance at a Paramount theater, Lasky confessed his youthful dream. He'd always hoped that Sousa and company would march down his street, hear him play his cornet and place him in the band. He even admitted to still keeping his old mouthpiece next to his bed at night—just in case movies didn't work out. The maestro laughed: "Well, since they have worked out too well, you'd better thank me for not walking down Santa Clara Street. If I had, you might be sweating in a band uniform out there on the Paramount stage today."

Unlike Mayer and Lasky who were riding high as the Academy was forming, Harry Warner was once again facing financial ruin. Despite the continued success of their canine star, Rin Tin Tin, Warner Bros. needed a major hit.

Knowing that the solvency of the family business rested on *The Jazz Singer*, Sam, who had the most experience with sound, took charge. Moving his wife and new daughter, Lita, back to Los Angeles, he put in long hours tending personally to the film's many details as headaches plagued him. By the time the film wrapped, Sam was exhausted and everyone around him noticed the physical toll that this latest production had taken on the forty-year-old. The pills he had been popping to keep him going were no longer effective.

The Warners planned to premiere their latest feature in New York on October 6, 1927—coincidentally Lita's first birthday. If this new talking picture revolutionized the film medium the way they hoped, Warner Bros. would once again be a major Hollywood contender. If the picture failed, the company and the brothers were finished.

Instead of heading to New York with his brothers, however, Sam was admitted to the hospital with a case of bad sinuses. Diagnosed with an "acute mastoid infection," he underwent surgery, but his condition did not improve. Doctors performed a second surgery and then a third. Abe was the first brother to arrive at the hospital, just before Sam's fourth surgery. Harry and Jack were en route from New York when a cerebral hemorrhage claimed Sam on October 5, 1927. None of the brothers were present for *The Jazz Singer's* triumphant premiere. Instead, they were in mourning.

Once family matters were attended to, Harry had to get back to business. It was only a matter of time until other production companies attained the same level of technology and released talkies of their own. In order to stay ahead of the game, Harry boldly borrowed $100,000,000 and bought controlling shares of First National Pictures who also owned one of the largest theater chains in the country. He then reorganized the company. Still the man on top, Harry remained in control of the overall budget. He put his only son, Lewis, now twenty, in charge of the recently acquired Warner Bros. Music. Abe headed up the theater division while Jack continued running the studio with producer Darryl Zanuck overseeing First National. By 1929, Harry Warner was considered one of the most powerful men in the film industry and Warner Bros. made a tidy profit exceeding $14,000,000.

That same year, Harry bought a twenty-two-acre farm in Mount Vernon, New York for his wife, Rea, and their three children. Betty, the youngest, recalled:

Mother . . . went back to the city, where they were dismantling famous homes, homes that had belonged to the original 400 families, like the Astors, and bought whole rooms—walls, ceilings, and floors—and transplanted them to Mount Vernon. . . .

. . . father loved the farm. He had all kinds of animals, pigeons, sheep, cows, dogs, and rabbits. He continued to practice and be proud of his butchering and breeding of prize chickens. He thought of himself as a first-generation Jewish cobbler and butcher turned movie mogul.

Harry also added a fourth child to the family, Sam's daughter, Lita. Convinced that Lina Basquette was an unfit mother, he took custody of the three-year-old and raised her as his own.

During this time, Harry was also grooming Lewis to one day take over the leadership of Warner Bros.—another thing that irritated Jack. Outgoing, smart and talented, Lewis loved music, had many friends and enjoyed the good times and privileges that came with being his father's son. That all changed in the spring of 1931 when the young man experienced an infected wisdom tooth. After having the tooth pulled and against his doctor's advice, the twenty-two-year old headed to Cuba for a vacation arranged by his father. Once there, the infection spread to his gum. Lewis' condition grew worse despite the best efforts of a Cuban dentist. Harry sent a plane to Havana and flew his son to Miami. From Florida, Lewis caught a train to New York where he was hospitalized and surgery performed. Five weeks later, he caught pneumonia and died on April 5, 1931. Harry's dream of passing the studio on to his son was gone and Jack was biding his time.

With the Great Depression taking hold in the early 1930s and box office sales down, Warner Bros., like many other companies, was feeling the pinch. Forced to let almost 1,000 employees go and impose pay cuts on those remaining, the studio continued releasing gritty gangster films like *Public Enemy* (1931) with the grapefruit friendly James Cagney and

Little Caesar (1931) featuring the tough-talking Edward G. Robinson. The studio also threw in an occasional western like *Somewhere in Sonora* (1933) with John Wayne or a musical such as *42nd Street* (1933) with its groundbreaking Busby Berkeley choreography. All proved popular with an economically challenged public.

By the end of 1934, flames claimed much of the Burbank studio with losses totaling more than $2,000,000. The Warner Bros. fire chief died from a heart attack after fighting the blaze. Aside from losing the chief, Harry was particularly distressed about the irreplaceable prints that were destroyed—twenty years worth of films were lost. Thankfully, 1935 was better. The studio finally turned a profit after several lean years. Harry moved his family from New York back to California to a home in Beverly Hills. He also purchased Jesse L. Lasky's lavish Santa Monica beach house as well as a 1,100-acre ranch where he, like Louis B. Mayer, raised racehorses. Abe remained in New York to handle the business there. For Harry, the downside to living and working in California meant more confrontations with Jack.

Without Sam to act as a buffer, the oldest and youngest Warner constantly quarreled. Harry loudly disapproved of Jack's many romantic dalliances and what he perceived as Jack's devil-may-care attitude toward the business. As for Jack, he still resented the power that Harry wielded and encouraged his brother to find a girl and have some fun. A devoted family man, Harry was appalled at the very idea.

By 1939, trouble was lurking in Europe prompting Harry to close their offices in Germany. He also gave the go-ahead for *Confessions of a Nazi Spy* (1939) with Edward G. Robinson as a G-man. The film's political statement condemned Germany and their Nazi nation. Harry and Jack both received death threats over their controversial picture. Even Congress dismissed the film, accusing Warner Bros. of "creating hysteria among the American public and inciting them to war."

After the bombing of Pearl Harbor, Harry, now vindicated for the backlash from *Confessions of a Nazi Spy*, and his studio joined the war effort.

He told his department heads that they were going to make training films for the U.S. government and further declared that he expected no profit from any of them. The studio went on to make a series of shorts—some strictly for training soldiers with others geared toward all U.S. citizens. Proud of these pictures, Harry was so delighted when a *New York Times* journalist wrote that Warner Bros. was "combining good citizenship with good picture making" that he had those very words stretched across a billboard near the studio.

During the war years, most of Warner Bros.' general movies maintained a patriotic theme. From Jesse L. Lasky's *Sergeant York* (1941) and the romantic drama of *Casablanca* (1942) to the spirited musical *Yankee Doodle Dandy* (1942), Harry kept his promise to make American films for Americans, but he also had to think about the future. In 1945, he announced:

> The motion picture industry would be shamefully remiss if it were not looking ahead to its task in the postwar world. The essence of the task can be stated in a single phrase, "To interpret the American Way." . . . One of our chief aims now in the postwar world will be to show Americans how millions of Chinese, Icelanders, Indians, Eskimos, and Russians live. I can think of no clearer, surer way to achieve a community of nations . . .

As World War II came to an end, Harry's life erupted. His daughter Doris divorced and remarried. The entire episode caused Harry great embarrassment over what he considered dirty family laundry aired in public. Then to make matters worse, Lina Basquette resurfaced after almost 20 years. Her tumultuous life included six more marriages as well as numerous affairs. Now she wanted one-fourth of all Warner Bros. assets, claiming that as Sam's widow, she was entitled to his share of the family goods. She settled for $100,000 in cash, but not before causing Harry further public shame.

As the House Un-American Activities Committee combed Hollywood for Communists, the Supreme Court ruled that movie studios could no longer own their theaters. More star players were going the independent route hiring agents to represent them and no longer tied to just one studio. Throw a new medium, television, in the mix and by 1950, the studios' golden era was quickly coming to an end with Warner Bros.' profits in a decided downspin.

Now in his seventies, Harry preferred life on his ranch among his prized horses to the studio. Besides it was also a place where he could avoid Jack. As age crept up on them, instead of mellowing the brothers out, Harry and Jack's mutual animosity deepened. Their arguments became louder and more heated. Jack now owned a home in Cap d'Antibes near the French Riviera where he indulged in one of his favorite pastimes, gambling—another activity that Harry frowned upon. Abe was still living in New York and wanted to retire. Harry, however, wasn't quite ready to give up the family business.

When Jack began talks with a Canadian conglomerate about selling the studio, he kept it from his brothers. Once the story leaked to the press, seventy-five-year-old Harry was irate. Jack insisted that he and Abe wanted out. They had all worked hard their entire lives and deserved a chance to "sit on our ass and watch sunsets." He also reminded Harry that Rea and his daughters wanted him to take it easy. It took time for Harry to come to grips with the sale, but he finally agreed as long as all three brothers left together.

In the spring of 1956, the Warner Brothers sold their studio to a group of investors. What Harry and Abe didn't know was that Jack made a deal of his own. Once the brothers signed over their shares, Jack would get his back and then be named president of the company—the position he always wanted and resented Harry for having. When Harry read about the underhanded deal in the paper, he collapsed—the victim of a stroke and his own brother's deception.

Harry suffered several strokes before he died on July 27, 1958 at the age of 76. The official cause of death was a cerebral occlusion, but family members insisted that Harry died of a broken heart.

Chapter Twenty-Three

ANCIENT SLAVES, BAD FACELIFTS AND BROKEN TOWEL BARS

B y 1928, Cecil B. DeMille was working with the Academy's Committee on College Affairs, as well as helming the presidency of the MPPDA. He also signed a contract with MGM to direct three films with which he had to please the brass—namely, Mayer and Thalberg—by making sure he did not overspend during production and still end up with quality films that would earn-out at the box office. This was an adjustment for the controlling filmmaker who was used to having the final word on all of his productions. After three mediocre films, beginning with DeMille's first talkie, *Dynamite* (1929), followed by his only musical, *Madam Satan* (1930) and ending with a remake of *The Squaw Man* (1931), neither DeMille nor MGM wanted to continue their relationship. But there was more . . .

In between these films, the stock markets crashed and DeMille lost one million dollars, but managed to hang on to the two million he had invested in California oil wells. He walked daughter Cecilia down the aisle when she married Los Angeles businessman Francis Edgar Calvin. In addition, he broke his ankle and also underwent an appendectomy.

After all that, he returned to the Paramount fold with the help of his old friend and partner, Jesse L. Lasky—much to Adolph Zukor's displeasure. "Creepy" Zukor warned DeMille that he had just one chance to prove himself. If his first film for Paramount were not a blockbuster bonanza, it would be his last.

Despite the fact that Lasky was let go during production, DeMille didn't disappoint. Relying on his tried and true formula, bible stories plus sex, *The Sign of the Cross* (1932) played to sellout crowds. With British actor Charles Laughton as arch fiddler Nero, and former banker Frederic March as Roman good guy Marcus Superbus, the film was a silver screen sensation. Between seductive slave dances, barely-there costumes and an unprecedented bathtub scene featuring an unclad Claudette Colbert submerged in donkey milk, the soon-to-be martyred Christians acted heroically as they faced a grisly death inside the Roman arena.

A typical DeMille day started at 6:30 a.m. on the aptly named DeMille Drive. By seven, he and Constance had breakfast together before he went to work. He arrived at the studio shortly after eight through his own entranceway—the aptly named DeMille Gate. He was on the set of his current production by nine where he filmed until after noon. He then ate lunch in the studio commissary with his staff who always waited for their leader's arrival before indulging. Then it was back to the set until seven. After that, the daily rushes were viewed and meetings held. Back home on DeMille Drive around eleven, he and Constance shared a late dinner before the director locked up the house and trudged off to bed with a book.

After a couple more not-so-successful films, Zukor prodded DeMille: "Better do another historical epic, Cecil, with plenty of sex." History and sex. For DeMille, that meant only one person—Egyptian Queen Cleopatra. Claudette Colbert, just back at Paramount after completing Columbia's *It Happened One Night* (1934) with Clark Gable, was tapped for the leading role. With over-the-top battle scenes, shimmying slaves who were half-naked and royal seductions aplenty, *Cleopatra* (1934) brought DeMille back—front and center.

Temporarily abandoning the ancients and their debauchery, DeMille took a turn at American history with Gary Cooper as Wild Bill Hickok in *The Plainsmen* (1936). Mexican-born Anthony Quinn, a newcomer to Paramount, was cast as a Cheyenne Indian. During this time, DeMille also started moonlighting for Lever Brothers' *Lux Radio Theater* pulling in two grand for his duties as host and director for each weekly broadcast. For the next nine years, DeMille ingratiated himself into private homes by introducing stars like Clark Gable and Barbara Stanwyck who read radio versions of popular movie scripts.

After the Wild West, DeMille turned his attention to the War of 1812 and the pirate Jean Lafitte in *The Buccaneer* (1938). Anthony Quinn had found his way into DeMille's good graces and gained a supporting role in the film. He also married into the family, taking daughter Kathleen as his first wife on October 5, 1937.

In early 1939, the director, now in his fifties, collapsed on the set of *Union Pacific* (1939). Production was shut down for three weeks while he recovered from prostate surgery. DeMille, packed in ice, returned to work on a stretcher and kept right on directing his movie while lying on his back. Due to the film's success, Paramount gave him a four-picture contract, his continued tension with Zukor notwithstanding.

Personal tragedy struck the DeMille family on March 15, 1941 when Katherine and Anthony Quinn's two-and-a-half-year-old son, Christopher, wandered away from home. While playing with a toy sailboat, the toddler accidentally tumbled into a pond that belonged to W.C. Fields who lived next door. The gardener found the boy and emergency personnel were summoned, but they could not revive him. DeMille arrived on the scene in time to help carry the child's body back to the house to wait for the coroner.

Later that year, America entered World War II while DeMille was running his own production unit inside Paramount. He had also transitioned from black and white film to Technicolor making movies like *The Story of Dr. Wassell* (1944) and *Unconquered* (1947)—both pretty much flops despite the casting of fan favorite Gary Cooper in both starring roles. The press reported on the personal side of DeMille during those war years:

> . . . The old tycoon of celluloid, bathtub and glamour, who for 30 years could obtain all the comforts of life by simply pressing a button, is now reduced to waiting on table at his house, tending the garden . . . washing his own socks . . . He has lost a valet and a writer to the draft, a butler, a maid and two gardeners to Lockheed, and the laundryman to a Japanese relocation center. . . .

After hosting more than 400 radio shows with millions of listeners around the country, DeMille resigned from the *Lux Radio Theater* in 1945 over a political dispute. He eventually returned to the bible for *Samson and Delilah* (1949)—another film filled with spectacle, skin and sin. The Academy honored the long-term director with a Special Award "for thirty-seven years of brilliant showmanship." DeMille then took a turn in front of the camera when he played himself in Billy Wilder's classic *Sunset Boulevard* (1950).

DeMille's circus drama, *The Greatest Show on Earth* (1952), featuring Charlton Heston in his first major screen role, earned an Academy Award for Best Picture. The director also claimed the much-coveted Irving Thalberg Memorial Award that same year. Back in his biblical element, DeMille had one more film left in his directorial bag of tricks—a remake of his 1923 blockbuster silent movie, *The Ten Commandments.*

This time DeMille bypassed California's Guadalupe Dunes and went directly to Egypt. While filming the famous Exodus scene there, he suffered a heart attack, but finished the picture in spite of his doctors' protests. The star-laden film was the culmination of all of the demanding director's previous work rolled into one—the biblical theme, the grandeur and the overwhelming spectacle that came to define DeMille. And yes, there was sex.

At home, a family drama played out when DeMille's older brother, William, died at Playa del Rey on March 5, 1955 from cancer. Shortly after the funeral, a secret shared by the brothers for over thirty years was revealed when DeMille spoke to his thirty-three-year-old adopted son, Richard:

> Before you were born, your Uncle William and I agreed that whichever
> of us died first, the other would tell you about your parents. Your father
> was your Uncle William. Your mother was a writer.

That writer was Lorna Moon—the friend of Frances Marion who had been stricken with tuberculosis and died in a New Mexico sanitarium on May 1, 1930 with funding from the sympathetic MGM producer Harry Rapf. The elder DeMille's affair with the novelist resulted in a son, whom Cecil and Constance agreed to adopt, claiming he was a foundling.

After completing his autobiography and in the midst of planning a new film, the 77-year-old suffered a second heart attack. He died on January 21, 1959 with daughter Cecilia at his side. His book, *The Autobiography of Cecil B. DeMille,* was published posthumously. DeMille once announced that he didn't write the bible and he didn't invent sex. Maybe not, but it was his idea to shuffle them together on the silver screen. From the barn on Selma and Vine to the spectacle in Egypt, nothing was too risky or too big for the man who marched with Moses and flirted with Cleopatra. William DeMille summed him up best: "One thing I have always admired about my younger brother is his ability to bite off more than he can chew, and then chew it."

Cedric Gibbons was also a director—an art director—who designed sets and sometimes awards. When the Academy decided to recognize outstanding achievements in the motion picture industry with what they called an "Award of Merit," a committee was formed with Gibbons in charge of making up the program's rules, as well as designing the award itself. The group considered all types of prizes—medals, certificates, plaques, etc. Gibbons felt a statuette would be more dignified and sketched a sleek, strong-looking knight with an imperial air of being the best—whom we now know as Oscar.

The dapper art director drove his Deusenberg to the studio every morning. After removing his fashionable hat and gloves, he got down to business—running the MGM Art Department. Gibbons ruled his realm much like an architectural firm. He was the man in charge, but coordinated various areas that also worked independently. While he took care of the budget, read scripts and sometimes provided rough designs to his staff, it was up to each Unit Art Director to pull all of the details together for their specific films. They worked with four separate factions covering special effects, set construction, set decoration and set painting. Within these divisions were professionals like wallpaper hangers, furniture-makers and interior decorators—all under Gibbons' studio umbrella.

It was also up to the Unit Art Director to dissect a script, making note of the number of scenes and sets along with their estimated cost. Details would always be discussed with Gibbons who would then give his final approval on production plans. Afterward, each scene was drawn out in detail. Draftsmen then took these sketches and determined the necessary elevations along with possible camera angles. Blueprints were produced and the set built in miniature. If Gibbons liked what he saw, he gave the go-ahead for the actual set construction. If not, it was back to the drawing board—literally.

Gibbons also established a studio library where staff consulted reference materials to ensure accuracy right down to the type of sword a Roman warrior might have carried or the hairstyle preferred by a French queen. At work, he kept things professional. He rarely fraternized with his subordinates who always respectfully referred to him as "Mr. Gibbons." An occasional "Gibby," however, could be heard in the hallways or seen on internal studio correspondence. His crew was a loyal bunch who appreciated "Gibby"—especially when he took the heat for their mistakes. Never reprimanding a member of his staff in front of anyone, he would call them out in private when necessary. By requiring his people to come to him for sign-off on every single model, sketch or idea they finalized, Gibbons maintained control.

He also had clout. With stories and settings becoming more complex and more movies in production, MGM's limited stage space became an issue. Gibbons requested and got approval for four more soundstages.

Outside of MGM, the divorced Gibbons fell hard for Mexican actress Dolores del Rio. María de los Dolores Asúnsolo y López Negrete was born to an upper class family in Durango, Mexico on August 3, 1905. At sixteen, she married the wealthy Jaime Martinez del Rio who was eighteen years older. Eventually the couple moved to Hollywood where Delores pursued acting while Jaime worked as a screenwriter. Her breakout role came when director Raoul Walsh cast her as the saucy Charmaine de la Cognac in his classic *What Price Glory* (1926). As her career blossomed, her marriage crumbled. She and Jaime divorced in 1928. He moved to Germany where he died from blood poisoning the following year. After a brief courtship, the actress married Gibbons on August 6, 1930 at the old Franciscan Mission in Santa Barbara.

Privately, Gibbons put his talents to good use. He designed his own home in the canyons of Santa Monica. The spectacular house was built in 1930 and had an ultra-modern and sleek look much like his MGM sets. Inside the white stucco structure, the floor plan was open with each room blending into the next. The first floor held a dining room, kitchen and guest suite along with a library whose winding staircase led to the strategically placed living room on the second floor. Here, white, black and gray dominated with a splash of occasional color for dramatic effect. Mirrors hung above the fireplace and recessed lighting made the room appear even larger.

Outside, terraces led to the swimming pool and tennis court. When the sun shone on the pool, the glimmer was caught in the sparkling living room mirror. At night, Gibbons turned on roof sprinklers and shined the garden lights on his self-made "rainfall" for a similar evening effect. The unusual Gibbons home was featured in many magazines. His designs also influenced many modern homemakers, who often wrote letters asking him about his eye-catching movie sets. He explained that a home, like a movie set, should reflect the people or characters in it—unlike trendy fads that had to be replaced as they went out of fashion.

In the spring of 1933, the Gibbons entertained a houseguest—his sister's twenty-year-old daughter, Veronica Balfe. When Uncle Cedric and Aunt Dolores threw a party for the young New York socialite, they invited lanky actor Gary Cooper. "Coop" was so smitten with "Rocky," he married her before the year was out. The couple had a daughter, Maria, and remained together almost thirty years until Cooper's death in 1961.

Longevity, however, was not in the cards for the Gibbons–del Rio union. After nine years, the couple separated. They divorced in 1941 with del Rio claiming mental cruelty. She told the court that her husband acted with "coolness" toward her that caused her to be "nervous and ill." While Gibbons remained mostly silent about the ordeal, it was duly noted by the press that del Rio was often seen keeping company with recently divorced filmmaker Orson Welles.

On October 25, 1944, Gibbons took a third wife, model-turned-actress Hazel Brooks, thirty years his junior. Born in Capetown, South Africa in 1924, Brooks signed on with MGM when she was just 17 where she played mostly uncredited roles. Two years later, she was married to Gibbons by a Beverly Hills justice of the peace. Not long after, his health deteriorated. He experienced a heart attack in 1946 followed by a series of strokes that slowed him down considerably although he continued to work. In 1950, the Society of Motion Picture Art Directors honored the legendary art director with an award for his many contributions to the filmmaking industry.

In poor health, Gibbons retired after 32 years with MGM—the studio he'd been with since it all began in 1924. He may not have personally designed sets for every movie that carried his name, but Gibbons defined the overall look of MGM while setting the standard for Hollywood glamour. Thanks to his Art Deco designs and outstanding managerial skills, he conjured up the class and elegance Louis B. Mayer envisioned.

On July 26, 1960, the long-suffering Gibbons died at home. He left no personal papers, but he did bestow a polished mark of excellence on the movies he touched. He once said:

> I don't claim that a good set can save a poor picture entirely, but it certainly can lift a good story into the realms of real triumph.

Director Frank Lloyd also strived for excellence. By 1928, he was back at First National where he filmed the historical drama *The Divine Lady* (1929) depicting the famous romance of the married British Navy Admiral Horatio Nelson and his also-married mistress, Emma Hart. For his efforts, Lloyd received an Academy Award. Known in the film business as a reliable director who delivered fine films, Lloyd was recognized a second time by the Academy for another romantic drama, *Cavalcade* (1933), which also took top honors as Best Picture.

Confusion reigned at the award ceremony that evening when another Frank was also nominated for Best Director. Host Will Rogers announced the winner by saying: "Come on up and get it, Frank." At that moment, Best Director nominee Frank Capra jumped up, waved for the spotlight and began making his way toward Rogers who then added: "The winner is Frank Lloyd."

A horrified Capra froze as the spotlight left him and swept the room to find Lloyd. Totally embarrassed, Capra slinked back to his seat amidst much jeering. He recalled the moment as "the longest, saddest, most shattering" of his life. Capra later triumphed, however, with multiple Oscars of his own, but most likely paused to make sure that he was indeed the right "Frank" before he stood up.

Despite his two Oscars, Lloyd's most memorable film was yet to come when he took on the challenge of directing two major Hollywood stars—Charles Laughton and Clark Gable, who didn't like each other one bit. Gable's outright disapproval of Laughton's homosexuality did nothing to improve their working relationship. Besides the fact that Gable did not want to film a period picture requiring him to wear knee pants and lose his world-famous mustache. His protests went nowhere, but he successfully drew the line at speaking with a British accent. Despite many tensions on the set and Gable's own doubts, *Mutiny on the Bounty* (1935) was a box office hit. The film went on to win an Oscar for Best Picture and remains a classic.

Whether he was working for MGM, First National or Republic, the always-dependable Lloyd brought his films in on time and within budget. He was well liked and learned to work with the many egos he faced on a daily basis. Never one to dictate how a scene should be filmed, he often asked his actors for their interpretation and then gave their recommendations a try. According to *Time* magazine, the director had a knack for showcasing ordinary people who found themselves living in the midst of extraordinary times:

> . . . [Lloyd] likes to take a few typical characters of the period, run them through the normal complications of normal people, silhouette them against a background of great dates, deeds, land marks. . . .

During World War II, Lloyd entered the service as a major. He made documentaries about bombings in the South Pacific for the U.S. Army Air Corps including the short, *Air Pattern-Pacific* (1944). The 42-minute film depicted the 13th Air Force Combat Camera Unit and their participation in several aerial battles under Lloyd's command. He earned the Air Medal as well as the Legion of Merit for his work. After his war service, he returned to his day job where he continued directing. Two films later, Lloyd quietly left Hollywood. When asked why, he gave a simple explanation:

> When I went into the Army, I was tired. When I got out, I was even more tired. I have traveled some 30,000 miles by air. That may be all right for the young privates, but it was a drain on the old colonel.

My wife suggested that I quit and enjoy for a while. I had always liked the country around Carmel so I bought a place there. I played golf and managed my farm and we traveled a bit. . . .

Lloyd's blissful life in Monterey came to an end on March 16, 1952. Alma, his wife of almost forty years, died after a battle with cancer. Her death prompted his return to Hollywood. He made two films at Republic Pictures, *The Shanghai Story* (1954) starring actress Ruth Roman and *The Last Command* (1955) about the Alamo—neither film memorable. Lloyd also married writer Virginia Kellogg who penned one of James Cagney's biggest hits, *White Heat* (1949). The couple wed on September 2, 1955 on a yacht as it sailed under San Francisco's Golden Gate Bridge. Lloyd once again retired—this time permanently.

Suffering from a heart and lung condition, the Scottish director died on August 10, 1960 with approximately 200 films to his acting, writing, directing and producing credits. A versatile showman and past president of the Academy, his career ran the gamut from silent films to modern movies that included a little romance and a lot of drama peppered with some very high adventure. He once said: ". . . a film should not be judged as a historical document, it should be judged purely and simply as an evening's entertainment."

If Cecil B. DeMille was the most demanding, Cedric Gibbons the most debonair and Frank Lloyd the most down-to-earth, producer Joseph M. Schenck was probably the most diverse. In addition to his day job as United Artists' top man, he was a banker, realtor and amusement park owner. Along with a good cigar and a bottle of whiskey, he also enjoyed an all-night round of poker with other Hollywood high rollers like Irving Thalberg, David O. Selznick and Sid Grauman. It was simply understood that the higher they bet, the more important they were.

In 1927, Schenck was pretty important. His life insurance policy was worth $1,250,000—so was his wife's. Under Schenck's leadership, UA ended 1928 with a profit and, despite the stock market crash in 1929, ended that year in the black as well. Like many of his contemporaries, however, Schenck was skeptical when it came to talkies. He once stated:

> Sound film will leave nothing to the intelligence of the picture going public. In the silent drama a certain gesture, a particular facial expression, will often convey more than a subtitle. But in talking films nothing will be left to the imagination and for that reason they must only be a passing phase.

By 1930, he knew he was wrong so, along with Douglas Fairbanks and Mary Pickford, Schenck traveled to San Francisco to take a look at the "Farnsworth Television device"—an odd little box that allowed spectators to view movies right in their own homes. Not wanting to make another mistake, Schenck declared: "Television motion pictures for the home are coming just as surely as the 'talkies' came to the screen."

Three years later, Schenck partnered up with another producer, Darryl F. Zanuck, to establish a new motion picture company. Zanuck, a World War I veteran, started out with Warner Bros. as a writer for Rin Tin Tin. He soon moved up the corporate ladder to producer and eventually became Head of Production under Jack L. Warner. Before long, the ambitious Zanuck realized that, as an outsider, he would never "inherit" the family studio so he started looking for other options. That's when Schenck made him an offer he couldn't refuse. While Schenck kept his position as head of UA, the two movie men co-founded Twentieth Century Pictures with UA distributing.

Shortly after, Schenck and brother Nicholas sold their interest in the Palisades Amusement Park for almost half a million dollars to another pair of brothers—Irving and Jack Rosenthal. Schenck's marriage to Norma Talmadge also came to an end. She and "Daddy" considered divorcing for several years, but until Talmadge decided to marry George Jessel, they kept their troubled marriage intact. Evidently, there were no hard feelings. In 1935, Schenck and Zanuck merged their company with the financially stressed Fox Film Corporation to form Twentieth Century Fox Film. With Schenck installed as chairman of the board and Zanuck as head of production, one of their first contracts went to George Jessel—now married to Talmadge.

By this time, organized crime was making inroads in the Hollywood hotbed. Chicago mobster Willie Morris Bioff, who had ties to Al Capone, was in charge of the International Alliance of Theatrical Stage Employees & Moving Picture Machine Operators (IATSE)—the union representing many professional studio workers, technicians and craftsmen. Bioff assured the studios that the only way to avoid "trouble" was by paying him, which ultimately meant handing over lots of dough to the Chicago syndicate.

Many studio executives complied, but in 1939 after an investigation by the National Labor Relations Board, indictments involving labor racketeering were made. For the most part, studio brass spread their costs over several of their current productions. Schenck, however, made the very bad decision of giving Bioff a $100,000 personal check that intrigued the IRS. Schenck was soon charged with income tax evasion and found guilty. Sentenced to three years in prison, he was free on appeal when he agreed to testify against Bioff and his partner in crime, George E. Browne, in exchange for a plea bargain.

In the meantime, Schenck resigned from his position as Twentieth Century Fox's Chairman of the Board. He pleaded guilty to one count of perjury admitting that he lied to government investigators by describing his $100,000 payoff to Bioff as a loan. As a result of his testimony, Bioff and Browne were convicted of extorting money from several major Hollywood producers and Schenck's original sentence was suspended. He was given a new, lighter one for the perjury—one year and one day. Schenck served only four months and five days in Danbury, Connecticut before being released on parole on September 7, 1942. Three years later, President Harry Truman pardoned him and Schenck returned to Fox.

Over the years, Schenck, who partied hard and gambled big, was linked to many dazzling women including actresses Merle Oberon, Jean Howard and Marilyn Monroe. Monroe, who became a regular at his house parties, was known as "Joe Schenck's girl." The upcoming starlet appreciated his position at Fox, his lavish surroundings and the VIP company he kept. She was fascinated by his ambiance as she once described him: "It was as much the face of a town as a man. The whole history of Hollywood was in it." He arranged for her small part in the comedy *Scudda Hoo! Scudda Hay!* (1948) and then used his influence with Harry Cohn to get her a contract at Columbia.

In 1949, Schenck submitted his resignation as executive producer at Twentieth Century Fox, but his superiors flatly refused to accept it saying he was indispensable. Current Fox president Spyros P. Skouras claimed that Schenck was the "father" of the company and Fox couldn't run without him.

Schenck received a special Oscar in 1952 for his "long and distinguished service to the motion picture industry." The following year, he resigned once more from Fox and this time, his resignation was accepted. He was then re-elected Chairman of UA. He also partnered up with producer Mike Todd to form the Magna Theater Corporation, which was primarily established to market the Todd-AO wide-screen system—a very profitable venture. He retired in 1957 after which he suffered a stroke and never fully recovered. Schenck, in his eighties, died at his home in Beverly Hills on October 22, 1961, living alone except for his house staff.

While Joseph M. Schenck was riding high, writer Carey Wilson, one of Hollywood's top paid penmen, had a run of bad luck in 1927. Earlier that year, Wilson pulled the plug on his nine-year marriage when he moved out of his Beverly Hills home and into the Ambassador Hotel. Mrs. Wilson claimed that her husband deserted her and their two children on July 29, 1927 when he packed up his clothes and refused to tell her where he was going. Wilson accused the Mrs. of cruelty when she kicked him with her shoe before cutting him with a broken glass towel bar from the bathroom. Never mind the blood drawing, he also complained that she spent grocery money on jewelry. In turn, Mrs. Wilson claimed that her husband liked women and that she once found him dancing a little too closely with a strange young woman who later showed up at their home. She further stated that Wilson hit her when she voiced her objections to the visitor.

As if all that commotion wasn't bad enough, Wilson broke his foot that fall while playing tennis. The injury laid him up for six weeks. Then there was the ill-fated magazine venture sponsored by the Academy. Acting as co-editor along with art director Cedric Gibbons and screenwriter Waldemar Young, grandson of Mormon leader Brigham Young, Wilson put his skills to good use when the Academy published a magazine called *Motion Picture Arts and Sciences* in November 1927. Written for film industry professionals, the publication was canceled after only one issue.

Two years later, the divorce was final with Mrs. Wilson gaining their $100,000 home, a car valued at $18,000 and custody of nine-year-old daughter Nancy and son Carey Anthony, Jr., age three. She also received a monthly alimony payment of $500 for the first year with an additional $250 in monthly child support. Wilson mistakenly thought he was done with the towel bar beater.

In 1934, he took a second wife, actress Carmelita Geraghty, the daughter of screenwriter Thomas J. Geraghty. Born in Rushville, Indiana in 1901, her ten-year acting career came to an end when she married Wilson. Their first twenty-four hours as man and wife were challenging. Right after the "I dos," matron of honor Jean Harlow dramatically announced the end of her marriage to cameraman Hal Rosson. The very next day, the first Mrs. Wilson was back in court demanding an increase in her child support causing the newlyweds to postpone their honeymoon. The judge turned down the request stating that "too much money sometimes spoils children."

Despite his troubles, Wilson continued penning movies such as *His Captive Woman* (1929) featuring Milton Sills, *Polly of the Circus* (1932) with Clark Gable and Marion Davis and *Bolero* (1934) starring George Raft and Carole Lombard. He was also one of three writers who worked on the screenplay for director Frank Lloyd's *Mutiny on the Bounty* (1935).

That same year, MGM formed a department devoted to shorts and it was there that Wilson did some of his most memorable work.

MGM writer Samuel Marx happened to see a play called *Skidding* about a small-town judge, James Hardy, and his all-American family that included a teenage son, Andy. Bringing the story back to MGM, the studio turned it into *A Family Affair* (1937) starring Lionel Barrymore as the judge and Mickey Rooney as Andy. Wilson then produced the popular Andy Hardy series while Mayer personally saw to it that Andy never disrespected his mother or got into serious trouble. If the script didn't meet with Mayer's approval, he simply crossed out the offending scenes. Mayer must have known exactly what he was doing. The Andy Hardy series won a special Oscar in 1942 "for its achievement in representing the American way of life."

Wilson also became fascinated with the French seer Nostradamus after reading a book about his many controversial predictions, which dated back to the mid-1500s. Between 1938 and 1955, Wilson produced, wrote and narrated several shorts detailing the life and mysterious quatrains written by Nostradamus. In addition, Wilson worked on the many Dr. Kildare films starring Lew Ayres as the young doctor and Lionel Barrymore as his mentor, the all-wise Dr. Gillespie.

In between these various series, he also produced features such as *The Postman Always Rings Twice* (1946)—a controversial film noir starring Lana Turner as a two-timing wife who prefers killing her husband to leaving him. The following year, Wilson produced the action-packed *Green Dolphin Street* (1947), which won an Academy Award for its spectacular earthquake and tidal wave scenes. His final production was a documentary called *This is Russia* (1957), which he also wrote and narrated.

After retiring from his Hollywood job, Wilson continued producing films for the U.S. Army and other government agencies. On February 1, 1962, Wilson died at Good Samaritan Hospital a few hours after suffering a stroke in his home. Although he thought of himself as a writer, he also played the role of producer and once said: "A producer in a movie factory is man who is ready for a good night's sleep when he gets home."

Handsome matinée idol Richard Barthelmess probably looked forward to a good night's sleep, too, after the heady success of his latest film, *The Patent Leather Kid* (1927). Now raising his daughter, Mary, and under contract with First National, he was working on his next film, *The Drop Kick* (1927), a drama about college football. Under his contract, First National paid him well—$375,000 annually for three pictures.

Barthelmess also found a new girl, actress Katherine Young Wilson. Born in Jacksonville, Florida, Wilson tested her stage presence in the local community theater before moving to New York. The couple announced their engagement in August 1927 and planned a New York wedding the following November. At that time, Wilson announced she was trading in her day job for full-time housewifery. She was already remodeling Barthelmess' Beverly Hills home. The short-lived engagement ended when Wilson decided she'd rather be a working girl.

Barthelmess had better marital luck in 1928 when he wed for the second time. His new wife, Jessica Stewart Sargent, from Selma, Alabama, was recently divorced and a single mother. Their April 21st wedding took place in Reno, Nevada followed by a Hawaiian honeymoon. Barthelmess later adopted her five-year-old son, Stewart. He also made a successful transition to sound under the direction of Frank Lloyd. In Barthelmess' first talking picture, *Weary River* (1929), he played a gangster who ends up in prison. When the jailbird sings on a radio show broadcast from the big house, the public demands more, dramatically changing his life—maybe.

As the thirties progressed, Barthelmess' career slowed down. He made fewer movies and his matinée idol status turned into character roles. That didn't deter Trinity College, Barthelmess' old academic stomping grounds, from recognizing his many achievements. The school invited him to "graduate" with the senior class of 1938 and receive his degree. According to the principle, it was customary for the college to give degrees to students who had dropped out, but were still considered successful twenty years later.

By 1939, Barthelmess hadn't made a movie in three years. His bad facelift didn't help either. The botched surgery left him with limited facial movement. He returned to the screen with a small role in *Only Angels Have Wings* (1939). When the film was shown to test audiences, they cheered when they saw him. Producers at Columbia Pictures were so impressed they expanded his part. At the time, Barthelmess was fishing off the coast of Guaymas, Mexico so the brass chartered a plane to pick him up and bring him back to Hollywood. The drama, starring Cary Grant and Rita Hayworth, was nominated for two Oscars.

When the United States entered World War II in early 1942, forty-six-year-old Barthelmess joined the Navy and as a Lieutenant reported for duty in Virginia. While stationed there, he also had the unusual opportunity of swearing in his son, Stewart, at Norfolk's naval recruiting station. Later that year, his final two movies were released, *The Spoilers* starring Marlene Dietrich and *The Mayor of 44th Street* featuring Anne Shirley with Barthelmess in supporting roles.

After the war, he never returned to filmmaking. Instead, he lived a privileged lifestyle based on his ample savings and savvy real estate investments. Barthelmess enjoyed tennis, swimming, horseback riding, and sailing on his yacht. In 1955, he sold The Dunes, his 50-acre oceanfront estate in Southampton, to automobile magnate Henry Ford II.

After battling throat cancer for several years and losing his ability to talk, Barthelmess died on August 17, 1963. Best remembered for saving Lillian Gish as she floated downstream in an icy river, he remains the handsome hero who exuded charm and made those matinée girls swoon. When asked why he left the business, he explained: "The fun had gone out of picture making. We used to go to the studio and we hated to leave at night. It doesn't seem to be that way anymore."

Chapter Twenty-Four

PRETZELS, LAWYERS AND POTENTATES

S cenarist Bess Meredyth was one of Hollywood's top penwomen in 1927. Recently divorced from her first husband, actor Wilfred Lucas, their only son, John, attended military school, but stayed with his mother most weekends. The quick-witted Meredyth remained under contract at Warner Bros. and was still enthusiastic when it came to her chosen profession. She once stated:

> Any work that varies is thrilling and writing for the stars is certainly full of variety. Stars differ so from each other. Stories differ. Directors and studios have such varied tactics. And the scenario writer must be wary enough to sense the situations.

During her tenure with Warners, she met Kertesz Kaminar Mihaly, a newly imported Hungarian film director who always wore a long black coat. After directing several minor films such as *The Third Degree* (1926) starring John Barrymore's future wife, Delores Costello, the brothers gave him a biblical story hoping to compete with DeMille. *Noah's Ark* (1928), also with Costello, featured newcomer Myrna Loy in the small part of a dancing slave girl. Now known as Michael Curtiz, the director, along with his overcoat, caught Meredyth's eye. She didn't mind his accent or that he always called her "Bessky," but the dark outerwear had to go.

While they were dating, Meredyth got creative. Riding in her chauffeur-driven Lincoln, she had the driver crank up the heat. Curtiz would eventually shed the coat for the evening and one day just stopped wearing it altogether—much to "Bessky's" secret delight.

At work Curtiz stayed with Warner Bros., while Meredyth left for MGM where she penned films for such super silent stars as Greta Garbo and John Gilbert. In 1929, she married Curtiz—his third, her second—and he joined Meredyth at her two-bedroom suite in the Roosevelt Hotel.

When MGM renewed the popular writer's contract in 1931, the lesser-known Curtiz continued working at Warner Bros. Meredyth began suffering from what her son referred to as probable "anxiety attacks"—possibly due to the stress brought on by a philandering husband. With various doctors and nurses in attendance, she stayed home for weeks at a time, sometimes bedridden, often crying, and occasionally fainting. She passed her days reading mystery novels, working on jigsaw puzzles and popping pills to sleep. Just as abruptly as her homebound spells started, they stopped and she would return to work as if nothing had happened.

Despite their infidelities and emotional insecurities, Meredyth and Curtiz remained together. The couple traveled to Europe in 1934 and visited Budapest where he received a hero's welcome and she met his mother and brothers. From Hungary, they went on to Vienna, Berlin and then to the French Riviera.

At home, the Curtizes entertained on the weekends, inviting friends over to their picturesque estate in the San Fernando Valley. Besides their fourteen-room English-manor-style house, the estate included a guest-house, servants' quarters, swimming pool and private stables. They often practiced skeet shooting and played polo on the grounds. Meredyth also enjoyed horseback riding. Her horse, Shadow, was so named because the steed was afraid of its own silhouette.

Meredyth even tended her own garden. Local rabbits thought her vegetables were planted just for them. Frustrated, she let her husband take charge of the situation—with one of his shotguns. Curtiz caught the hopping intruder red-handed and shot it, but only clipped its leg. Horrified by what he'd done, Curtiz took the injured rabbit to a veterinarian who fixed the damage. From then on, vegetables were bought from the store.

By the mid-thirties, Curtiz hit his stride with films like the adventure-filled *Captain Blood* (1935) starring Errol Flynn in his breakout role and *The Charge of the Light Brigade* (1936), another popular Flynn feature. Meredyth was now working at Twentieth Century Fox and, tired of her husband's indiscretions, wanted to end the marriage. She claimed that Curtiz refused to talk to her and often drove her to the brink of hysteria. The couple divorced in 1936, but soon remarried.

Two years later, Meredyth was earning more than $77,000, but her career was waning, most likely due to her anxiety attacks, which kept her home. Curtiz, however, continued directing big box office films such as the toe-tapping *Yankee Doodle Dandy* (1942) starring a fleet-footed James Cagney and the crowd-pleasing *Mildred Pierce* (1945) with Joan Crawford. Curtiz also won an Academy Award for directing the wartime drama *Casablanca* (1942).

It was often said around the studio that Meredyth provided most of the brains behind Curtiz's productions—although he would never admit it. According to screenwriter Julius Epstein: "We knew they were Bess Meredyth's ideas, not his, so it was easy to trip him up. We'd make a change and say, 'What do you think, Mike?' and he'd have to go back and ask Bess."

Mark of Zorro (1940) starring Tyrone Power was Meredyth's last picture at Fox. In 1946, she and Curtiz established their own production unit at Warner Bros. where she acted as his story editor. Their first film was *The*

Unsuspected (1947) with Claude Rains. They sold their ranch and moved to Encino where Meredyth discovered that Curtiz was once again cheating. She left him for a short time, but soon returned home.

Just before he began filming *The Proud Rebel* (1958) with Alan Ladd, Curtiz was struck with appendicitis. During emergency surgery, doctors noticed a small lump on his prostate. After a biopsy, they determined it was cancerous. The diagnosis was shared with Meredyth and all agreed that it was best not to tell Curtiz. They didn't want to worry him. Not knowing he was terminally ill, he went on to direct Elvis Presley in *King Creole* (1958) and *The Hangman* (1959), a western with Robert Taylor.

When Curtiz traveled to Italy to work on *Francis of Assisi* (1961), he wrote "Bessky" a letter. He told her that he didn't want a divorce, but he would not return to their home. True to his word, Curtiz, often visited his wife, but never stayed. According to her son:

> . . . Despite all the help she gave him with his scripts, her wonderful sense of humor and his repeated infidelity, he had remained married to a voluntarily bedridden woman for 30 years.

Now, Meredyth spent even more time in bed. She wasted money on superfluous redecorating, needless servants and uncalled for lavish gifts.

While filming *The Comancheros* (1961) with John Wayne, doctors found that Curtiz's prostate cancer had spread. He died on April 10, 1962 leaving Meredyth a large piece of property north of Los Angeles. She promptly sold it and continued spending money paying salaries for a team of nurses to sit with her around the clock as she watched television from her bed.

Just before her 77th birthday, Meredyth mentioned to her son that she'd always wanted a mynah bird. John bought her one by the name of Ronald Raven. When the bird met Meredyth, it croaked out "Hello, Dolly!" Delighted, she soon taught her pet to swear. Whenever the phone rang, it wasn't uncommon for the bird to screech: "Somebody get the fucking phone!"

By the time she reached her late seventies, Meredyth's money was gone and her health truly failing. She really did need specialized care. With her finances depleted, John had no choice but to take his mother to the Motion Picture Country House and Hospital. After experiencing kidney failure, Meredyth died there on July 14, 1967, but not before teaching her granddaughters how to cheat at cards.

Another contemporary of Meredyth's, who also successfully made the transition from silence to sound, was actor Conrad Nagel. Too busy for a game of cards, he was one of the hardest working matinée idols in the business. Between 1928 and 1929, he played in sixteen movies including Warner Bros.' second talking picture, *Glorious Betsy* (1928), opposite Dolores Costello. Nagel successfully made the transition from silence to sound with his classically trained baritone voice. Unlike other silent film stars who were felled by talkies, Nagel kept up his steady pace with another ten movies in 1930.

In addition to his film work, Nagel served as president of the Academy from 1932–1933. He also belonged to both the Lambs' and Friars' Clubs. A popular member of the Hollywood colony, his easy stage presence made him a favorite master of ceremonies. He hosted many banquets and award ceremonies and was even called upon to deliver an occasional eulogy. His hectic schedule didn't help his marriage. Wife Ruth obtained a divorce in Juarez, Mexico in 1934 stating that she and her husband were no longer compatible.

Nagel then had an on-again-off-again affair with actress/writer Kay Linaker. They met while filming *The Girl from Mandalay* (1936). Engaged four times, the couple never quite made it to the altar. Linaker worked in many films including *Drums Along the Mohawk* (1939) as well as several Charlie Chan movies. She is best remembered for a film she didn't appear in, but co-wrote—*The Blob* (1958), which featured a handsome young fellow named Steve McQueen.

By the end of the thirties, Nagel's matinée idol days were over. He made fewer films and played character roles. Nagel believed that overexposure killed his career. With too many movies in too short a time, he felt that spectators simply became bored with him. In the forties, he infiltrated radio as host of *Radio Reader's Digest* featuring a series of independent short stories. He also went back to the boards, starring in several plays including *The Skin of Our Teeth* and *Goodbye, My Fancy.*

In 1945, Nagel took a second wife—Texas-born actress Lynn Merrick, twenty-four years his junior. Instead of celebrating their first anniversary, however, the couple separated and ultimately divorced. According to Merrick, Nagel told her he "had been a bachelor for too long to fit into married life." She further claimed that he made her feel like a guest in her own home and didn't allow her to shop or give orders to the house staff.

Single again and not making movies, Nagel still had little downtime. The *Pittsburgh Post-Gazette* reported that he ". . . has participated in four entertainment mediums: silent pictures, talking pictures, radio and the stage." He was soon to add a fifth—television. By the end of the decade, Nagel was hosting TV's *The Silver Theater.* During the fifties and sixties, the former matinée idol continued working in television, guest starring in such TV classics as *Bat Masterson, Car 54 Where Are You?* and *Route 66* where he was rediscovered by a new generation. He even tried the game show circuit, making appearances on *To Tell the Truth* and *What's My Line?.*

On August 31, 1955, Nagel married for the third time to Canadian girl Michael Coulson Smith, who was twenty-six years younger. That same year, he returned to Hollywood to work with actress Jane Wyman and current matinée idol Rock Hudson in *All That Heaven Allows* (1955). Soon after filming, Nagel filed for divorce claiming that Smith had physically threatened him. She denied any wrongdoing, but gave him a son, Michael, before their union ended.

In 1960, Nagel along with Mary Pickford and Harold Lloyd were present at the unveiling of the Beverly Hills Film Monument to the Stars dedicated to those celebrities who had once saved the city from annexation to Los Angeles due to a water supply shortage in 1923. Of the eight so honored only Nagel, Pickford and Lloyd were still alive.

Nagel retired in 1967. He lived in New York and remained active with the Lambs' and Friars' Clubs. In past years, he had also been an active member of the Associated Actors and Artists of America, as well as the Screen Actors Guild and the American Federation of Television and Radio Artists. He also earned a Special Oscar for his tireless efforts involving the Motion Picture Relief Fund. As late as 1961, the Screen Actors Guild appointed Nagel fourth vice president—a position they created just for him, which gave the Guild an official on the East Coast.

On February 24, 1970, when Nagel missed a meeting of the Lamb's Club's admission committee, which he chaired, a fellow member went to his New York apartment. Nagel, who suffered from emphysema, was found sitting in a chair wearing a smoking jacket—dead of a heart attack.

Wholesome and handsome with his all-American appeal, Conrad Nagel rarely got a break during his busiest years in Hollywood. Filming movies back to back, vacations were out of the question, but Nagel was a trouper who didn't mind the long hours—as long as he had a good pretzel to crunch.

California attorney Edwin J. Loeb also worked hard. Still in a partnership with his older brother, Joseph, Loeb devoted most of his time to legal issues concerning the film industry.

In 1928, he took a temporary break from the movies to work with the California Development Association when they questioned the validity of the state's pricey earthquake insurance. California required that proof of the insurance must be submitted in order to obtain building permits. Developers believed that the possibility of an earthquake was overhyped and the high cost of the specialty insurance discouraged builders from developing just about any area in the Golden State. It was also noted that more than 95% of all earthquake insurance was purchased in California even though several other states experienced tremors and quakes as well. Ultimately, the requirement was abolished and insurance companies admonished for their exorbitant rates based on one or two scientists' questionable theories.

In 1932, Loeb was appointed Western Arbiter over the motion picture industry by movie czar Will Hays. This appointment was given with the consent of many major Hollywood leaders including Louis B. Mayer, Joseph M. Schenck and Adolph Zukor. They felt that since Loeb had worked for all of them in the past, settling issues via arbitration, he should be recognized as the authority over disputes involving contracts, story rights and various other agreements between studios. He would also assist with the "establishment of practice and ethics" for the industry. The press, however, had different thoughts when they described Loeb's new position as a dictator, which he strongly refuted:

> Any talk about my being the arbiter or dictator over the Western activities of the amusement business is ridiculous, untrue and without any foundation in fact . . . Further in any matters of dispute which may arise between the various producing companies, and into which I am called as arbiter, my word is not final. Either party to such a dispute has the right of appeal to a committee of our companies' executives.

Loeb also sat on the First Board of Governors of Friends of Claremont Colleges. In addition, he and brother Joseph were among the founders of the local chapter of the American Jewish Committee (AJC). When he wasn't working or performing civic duties, Loeb liked nothing better than pulling an all-nighter with a high stakes card game. His gambling buddies included Schenck, Mayer and Irving Thalberg.

The young MGM producer was one of Loeb's closest friends. When Thalberg died in 1936, Loeb not only acted as a pallbearer at the funeral, he also handled estate matters for Thalberg's widow, Norma Shearer. In addition, he was actively involved in real estate, divorce proceedings, wills and the occasional criminal charges involving various Hollywood celebrities who called upon him for legal assistance.

After a long career of tending to the stars and their studios, Edwin Loeb died on November 3, 1970 at the age of 83. The law firm of Loeb and Loeb that he and his brother founded over 100 years ago remains successful and continues to carry out their vision.

Edwin Loeb wasn't the only Hollywood heavyweight who made a good living. In 1927, funny man Harold Lloyd was one of the top paid players in the film industry. His current project was a silent movie called *Speedy* (1928). Filmed on location in New York's Coney Island, baseball greats Babe Ruth and Lou Gehrig each had cameo roles. In keeping up with the times, Lloyd's next film, *Welcome Danger* (1929), was originally shot as a silent movie, but half of the footage was reshot with sound before it was released. It also marked the first time that Lloyd worked with a script. The novelty of hearing "The Boy" speak drew large audiences, but the exorbitant cost of filming and refilming didn't allow for much profit. *Welcome Danger* was released on October 12, 1929—eleven days later the stock market crashed.

Economic hard times and sound didn't mix well with "The Boy" and Lloyd made only six films between 1930 and 1938. He sold the property where his production company stood to the Church of Jesus Christ of Latter Day Saints for their Los Angeles Temple. He produced a couple of films for RKO, *A Girl A Guy and A Gob* (1941) featuring comedienne Lucille Ball and *My Favorite Spy* (1942) with actress Jane Wyman, before retiring from the business.

Lloyd may not have been making films, but he found work on the radio as host of *The Old Gold Comedy Theater*. The weekly anthology series featured half-hour adaptations of recent movies. Guest stars included such big names as Claudette Colbert, Gary Cooper and Edward G. Robinson. Lloyd briefly returned to filmmaking in 1947 with *The Sin of Harold Diddlebock* (1947), which was written and directed by Preston Sturges—a partner of Howard Hughes at the time. Dissatisfied with the final result, Lloyd once again withdrew from Hollywood.

Two years later, Lloyd made the cover of *Time* magazine, but not for his movie work. He was recognized for being the Imperial Potentate of the Ancient Arabic Order of the Nobles of the Mystic Shrine—in other words, the Masons' top man. In this position, he spoke to hundreds of thousands of Shriners across the country. For the last two decades of his life, he also worked for various Shriner Hospitals and their young patients, eventually taking on the role of President and Chairman of the Board.

Besides his dedication to the Shriners, Lloyd enjoyed an assortment of hobbies. He still played handball and bowled, but he also added painting and photography—especially 3-D stills—to his interests. Over the years, he took hundreds of thousands of photos. Many of his stills depicting nude models became popular as they appeared in various men's magazines. He even photographed actress Marilyn Monroe as she lounged in a bathing suit near his pool. In 2004, Lloyd's granddaughter selected some of his finest work for a book, *Harold Lloyd's Hollywood Nudes in 3D!*.

In 1952, the Academy gave Lloyd a special Oscar for being a "master Comedian and Good Citizen." He was also honored by the television series *This is Your Life* in 1955. In addition, he guest-starred on several TV shows such as *What's My Line?* and *Hedda Hopper's Hollywood*.

Lloyd owned and carefully guarded his body of movie work. He released and narrated *Harold Lloyd's World of Comedy* (1962)—a compilation of many of his famous silent scenes. The film was shown at the Cannes Film Festival where the sometimes hard-to-please audience gave Lloyd a standing ovation. He followed up with another called *Funny Side of Life* (1963). Four years later, he worked as an uncredited supervisor for director Mike Nichols on *The Graduate* (1967).

Lloyd lived out his years in movie-star style on his beloved Greenacres. The opulent estate was designed by Michigan-born architect Sumner Spaulding and included a nine-hole golf course as well as a handball court. Inside the sunroom, Lloyd kept a fully decorated Christmas tree on display year round with ornaments he received from all over the world.

After experiencing kidney problems, he was ultimately diagnosed with cancer. Lloyd died at home on March 8, 1971, two years after his wife, Mildred. Greenacres was briefly run as a museum until 1975. The surrounding property was eventually sold, but the mansion still stands on six acres of land. It was recognized by the National Register of Historic Places in 1984.

Lloyd once said: "It has been amazing to me that these comedies can still strike a responsive note of laughter with audiences of all ages and in all parts of the world. Laughter is the universal language. It establishes a common identity among people—regardless of other differences. It is the sweetest sound in the whole world."

George W. Cohen may not have been a funny man like Lloyd, but he took his work just as seriously. After developing the Academy's constitution and by-laws along with Edwin J. Loeb, Cohen continued practicing law and working in the motion picture industry. At home, he and his wife, Carolyn, welcomed their second son, Richard, in 1928. Two years later, Cohen's father, Isaac, died unexpectedly at the age of 82. He had been a well-respected resident of Los Angeles for over sixty years.

Cohen spent two decades at Loeb & Loeb where he personally represented many celebrities such as Jean Harlow, Greta Garbo and Clark Gable. In addition to their professional needs, he also handled their private issues when they got into a spot of trouble. Aside from the individual stars, he also represented top studios, such as MGM, Universal and Warner Bros. He even worked as an attorney on specific films like *Gone With The Wind* (1939). In addition, he handled the Hollywood legal business for songwriter Irving Berlin.

By 1944, Cohen left Loeb & Loeb and joined Kaplan, Livingston, Goodwin, Berkowitz & Selwin of Beverly Hills. With his expert understanding of entertainment legalities, he became known as the "dean of motion picture lawyers." He also accrued a keen knowledge of the many types of Hollywood employment agreements and was often called the "father of the motion picture contracts." He was president of the L.A. Copyright Society as well as the secretary of the Beverly Hills Bar and later served as committee chairman for its constitution and by-laws. Cohen was also a board member of the L.A. Legal Aid Foundation.

When he wasn't practicing law, Cohen enjoyed cooking. The "Chicken Salad a la Cohen" served at Perino's, a popular restaurant that opened on

Wilshire Boulevard in 1932, was named after him. At one point, Cohen also tried his hand at winemaking and went so far as growing his own grapes in the backyard. Eventually, he gave up the private winery, but remained a strong supporter of California wines.

After suffering from heart trouble and a stroke, Cohen had a heart attack and died at Cedars of Lebanon Hospital on December 27, 1971. He left his widow, Carolyn, two sons, Donald and Richard, and his piano-playing sister, Gertrude.

Film executive M.C. Levee may not have been a lawyer, but he inspired confidence with his knack for fundraising and budgeting. He had already acted as treasurer for the Motion Picture Relief Fund and Hollywood's elite social society, the Mayfair Club, as well as the first chairman of the Community Chest Drive. It's no wonder Levee was chosen as the Academy's first treasurer, chairman of their Contracts Committee and a member of their Producers-Technicians Joint Committee.

Professionally, Levee joined Joseph M. Schenck at United Artists where he acted as General Studio and Business Manager. Always good with numbers, Levee knew exactly how film money was utilized—right down to the penny. He told a group of UCLA students that out of every dollar spent to make a movie 25 cents went to actors' salaries; 20 cents was applied to studio overhead; 19 cents for the sets; ten cents each on crew and story; eight cents for location expenses; five cents on the film itself and finally, three cents for costumes.

During his tenure at UA, Levee was also in charge of sound. True to form, he approached the problem logistically. Science had determined what normal eyesight should be, but not normal hearing. Therefore, it was hard to figure just what, and how much, spectators heard when they sat in front of a movie screen. Levee explained:

> One of the greatest weaknesses in talking pictures today—a weakness that will never be overcome as long as talking pictures are made—is the difference in the hearing of people.

You are capable of receiving 2000 or more cycles than I. You will hear the faintest whisper, where it cuts off as far as I am concerned. We are in the monitor room of a studio, listening to a "playback" of a record. I say, "That's too loud." You say "That's perfect." Which is right?

Two years later, as sound became the norm instead of another ticket-selling novelty, Levee accepted a position of Executive Manager at Paramount. He also served as the Academy's president from 1931 to 1932. When his Paramount position was eliminated in 1932, he was let go.

That spring, Levee went on to establish the Screen Guild—a non-profit organization similar to the east coast Theater Guild. Like its New York cousin who produced plays, the west coast Screen Guild was meant to produce movies. According to Levee:

> The Screen Guild will aim to create an opportunity for accomplishing for screen entertainment in a measure what the Theater Guild has accomplished for the stage. It will be an entire independent producing organization not designed as an opponent of existing production companies but rather as a means of filling a recognized gap in the industry whereby higher creative talent will be offered for unhampered development and expression along lines that will meet public approval.

This private cooperative was expected to realize substantial savings, while encouraging creativity because it did not have the same overhead as the larger studios. Guild members who backed the endeavor would be entitled to a share of the profits. Any subsequent earnings of the Guild itself would be put right back into other productions. The Bank of America agreed to act as trustee and dole out the dollars.

Not long after, Levee left the filmmaking side of Hollywood. He opened his own business, the M.C. Levee Agency, where he ran a one-man show. With no staff or co-agents, he single-handedly represented many of Hollywood's top celebrities including Bette Davis, Merle Oberon and

Paul Muni. Recognized for his insider's knowledge and for having the wherewithal to negotiate fair contracts, Levee remained a popular figure in the film community.

As an agent, he often defended the big salaries that came with big stars. For many, fame was fleeting and the oversized paydays didn't last long, but to a financially stressed public, the high dollars were obnoxious. Levee attempted to explain:

> Those who challenge the salaries of famous stars do not give them credit for much except luck in winning out as they do; they don't consider the brevity of the whole thing. They don't give proper credit for the gifts and ability that go into the success, and the short time in which the great revenue may be gained. You never hear anybody condemn the owner of land on which an oil gusher is found, because of the great wealth that he accumulates through petroleum royalties. . . . In nine cases out of ten, the person who acquires it hasn't a thing to do with it. He just happened to hold onto that particular piece of land by sheer luck.

Consequently, many who were once on top of their game suffered financially when they couldn't find work. Levee's efforts with the Motion Picture Relief Fund attempted to help many filmmakers who were down on their luck.

As an agent, he specialized in high-maintenance. When he took over the representation of Douglas Fairbanks, Jr. and his new wife, Joan Crawford, Levee also tended to Fairbanks' mother, paying her bills and ensuring she had enough money to live on. He also intervened when a couple from Denmark attempted to blackmail the actor. When Crawford decided on divorce, it was Levee who broke the bad news to Fairbanks.

Throughout the years, he continued acting as a super agent to the stars taking care of business—professionally and sometimes personally. He was also a founder and the first president of the Artists Management Guild—a trade organization for talent agents. Stricken with cancer, Levee died on May 24, 1972 in Palm Springs at the age of 81. Valued for his honesty, smarts, loyalty and friendship, the innovative producer-turned-top-notch-agent maintained his well-respected position in the filmmaking community for decades.

Chapter Twenty-Five

LAST FOUNDERS STANDING

The unexpected loss of Sam Warner in 1927 sent his youngest brother, Jack, reeling. Sam was the champion behind Warner Bros.' talking picture *The Jazz Singer* (1927), which changed movies forever, but he never lived to see the movie's premiere nor its legacy endure. None of the brothers saw the premiere. Instead, they were busy making funeral arrangements. While Harry and Abe mourned their brother, Jack grieved for his best friend. Now, there was no one to maintain a semblance of peace between him and his older siblings. In the meantime, the success of *The Jazz Singer* brought the studio back from the brink of bankruptcy—much like Rin Tin Tin had done in the past. Ticket sales proved that Hollywood had reached a pivotal turning point and sound was here to stay.

While Harry ran the business, scooping up controlling interest in First National, he also took time to scold his little brother. He made it very clear that Jack's loose living was not acceptable to the family, nor were his many affairs conducive to the good name of their company. A livid Jack snapped back: "Talk to me all you want about holding down production costs, but my personal life is damn well my own."

As the Great Depression strangled the country, Warner Bros. remained profitable. Sparked by the novelty of talking pictures and a need to escape their misfortunes, financially strapped spectators continued buying movie tickets. The studio owned several subsidiaries as well as film exchanges and theaters. They employed over 18,000 people and funded a multi-million-dollar payroll. By the end of 1931, however, even the mighty Warners were feeling the pinch. With unemployment rates skyrocketing, many moviegoers had to choose between feeding or entertaining their families. Groceries won, and the studio ended the year in the red.

None of the country's woes, however, kept Jack from running wild, much to Harry's dismay. Loud and brash, Jack relished the spotlight, living large with flashy clothes, bawdy jokes and fast women. Without Sam to reel him in, Jack grew even more obnoxious, gleefully watching Harry smolder over his little brother's not-so-discreet indiscretions. Despite his bad behavior, Jack knew good material and fine talent when he saw it. He was also savvy enough to hire the right people—like producer Darryl Zanuck who successfully juggled multiple productions on a daily basis. When Zanuck left the studio to join Joseph M. Schenck at Twentieth Century, Jack replaced him with another talented producer, Hal Wallis. No matter how much good business sense Jack displayed or how many outstanding movies he made, Harry couldn't see past his brother's faults. As for Jack, he took a keen delight in making Harry mad. Cain and Abel had nothing on the warring Warners.

Jack's extramarital fun was just that. None of his relationships were serious and leaving his wife, Irma, was not on his mind—until 1932 when he met the also-married Ann Paige. The attractive brunette was the wife of former Warner Bros. player Joseph Paige whom Jack had christened Don Alvarado hoping to give Valentino a little competition. By the time

Jack met Ann, she had a young daughter, Joy, and her husband's career was floundering now that Latin lovers were no longer in vogue.

With their blissful days behind them, Ann left Alvarado. Jack then set her up in a Malibu beach house where he stayed whenever he could get away from the studio and Irma. He even helped Ann obtain a divorce in Mexico, but all the while, Jack himself remained legally married. As he spent more and more time in Malibu, his frequent absences from home forced Irma to face the truth. After a tearful confrontation, Jack left his wife. Ann soon admitted that she was pregnant and their daughter, Barbara, was born on September 10, 1934—something Jack kept from almost everyone since his divorce wasn't yet final. When his marriage to Irma officially ended in 1935, the divorce decree ordered that neither party could remarry for at least one year.

Despite her hopes for a reconciliation, Irma and her son, Jack, Jr., moved out of their Beverly Hills home. In a bold move, Jack quickly moved Ann in, along with his stepdaughter Joy and the new baby. Finally, in 1936, after the waiting period required by the divorce, Jack and Ann were married in New York. Irma's hopes for a happy ending were shattered. The outraged Warners read about the wedding in the newspaper. An angry Harry wrote to Jack: "The only thing good that has come on this day is that Mama and Poppa did not live to see it." The animosity between the two men deepened and now spread throughout the entire family. Brothers and sisters alike voiced their strong aversion to Jack's new bride. Ann wisely stayed away from Warner family gatherings, knowing she wasn't welcome.

Family relations didn't improve when Jack and Ann suddenly announced their adoption of a two-year-old girl. Nor did the Warners approve when Ann overhauled the mansion to suit her own taste. The end result was so extravagant that the place was dubbed "San Simeonette"—after Hearst's spectacular castle in northern California.

Jack's typical day at the studio began around 9:30 a.m. with a phone call to his secretary asking if there were any pressing matters. He usually arrived at his office by noon, read the mail and met with various production heads. Once he was told that brother Harry had left the dining room, he'd have lunch. Most afternoons, he viewed rushes filmed the day before. During the latter part of the day, he'd read the daily papers and any new story ideas submitted by studio readers. He then treated himself to a shave by his own private barber. Around eight, his secretary usually made a pot of coffee and Jack often remained at the studio until midnight.

Over the next several years, Jack supervised productions for such major films as *The Adventures of Robin Hood* (1938), starring the sound era's favorite swashbuckler, Errol Flynn, as well as the edgy drama *The Dawn Patrol* (1938)—another Flynn vehicle. The war years followed with training films like *Winning Your Wings* (1942) featuring Lieutenant James Stewart and the musical *Yankee Doodle Dandy* (1942) along with the wartime classic *Casablanca* (1942), considered by many to be one of the best films ever made.

After the war, another national pastime emerged—hunting for Communists. The House Un-American Activities Committee (HUAC) called Jack to Washington for his testimony concerning a suspect Warner Bros. movie, *Mission to Moscow* (1943). The film, originally made at the suggestion of U.S. President Franklin Delano Roosevelt, put a positive spin on Stalin's Russia in order to gain the sympathy of Americans during World War II. Now the film seemed like a nod to Communism, which the HUAC would not tolerate. A nervous Jack tried to explain the wartime situation to committee members who didn't seem to believe him. To protect himself and his studio, he offered names. Immediately afterward, he knew what he did was wrong, but the damage was done. Jack even tried to retract his statements at a second hearing, but it was too late. The blacklisting had begun.

The following year, Jack purchased a villa in southern France on Cap d'Antibes near the French Riviera's famous casinos. Far from the judgmental eye of his eldest brother, Jack indulged in one of his favorite pastimes— gambling. The games provided an intriguing escape from the producer's hectic life, as well as his frowning family. Maybe it was a way to remove himself from the HUAC debacle as well. And the attention of European royalty suited him.

After HUAC, Hollywood had another battle to face—television. During the early fifties, more and more moviegoers chose to stay home huddled around a small black-and-white screen that offered entertainment minus the price of an admission ticket. At first, studio executives bristled at the very word "television," but as their profits fell and TV's popularity rose, they gave in and joined forces with the new medium.

In 1956, Warner Bros. sold the rights to many of their films to television. They also developed several series for a new network known as ABC. Some of their early shows included westerns such as *Maverick* starring James Garner and dramas like *77 Sunset Strip* with teen favorite Edd "Kookie" Byrnes.

It was about that time that brother Abe, now in his seventies, decided he'd had enough and wanted to retire. Harry, with no son to leave the business to, was more reluctant. It was Jack who ultimately talked his siblings into selling only to turn around, retrieve his shares and appoint himself as President. Jack's underhanded strategy caused Harry's collapse and a final rift between the brothers that never closed.

The last time the two men saw each other was at Harry and Rea's golden wedding anniversary party. Suffering from the aftereffects of several strokes, Harry was unable to communicate and too ill to participate in the festivities. He simply sat in a chair watching. Jack, who made a boisterous entrance, downed a drink and went looking for his brother. Jack, Jr. described the final meeting between his father and uncle:

> [Jack] stepped close to his brother and tried to say something of little consequence, hoping Harry would perhaps notice him. Harry did notice . . . and he did the only thing he could still do. He closed his eyes tightly, shutting his brother from sight—and two big tears slowly rolled down his sunken cheeks . . . Then, with his face suddenly gone bright

red, my father turned and almost ran out of the silent room. I reached over to hold my uncle's hand for a while until the tears stopped.

Harry Warner died the following summer while Jack was living the life on the French Riviera. He declined to attend his brother's funeral. Four days later, after a late-night session of baccarat in Cannes, Jack collected his winnings and headed home. As he drove along the winding road in his sporty Alfa Romeo, it is believed that he fell asleep at the wheel. His car crossed the center line and collided with a parked coal truck. The car flipped, caught fire, and Jack was tossed forty feet.

He was picked up by a group of fellow gamblers who happened by in a Volkswagen. They literally shoved his broken body into the back seat and took him to a hospital in Cannes. As Jack hovered near death, Ann was notified. Jack, Jr. was not. He heard about his father's accident on the radio. After four months of convalescence in France, Jack returned to the states. In late 1958, he made his way back to work, but not before he had his only son fired and banned from the premises. When the shocked Jack, Jr. asked for an explanation, he was simply told that he reminded his father too much of Irma. Jack Warner penned his autobiography, *My First Hundred Years in Hollywood*, in 1964. There was not one mention of his son or his first wife. He recorded that he was a single man when he met Ann.

By the end of 1966 even the seventy-two-year-old Jack was getting tired. He sold his shares of Warner Bros. for $32,000,000 and a promise that he could continue working as an independent producer. The following year, Brother Abe, struck by a stroke, died in his Miami home after a good day at the track on November 26, 1967. Jack was now the last surviving Warner brother.

It was another two years before he, too, left the company that he and his brothers had built. In 1973, not long after his eightieth birthday, Jack took a fall while playing tennis. His health declined and he grew disoriented. Four years later, he suffered a major stroke and was wheelchair-bound, leaving Ann to care for him. Another stroke later claimed his eyesight. Warner died of edema on September 9, 1978 at the age of 86—the final Warner and the last of Hollywood's original movie moguls.

"America's Sweetheart" Mary Pickford may not have been a movie mogul like the Warners, but she was a Hollywood powerhouse in her own right. When she received the call telling her that her beloved Douglas Fairbanks was dead, she claimed that she intuitively knew before she even picked up the phone. Even though she was now wed to her leading man in *My Best Girl* (1927), Charles "Buddy" Rogers, Pickford still mourned the loss of Fairbanks the rest of her days. *My Best Girl* had been her final silent film, not counting an uncredited role as the Virgin Mary in Fairbanks' adventure film, *The Gaucho* (1927).

Pickford made a total of five talking pictures—the first, *Coquette* (1929), garnered her a Best Actress Academy Award. In her final film, *Secrets* (1933), she appeared opposite British actor Leslie Howard. Pickford had been making movies and playing children since 1909. At the age of forty-one and with over 200 films to her credit, she retired from filmmaking. She later explained:

> I left the screen because I didn't want what happened to Charlie Chaplin to happen to me. When he discarded the little tramp, the little tramp turned around and killed him. The little girl made me. I wasn't waiting for the little girl to kill me.

Just as her moviemaking days were coming to a close, Pickford's personal life unraveled. Breast cancer claimed her beloved mother, Charlotte, in 1928 ending a terrible three-year battle that Mary could only watch—terrified and helpless. Three months after Charlotte's death, perhaps in a fit of rebellion, Pickford ordered her hairdresser to cut off her famous curls. Her new bob set off a national frenzy. For the first time in more than twenty years, "America's Sweetheart" fell from favor. With her maternal anchor gone, her marriage to Fairbanks coming unglued and her career floundering, Pickford took comfort in the bottle—an unfortunate practice the Pickfords all shared.

By the time she married Rogers in 1937, she had experienced even more family loss. Brother Jack, who lived in a world of excess, fell ill and died in Paris on January 3, 1933 at the age of 37. On December 9, 1936, sister Lottie, 41, was felled instantly by a heart attack. The family Pickford had so dutifully cared for, supported and loved her entire life was gone.

After their marriage, Rogers and Pickford settled at Pickfair—Mary's part of the divorce settlement. Despite their new spouses, Fairbanks and Pickford never lost their connection or the sadness they shared over their failed marriage. He often visited, and together they sat by the pool lamenting their past mistakes.

Despite her personal melancholia, Pickford remained duty-bound. In 1941, she was still a partner at UA and continued her charity work. She was also a decision maker on the board of the Motion Picture Relief Fund. Twenty years earlier, she helped establish the fund intending to provide assistance to filmmakers in need. She was also the force behind the "Payroll Pledge Program" whereby studio employees earning more than $200 each week could give one half of one percent to the fund. As a result, the group was able to purchase property in Woodland Hills, California where they built the Motion Picture Country House. It was Pickford who picked up a shovel and broke ground.

At the age of 51, the former actress gave in to a temporary maternal desire and adopted six-year-old Ronald Charles. The following year, she acted on a whim and brought home five-month-old Roxanne. As the children grew, the novelty of motherhood wore off and their care was mostly left to the servants or private boarding schools. As for Pickford, she continued drinking and was prone to outbursts that when sober she could not remember.

In 1955 Pickford penned her autobiography, *Sunshine and Shadows*, picking and choosing her own version of events. The following year, she sold all of her UA shares for $3,000,000—the last of Hollywood's original big four to move on. Chaplin had already gotten out of the company, as well as the country, a few years earlier, while both Griffith and Fairbanks were long since dead.

Her marriage to Rogers was a lasting one, but she was not easy to live with. She often called him "Douglas" and took out her frustrations on him—whether she was in a drunken rage or a lucid moment of animosity. Not one to complain, Rogers took most of her abuse in stride—always ready to protect and defend her when he felt it was necessary. As the years passed, Mary grew more and more reclusive, rarely leaving Pickfair and some days not even getting out of bed. She took phone calls, but admitted fewer and fewer visitors to her inner sanctum.

Among those allowed inside were her stepson, Douglas Fairbanks, Jr., and old friends such as writer Adela Rogers St. Johns and actress Lillian Gish. Pickford liked to reminisce about the early days of Hollywood and her marriage to Fairbanks. On one visit with St. Johns, a tearful Pickford asked her: "Will Douglas ever forgive me?" After all those years, her guilt over their unhappy ending still consumed her.

When she received an honorary Oscar in 1976, a film crew went to Pickfair where she said a few words of thanks in front of the camera. After that her mental and physical state declined to the point where she thought she was young again and still the Queen of Hollywood. Eighty-seven-year-old Pickford died on May 29, 1979 after suffering a stroke a few days earlier. Rogers, her loyal husband of more than four decades, was at her side.

Pickford's petite frame and sausage-like curls belied the shrewd businesswoman that hid behind a façade of innocence. Her fans never accepted her any other way, but Mary had to eventually grow up and when she did her long Hollywood reign ended. Her influence, however, remains. With every Academy Award presented, along with each new resident welcomed at the Motion Picture and Television Country House and Hospital, the aura of Mary Pickford lingers on.

If the delicate Pickford represented the feminine face of Hollywood, director Raoul Walsh went for the macho. While he was busy establishing the Academy, Walsh also found time to marry his second wife, Lorraine Helen Walker, in Tijuana, Mexico. Following their nuptials, he got sidetracked with a rousing round of roulette. The gambling groom walked away with $18,000 in winnings on his wedding night.

He also directed his final silent film, *Sadie Thompson* (1928), which was based on author W. Somerset Maugham's play *Rain*. Gloria Swanson was cast as lady of the night Sadie, with Lionel Barrymore as the self-righteous missionary who gives in to her dubious charms. Walsh himself took on a supporting role as a marine officer—his first in more than ten years. It was also his last, but he didn't plan it that way.

With sound entering the pictures, Walsh didn't want to be left behind. He agreed to direct and star in the talking western *In Old Arizona* (1929). Playing the Cisco Kid, Walsh sported a moustache and a Mexican accent. Filming took place on location in Utah until the company's sound van broke down. Nearly done with their scenes, the group packed up and headed back to the studio where they planned to finish the job. Driving through the desert at night, a jackrabbit vaulted through the windshield smashing into Walsh. Severely cut by the shattered glass, he was taken by train to a Salt Lake City hospital. The cuts and scrapes eventually healed, but Walsh lost his right eye. When doctors offered him a glass one, he declined: "No, I'd get drunk and lose it."

In Old Arizona was reshot with actor Warner Baxter taking Walsh's role as the Cisco Kid under the direction of Irving Cummings. Baxter won an Academy Award for his performance and went on to play the Cisco Kid in several sequels. Walsh may have lost out on the movie, but he gained his most defining accessory—the black eye patch.

Nothing kept Walsh down for long—not even a missing eye. He returned to work and in 1930 directed a western called *The Big Trail*. The film featured former prop man Marion Morrison, in his first major role. Fox brass agreed that a feminine name like "Marion" was not manly enough for one of their rugged cowboys. At the same time, Walsh had taken a shine to Revolutionary War General "Mad" Anthony Wayne.

Anthony or Tony Wayne didn't cut it, but they all agreed on just plain "John." It was all-American, masculine and perfectly fit the tall, strapping young man. Unfortunately, the movie flopped and John Wayne had to wait a bit before landing his breakout role.

Walsh directed mostly unmemorable films for the rest of the decade. Anyone else might have thought about retiring or at least changing their line of work. Not Walsh. At 52, he signed on with Warner Bros. and began a period of brilliance. Walsh's first film for the Warners starred two heavy hitters, James Cagney and Humphrey Bogart. *The Roaring Twenties* (1939) was not only box office dynamite, it was a crowning achievement in the gritty gangster genre, allowing Walsh to reclaim his top director status.

That same year, the first Mrs. Walsh resurfaced. In their original divorce agreement, Miriam Cooper was to receive $500 worth of weekly alimony. In 1934, she agreed to a reduced payment of $325 with one stipulation— if her ex-husband missed three consecutive payments, she could come after him under the terms of the first agreement. Confused? Walsh must have been. He failed to make three payments in October resulting in Cooper's claim that Walsh now owed her $46,650. She figured that under the original $500 agreement, she should have gotten a total of $130,500 over the years. Instead she only received $83,850—hence the difference. Who said high finance was easy?!

Their sons, John, now 25, and Robert, 17, had been living with their mother. Robert, still a minor, petitioned the court asking that his guardianship be given to his father. The court granted his request and in late 1941, the battling Walshes finally reached a settlement. Cooper collected $25,000 in cash, $225 per week for four years and then $200 a week for the rest of her life or until she remarried—something she never did.

With the court drama behind him, Walsh renewed his successful partnership with Bogart with *They Drive by Night* (1940) and *High Sierra* (1941). In a change of pace, he reteamed with Cagney for a sentimental look at the early 1900s in *The Strawberry Blonde* (1941)—Walsh's personal favorite of all his sound pictures. His final film of 1941 starred Errol Flynn as General George Custer. *They Died with Their Boots On* was the first of several movies that Flynn and Walsh would make together.

Walsh went on to direct a variety of films during the forties. He helmed the biopic *Gentleman Jim* (1942) with Errol Flynn as boxer James J. Corbett, war drama *Objective Burma!* (1945) also with Flynn and *The Horn Blows at Midnight* (1945), a comedy featuring comedian Jack Benny as an angel.

His professional winning streak, however, didn't extend to the home front. After a brief separation, wife Lorraine filed for divorce on the grounds of mental cruelty. She stated that: "For the last five years, Mr. Walsh has been very rude. He refuses to talk. When friends called at our home he refused to talk to them. His only explanation was that he wanted to live alone." For her trouble, the second ex-Mrs. Walsh was awarded $200 a week in alimony for the rest of her life or until she married again—which she did.

In 1947, Walsh wed for the third time. His bride was Mary Edna Simpson, the daughter of a Kentucky horse-breeder whom the director met while visiting Lexington. He was 60; she was 23. The couple married in Mexico, but two years later decided to do it again in Tucson—just in case their south-of-the-border union wasn't legal.

In 1949, Walsh once again reached another peak in his long career with *White Heat*. Back with James Cagney as the thoroughly contemptible mama's boy, Cody Jarrett, Walsh directed one of his finest films and Cagney gave one his greatest performances. In the final climactic scene, as the despicable Jarrett reaches the top of a jumbo gas storage tank, he goes out in a fiery blaze, hollering: "Made it, Ma! Top of the world!"

Walsh spent the last twelve years of his career freelancing. He worked and played with many Hollywood greats: "They were all marvelous people. The sad part about it, I lost four of them—Bogey, Flynn, Gable and Cooper, all within four years. . . . One right after another—all great friends of mine. Between pictures we used to pal around. I used to go fishing and hunting with Cooper and I used to go hunting down in Utah and Arizona with Gable. And I used to go out drinking with Flynn."

He even sold his three-bedroom home in Encino to Gable just before the actor married Carole Lombard. Later, the two men teamed up to bid on the Detroit Tigers baseball franchise. Their intention was to eventually move the team from Michigan to the west coast. That deal didn't pan out, so Gable and Walsh continued making movies and the Tigers continued playing baseball in Motown.

After more than half a century, Walsh finally retired from films. His last movie was the western *A Distant Trumpet* (1964) featuring Troy Donahue and Suzanne Pleshette. The former director lived out his years with his wife, Mary, on his 1500-acre ranch north of Los Angeles where he tended his orange trees, cattle and racehorses. In 1974, he published his autobiography, *Each Man in His Time: The Life Story of a Director.* Of course, he took the opportunity to do what he did best—embellish.

When glaucoma claimed the sight in his left eye leaving him blind, he never complained. He once told a visitor that he could still ". . . sit on my porch and enjoy the bird-calls and the aroma of the flowers and detect the footsteps of the approaching internal revenue agents."

Walsh was a tough Irishman who could tell an enthusiastic tale—a dozen different ways—none of which would ever bore his listener. Luckily, he chose to tell many of his stories on the silver screen. Known best for his adventure films and action-packed gangster movies, Walsh was considered a man's director. He worked hard, played even harder and wore his eye patch with panache. Walsh died of a heart attack on New Year's Eve in 1980 at the age of 93. Mary, his wife of 35 years, was with him at Simi Valley Adventist Hospital. Not one to dwell on his many achievements, he once said: "I just did my job. I let others make up the theories."

Like Walsh, Henry King was also a distinguished Hollywood director who had been involved in filmmaking almost from the beginning. While forming the Academy, King was busy making his final movie for Goldwyn, *The Magic Flame* (1927). The circus drama starred Ronald Colman as a clown and Vilma Banky as a daring trapeze artist. For King, the transition to sound posed little problem. His first all-talking picture was a pirate adventure with Lupe Velez called *Hell Harbor* (1930) and filmed on location in Florida.

King was also raising a family with his wife, Gypsy. His stepdaughter, Ruth, was now a teen while Henry, Jr., was just six and son John only three. Their daughter, Martha Ellen, arrived in 1930, shortly after King joined Fox.

He stayed with the company through the merger with Twentieth Century Films and was recognized as one of their top directors. During the early thirties, he found success with sentimental films like *State Fair* (1933) featuring Will Rogers and Louise Dresser, as well as the poignant Depression-era drama *One More Spring* (1935), a tale of three homeless people forced to move into a shed in New York's Central Park.

The following year, King filmed a biopic about the Canadian physician who delivered the Dionne Quintuplets, Dr. Allan R. Dafoe. The five girls, Cecile, Yvonne, Annette, Emilie and Marie, were also featured in the film *The Country Doctor* (1936). The troupe traveled to Ontario where the toddlers lived and had to abide by the many rules set forth by Dafoe. Filming could only be done inside the children's sterile play area for less than an hour each day. Anyone entering the room had to wear a surgical mask—except for the actors, Jean Hersholt and Dorothy Peterson. They submitted to daily throat checks and spray instead. In addition, the girls could not be awakened if they were sleeping and never coerced into laughing or crying. As result, King discarded his script and just filmed the children for more than two weeks. The footage was later edited into the final film.

Over the next few years, King directed *In Old Chicago* (1936), the story of the O'Leary's and their troublesome cow, the musical *Alexander's Ragtime Band* (1938) featuring Tyrone Power, and *Jesse James* (1939) also with Tyrone Power as Jesse and Henry Fonda as his no-good brother, Frank.

As America entered World War II, King put his pilot's license to good use. He helped form the California Civil Air Patrol comprised of several volunteer flyers who flew with the Ferry Command. The group took part in search and rescue missions whenever aerial assistance was required. They also guarded power and water supplies and sometimes acted as a courier service. King ultimately obtained the rank of colonel.

In 1943, the director, who had converted to Catholicism after making *The White Sister* (1924), filmed *The Song of Bernadette*. The movie starred dark-haired actress Jennifer Jones who won a Best Actress Oscar for her saintly performance while King received a nomination for his heavenly direction. Due to the movie's success, King was also voted best director of 1943–1944 in a nationwide poll beating out such big names as Victor Fleming and Alfred Hitchcock.

The following year, King saw his eldest son off to war. The director flew to Arizona and pinned pilot wings on the young U.S. Air Force Second Lieutenant as part of the graduation ceremony. Later that year, Henry, Jr. was reported missing. It was several weeks before his anxious parents got word that their son had been shot down by the Germans and was now a prisoner of war where he remained until Germany surrendered in the spring of 1945.

After World War II, King had a hit with another sentimental favorite, *Margie* (1946), a look at life during the 1920s—a decade that was now perceived as simpler times. His next few pictures were not as successful, but that changed in 1949 when he helmed the war drama *Twelve O'Clock High* starring Gregory Peck. The air battles shown in the film were taken from actual World War II combat footage. It was also one of the first films to concentrate on the psychological effects of war instead of the conflicts.

During the fifties, King lost his wife, Gypsy, and later remarried. He also continued churning out films like *The Snows of Kilimanjaro* (1952), *Carousel* (1956) *and Beloved Infidel* (1959). At 76, he ended his four-decade career with *Tender is the Night* (1962)—a biopic about the colorful life of writer F. Scott Fitzgerald.

A reserved southern gentleman and dependable studio director, he was content to simply go to work and make the best movies he could. Given a story and a budget, he did his job without complaint or excuse. Always in a proper business suit, he commanded an executive-type respect and was usually called "Mr. King" by his subordinates. His movies covered all genres—westerns, musicals, dramas, adventures and comedies—some sentimental, some funny, and some edgy. With more than 100 films to his directing credit, many stand as a tribute to a man who never personally sought the spotlight. He much preferred the sky to flamboyance or publicity. He once explained his passion for flying:

> In the limitless reaches of the sky, a man is really alone. The problem, which seemed so difficult to master in the turmoil of the office and the studio resolve themselves when one is alone.

As late as 1978, ninety-year-old King was still clocking in over 10,000 miles annually in his private plane. At the time, he was recognized as the oldest active pilot in American aviation history until his age and health no longer permitted his personal access to the skies. He died in his sleep after a heart attack on June 29, 1982—the last surviving member of the Academy's original 36 founders.

As he drew his final breath, director Henry King, in his usual quiet fashion, marked the end of an extraordinary time that began when an enterprising soul unfurled a sheet, hung it from the ceiling and, for a nickel or so, invited curious spectators to witness pictures that moved.

THAT'S A WRAP!

The Academy of Motion Picture Arts and Sciences remains one of, if not the most, significant organizations in the film industry today. Although it's best known for the awards it bestows, the Academy has accomplished so much more than the delivery of a coveted statuette or an annual red-carpet bash. Its founding members revolutionized entertainment and, in the process, created, influenced and preserved the premier art form of the Twentieth Century.

From its inception, the Academy encouraged the next generation of filmmakers to get a formal education and learn the art of this new craft. The founders not only helped design college-level curriculum, but many personally lectured in the classroom to ensure that their industry would one day pass into capable hands. Regardless of their studio affiliation, they also united to address common issues such as the various challenges presented by the coming of sound, censorship dos and don'ts, as well as the resolution of workers' grievances. Most importantly, the Academy's 36 founders put their best faces forward and their differences aside and gave a troubled industry a united front during turbulent times. In the midst of two world wars, several recessions, one Great Depression and the speakeasy era of Prohibition, they ensured that their beloved art form would continue to evolve and grow long after they were gone.

These hardworking men and women were also mere mortals who coped with personal issues much like the rest of us. Some were widowed while others suffered the agonizing loss of a child or grandchild. Many cared for overbearing mothers or dealt with the aftereffects of disappearing fathers. Troubled siblings demanded attention, jobs, and in many cases, financial handouts. The founders also dealt with failed marriages, depleting bank accounts, mental illness, alcoholism, and in at least one case, jail time.

Perhaps they also met with a little luck and happenstance, but their talent, passion, tenacity, and commitment brought this motley crew together in early January 1927. Now top actors, writers, directors, producers and technicians, they simply saw a need, rose to the occasion and took command. In their unique way and with their distinctive contributions, these former gold miners, cowpokes and junk dealers shaped an art form and showed the rest of us what could be if only we had the courage to dream big.

As for their golden child—no matter what you call him, Oscar still represents the best in motion pictures, and with 36 parents, all high achievers themselves, the little man remains a powerhouse. It must be in the genes.

SOURCES

WEBSITES

www.ancestry.com

www.boxoff.com/oct97story3.html

www.centralcasting.org

www.filmsite.org

www.filmsofthegoldenage.com/foga/1998/winter98/nshearer.html

www.franklloydfilms.com

www.help.acusd.edu/History/classes/media/thalberg.html

www.historycentral.com/Navy/cruiser/seattleI.html

www.hollywoodmovie.about.com/entertainment/hollywoodmovie/library/
weekly/aa020899.html

www.imdb.com

www.jesse-l-lasky.com

www.mdle.com/ClassicFilms

www.measuringworth.com

www.nybooks.com

www.osann.org

www.ocarataglance.wordpress.com

www.oscars.org

www.pompress.com/titles/film/hollywood1.html

www.seeing-stars.com

www.silentsaregolden.com

www.taylorology.com

http://teaching.arts.usyd.edu.au/history/hsty3080/3rdYr3080/3080site/
don'ts:2fbe%20carefuls

www.time.com
www.youtube.com, Jesse L. Lasky—This is Your Life Parts 1–3
www.youtube.com, Douglas Fairbanks Documentary Parts 1–9
www.youtube.com, Early Years of Hollywood Parts 1–5
www.youtube.com, Hollywood: Early Directors Parts 1–5
www.youtube.com, Silent Clowns Parts 1–7
www.westegg.com/inflation

BOOKS

70 Years of the Oscar by Robert Osborne. Published 2002 by The Southern Illinois University Press, Carbondale and Edwardsville.

A Historical Study of the Academy of Motion Picture Arts and Sciences (1927–1947) by Pierre Norman Sands. Published 1973 by Arno Press, New York.

American Silent Film, Discovering Marginalized Voices edited by Gregg Bachman & Thomas J. Slater. Published 2002 by The University Press of Kentucky, Lexington.

An Empire of Their Own, How the Jews Invented Hollywood by Neal Gabler. Published 1988 by Crown Publishers, Inc., New York.

Back Lot: Growing Uup With the Movies by Maurice Rapf. Published 1999 by Scarecrow Press, Inc., Lanham, Maryland.

Behind the Motion-Picture Screen by Austin C. Lescarboura. Published 1919 by Munn and Company, New York.

Cecil B. DeMille: A Life in Art by Simon Louvoish. Publsihed 2007 by Thomas Dunne Books, New York.

Cedric Gibbons: Pioneer in Art Direction for Cinema by Lindy jean Narver. Published 1988 as a thesis for the University of Southern California.

Damned in Paradise, The Life of John Barrymore by John Kobler. Published 1977 by Athenium, New York.

D. W. Griffith: The Years at Biograph by Robert M. Henderson. Published 1970 by Farrar, Straus and Giroux, New York.

Eighty Odd Years in Hollywood: Memoir of a Career in Film and Television by John Meredyth Lucas. Published 2004 by McFarland & Company, Inc., Jefferson, NC.

Encyclopedia of the Great Plains edited by David J. Wishart. Published 2004 by The University of Nebraska Press, Lincoln.

Engulfed: The Death of Paramount Pictures and the Birth of Corporate Hollywood by Bernard F. Dick. Published 2001 by The University Press of Kentucky, Lexington.

Film Production Theory by Jean Pierre Geuens. Publlished 2007 by State University of New York Press, New York.

Film Study: An Analytical Bibliography Volume I by Frank Manchel. Published 1990 by Associated University Presses, Crabury, NJ.

Framework, A History of Screenwriting in the American Film by Tom Stempel. Published 1988 by First Syracuse University Press, Chicagoe and New York.

Gable, A Pictorial Biography by Jean Garceau. Published 1961 by Grosset & Dunlap, New York.

Goldwyn: A Biography by A. Scott Berg. Published 1989 by The Berkley Publishing Co., New York.

Gone Hollywood, The Movie Colony in the Golden Age by Christopher Finch & Linda Rosenkrantz. Published 1979 by Doubleday & Company,Inc., New York.

Hollywood and the Academy Awards by Nathalie Fredrick. Published 1970 by Hollywood Awards Publications, Beverly Hills.

Hollywood Anecdotes by Paul F. Boller, Jr. and Ronald L. Davis. Published 1987 by Ballantine Books, New York.

Hollywood at Your Feet by Stacey Endres & Robert Cushman. Published 1992 by Pomegranate Press, Ltd., Universal City.

Hollywood Be Thy Name, The Warner Brothers Story by Cass Warner Sperling and Cork Millner. Published 1994 by Prima Publishing, Rocklin, CA.

Hollywood Censored: Morality Codes, Catholics, and the Movies by Gregory D. Black. Published 1996 by Cambridge University Press, Cambridge, UK.

Hollywood Dreams Made Real, Irving Thalberg and the Rise of MGM by Mark A. Vieira. Published 2008 by Harry N. Abrams, Inc., New York.

Hollywood's Master Showman, The Legendary Sid Grauman by Charles Beardsley. Published 1983 by Cornwall Books, London.

I Blow My Own Horn by Jesse L. Lasky. Published 1957 by Doubleday & Copany, Inc., Garden City, NY.

Irving Thalberg: Boy Wonder to Producer Prince by Mark A. Vieira. Published 2010 by University of California Press, Berkeley and Los Angeles.

Los Angeles From the Moutains to the Sea, Volume 3, by John Steven McGroarty. Published 1921 by The American Historical Society, New York.

Love, Laughter and Tears, My Hollwood Story by Adela Rogers St. Johns. Published 1978 by Doubleday and Company, Inc., New York.

Marilyn Monroe: A Life of the Actress, by Carl Edmund Rollyson, Jr. Published 1993 by Da Capo Press, Cambridge, MA.

Mayer and Thalberg, The Make-Believe Saints by Samuel Marx. Published 1975 by Samuel French Trade, California.

Merchant of Dreams: Louis B. Mayer, MGM and The Secret Hollywood by Charles Higham. Published 1989 by Abbeville Press, New York.

MGM, When the Lion Roars by Peter Hay. Published 1991 by Turner Publishibng, Inc., Atlanta.

Movies and American Socity edited by Steven J. Ross. Publlished 2002 by Blackwell Publishers, Ltd., Malden, Mass.

My Autobiography by Charles Chaplin. Published 1964 by Simon and Schuster, New York.

My Secret Mother, Lorna Moon by Richard DeMille. Published 1998 by Farrar, Strauss and Girous, New York.

One Thousand Laughs From Vaudeville (no author given). Published 1908 by I. & M. Ottenheimer, Baltimore.

Palisades Amusement Park by Vince Gargiulo. Published 2005 by Arcadia Publishing, Charleston.

Pickford, The Woman Who Made Hollywood by Eileen Whitfield. Published 1997 by The University Press of Kentucky, Lexington.

Silent Players by Anthony Slide. Published 2002 by The University Press of Kentucky, Lexington.

Silent Stars by Jeanine Basinger. Published 1999 by Alfred A. Knopf, New York.

Silent Topics: Essays on Undocumented Areas of Silent Film by Anthony Slide. Published 2005 by Scarecrow Press, Inc., Lanham, MD.

Stanwyck by Axel Madsen. Published 1994 by HarperCollins Publisher, Inc., New York.

Stardust and Shadows: Canadians in Early Hollywood by Charles Foster. Published 2000 by Dundern Press, Ltd., Toronto, Ontario, Canada.

Thalberg, Life and Legend by Bob Thomas. Published 1985 by Doubleday and Company, Inc., New York.

Thalberg, The Last Tycoon and the World of MGM by Roland Flamini. Published 1994 by Crown Publishing, Inc., New York.

The Academy Awards: A Pictorial History by Paul Michael. Published 1968 by Bonanza Books., New York.

The American Theatrical Film: Stages in Development by John C. Tibbetts. Published 1985 by Bowling Green State University Popular Press, Bowling Green.

The First 100 Noted Men and Women of the Screen by Carol Lowrey. Published 1920 by Moffat, Yard and Company, New York.

The Grove Book of Hollywood edited by Christopher Sylvestor. Published 1998 by Grove Press, New York.

The Lion of Hollywood: The Life and Legend of Louis B. Mayer by Scott Eyman. Published 2005 by Simon and Schuster, New York.

The Master by Hermann Bahr and Benjamin Floyer Glazer. Published 1918 by Nicholas L. Brown, Philadelphia.

The Men Who Made Movies by Richard Schickel. Published 1975 by Atheneum, New York.

The Movies, Mr. Griffith and Me by Lilliamn Gish. Published 1969 by Prentice-Hall, Inc., Englewood Cliffs, New Jersey.

The Parade's Gone By by Kevin Brownlow. Published 1968 by University of California Press, Berkely and Los Angeles.

The Salad Days by Douglas Fairbanks, Jr. Published 1988 by Doubleday, New York.

The Speed of Sound: Hollywood and the Talkie Revolution 1926–1930 by Scott Eyman. Published 1997 by Simon and Schuster, Inc., New York.

The Times We Had, Life with William Randolph Hearst by Marion Davies. Published 1975 by Bobbs-Merrill Company, Inc., New York.

The Valentino Mystique: The Death and Afterlife of the Silent Film Idol by Allen R. Ellen-
berger. Published 2005 by McFarland & Company, Inc., Jefferson, NC.

The Warner Brothers Story by Clive Hirschhorn. Published 1979 by Crown Publishers, Inc., New York.

What Happens Next: A Hisotry of American Screenwriting by Marc Norman. Published
2007 by Crown Publishijg Group, New York.

Without Lying Down: Francis Marion and The Powerful Women of Hollywood by Cari
Beauchamp. Published 1997 by University of Calilfornia Press, Berkeley and
Los Angeles.

World Film Directors Volume One 1890–1945 Edited by John Wakeman. Published
1987 by The H.W. Wilson Company, New York.

Writing the Photoplay by J. Berg Esenwein and Arthur Leeds. Published 1913/1919 by
The Home Correspondence School, Springfield, Mass.

QUOTES

Preface
The Academy is the . . . *The Academy Bulletin*, April 2, 1928.

Chapter One: The Flickers
I went to a 100 schools . . . *Time* Magazine, 3/1/1943, Theater: Back Where
He Started (No author), http://www.time.com/time/magazine/
article/0,9171,932975,00.html.

Don't let even the wind . . . *Time* Magazine, 3/1/1943, Theater: Back Where
He Started (No author) http://www.time.com/time/magazine/
article/0,9171,932975,00.html.

One day, a man came around . . . *Hollywood Be Thy Name, The Warner Brothers Story*,
pp. 39–40.

What I saw in front of me . . . *Lion of Hollywood: The Life and Legend of Louis B. Mayer*,
p. 31.

Chapter Two: Welcome to Hollywood!
We were more concerned . . . *Stardust and Shadows: Canadians in Early Hollywood* by
Charles Foste, p. 30.

I know a business . . . *Goldwyn: A Biography*, p. 32.

Kindhearted publicisits who have . . . *Cecil B. DeMille: A Life in Art*, p. 20.

Jesse, I'm pulling out . . . *Cecil B. DeMille: A Life in Art*, p. 49.

If that's pictures . . . *Wolrd Film Directors Volume I*, p. 208.

Flaggstaff no good . . . *Grove Book of Hollywood*, p. 9.

Authorize you to rent . . . *Grove Book of Hollywood*, p. 9.

Welcome to Hollywood, Jesse! . . . www.youtube.com "This is Your Life Jesse L.
Laskey Part 2.

Chapter Three: Team Biograph
Mr. Griffith wasn't in . . . *Photoplay* Magazine, Volume 10, June 1916, p. 96.
A determination was born . . . *Pickford, The Woman Who Made Hollywood*, p. 19.
Who's the dame? . . . *Pickford, The Woman Who Made Hollywood*, p. 78.
How dare you sir insult me . . . *Pickford, The Woman Who Made Hollywood*, p. 78.
Our stage consisted of . . . *D. W. Griffith: The Years at Biograph*, p. 97.
Motion pictures are at last . . . *Film Study: An Analytical Bibliograph Volume I*, p. 123.
Frank Woods, a kindly . . . *Lillian Gish, The Movies, Mr. Griffith and Me*, p. 122.
The Makers of the Picture . . . *Writing the Photoplay*, p. 226.

Chapter Four: The Scribes
. . . a story told largley in pantomime . . . *Writing the Photoplay*, p. 2.
. . . Mr. Wilson is as close to . . . *Dynamic Carey Wilson Refused to Rest Until the Studio Locked Him Out* by Theodore Strauss, *New York Times*, 6/1/1941, p. X3.
. . . Characterization in pictures is . . . *Here Are Rules for Scenario Writing, But It's a Hopeless Task for Amateur* by Carey Wilson, *Pitttsburgh Press* 4/24/1924, p. 5.
One actor, who had left his . . . *The Master, 1918*, p. 8.
If it were not for . . . *The Parade's Gone By*, p. 299.
The sub-title should be . . . *Writing the Photoplay*, p. 226.
Many people believe that . . . *The Los Angeles Times*, 10/30/27, p. 29.

Chapter Five: The Silent Types
The motion picture enables . . . *Movies and American Society*, p. 94.
The walls are literalliy lined . . . *Photoplay* Magazine, Volumes 13–14, December 1917, p. 87.
. . . For the survival of the . . . *Film Production Theory*, pp. 58–59.
. . . The other day at the studio . . . *The Los Angeles Times*, 4/26/25, p. 19.
. . . I didn't know whether to go . . . *The Parade's Gone By*, p. 458.
Whatever the plot . . . *The New York Times*, 3/9/1971, p. 40.
From the time we made . . . *An American Comedy*, p. 122.

Chapter Six: The Idols
[Douglas] was always on . . . *Love Laughter and Tears*, p. 108.
Bounding, spinn, diving . . . *New York Review of Books*, Volume 56, Number , Februry 26, 2009; *The Silent Superstar* by Robert Gottlieb (www.nybooks.com).
I ran a car off a cliff . . . *Silent Stars*, p. 105.
Grey Duck arrived late today . . . *The New York Times*, 12/15/1919, p. 1.
Not once, but twenty times . . . *Hollywood Anecdotes*, pp. 18–19.
He started his vactionless . . . *The Los Angeles Times*, 5/11/1924, p. 36.

Chapter Seven: Calling the Shots
I got the company together . . . www.youtube.com "Hollywood: Early Directors"
    Part 1.
Once the director is satisfied . . . *Behind the Motion-Picture Screen*, p. 26.
. . . I got off the horse and looked . . . *New York* Magazine, 4/5/1974, p. 73.
I thought to myself . . . *The Men Who Made Movies*, p. 25.
Director Frank Lloyd will . . . *New York Times*, 10/3/1915, p. 91.
earned himself a place . . . *World Film Directors, Volume I: 1890–1945*, p. 684.
We spend hours discussing . . . *The Los Angeles Times*, 3/11/1923, p. vii.
[Stahl] was trying to imitate . . . *Lion of Hollywood*, p. 66.
We are at the stage . . . *L.A. Times*, 9/18/1921, p. 1013.
All the Americans . . . *One Thousand Laughs from Vaudeville*, pp. 28–29.
By this time my father was . . . *World Film Directors, Volume I: 1890–1945*, pp. 535–536.
At that time San Fernando . . . www.youtube.com "Hollywood: Early Directors" Part 1.

Chapter Eight: How Did They Do That?
Any art which makes its . . . *The American Cinemtographer, Volumes 3–4*, August,
    1923, p. 4.
. . . the audience must be made . . . *Behind the Motion-Picture Screen*, p. 110.
The technical director must . . . *Behind the Motion-Picture Screen*, p. 118.
. . . art directors have a great . . . *The Los Angeles Times*, 12/16/1920, p. III16.
Never let a motion-picture set . . . *The Los Angeles Times*, 12/16/1920, p. III16.
. . . a fairy would appear in a . . . *Behind the Motion-Picture Screen*, p. 194.
We had discovered Pomeroy . . . *Grove Book of Hollywood*, pp. 106–107.

Chapter Nine: Head of the House
My father's early movies . . . *Back Lot: Growing Up With the Movies*, p. 1.
Almost everyone wants to get . . . *The Los Angeles Times*, 8/14/1927, pp. C15–16.
I would never bet on . . . *New York Times*, 10/23/1962, p. 29.
Lou Anger, my friend and . . . *The Los Angeles Times*, 2/1/1923, p. II1.
The properties consisting of . . . *The Los Angeles Times*, 1/3/1922, p. II5.
The Motion-Picture Exposition . . . *The Los Angeles Times*, 7/2/1923, p. IV5.
Many producers who have . . . *The Los Angeles Times*, 10/13/1924, p. A16.
With his personality there is no . . . *The Moving Picture World, Volume 18, Isses 8–23*,
    December 6, 1913, p. 1156.
When I was with Universal . . . *Silent Players*, p. 141.
Never hold an unassailable . . . *The Los Angeles Times*, 10/15/1922, p. III38.

Chapter Ten: The Guardians
Spain when she blew up . . . *The Los Angeles Times*, 7/3/1898, p. B5.
My brother Edwin handled the . . . Oral History of Joseph P. Loeb taken by Claremont Graduate School on February 19, 1965.

Had motion pictures been in . . . *The Los Angeles Times*, 7/7/1926, p. A5.

I believe we are on the right . . . *The Los Angeles Times*, 1/251924, p. A1.

To do away with . . . The 22nd Biennial Bureau of Labor Statistics of California for the State of California, 1926, p. 149.

Chapter Eleven: On Top of the Mountain

a very convenient . . . *World Film Directors, Volume I: 1890–1945*, p. 208.

This will be my first trip . . . *The Los Angeles Times*, 8/20/1919, p. H14.

. . . I should like to say a good . . . *The Los Angeles Times*, 9/15/1921, p. 16.

The pictorial qualities . . . *The Los Angeles Times*, 10/14/1922, p. H1.

He is a picture technical . . . *Silent Topics: Essays on Undocumented Areas of Silent Film*, p. 77.

Chapter Twelve: Lions and Tigers and Brothers, Oh My!

[The representsative] said . . . *Hollywood Be Thy Name, The Warner Brothers Story*, p. 46.

Soap I can sell . . . *Hollywood Be Thy Name, The Warner Brothers Story*, p. 53.

If effervesence of spirits has . . . *The Los Angeles Times*, 3/1/1925, p. 17.

Perfection of a new appartus . . . *New York Times*, 4/26/1926, p. 7.

Who the hell wants to hear . . . Personal quote taken from wwwimdb.com.

Chapter Thirteen: The Lunatics

The lunatics have taken charge . . . *Pickford, The Woman Who Made Hollywood*, p. 192.

From Constance I had heard . . . *My Autobiography*, p. 199.

They intended putting . . . *My Autobiography*, p. 222.

We believe [United Artists] is . . . *Pickford, The Woman Who Made Hollywood*, pp. 191–192.

Douglas Fairbanks and Mary . . . *Silent Stars*, p. 117.

Here is magic . . . *Douglas Fairbanks (Vance)*, p. 177.

the same old melodramatic . . . *World Film Directors, Volume I: 1890–1945*, p. 1151.

Chapter Fourteen: In The Zoo

Louis B. chose the . . . *Hollywood Dreams Made Real Irving Thalberg and the Rise of MGM*, p. 19.

That's the kind of people . . . *Lion of Hollywood: The Life and Legend of Louis B. Mayer*, p. 57.

To me, the ideal picture . . . *New York Times*, 12/14/1924, p. C29.

Tell him if he comes to work for . . . *Lion of Hollywood: The Life and Legend of Louis B. Mayer*, p. 69.

The merger greatly . . . *The Los Angeles Times*, 4/28/1924, p. A1.

This is a great moment for me . . . *Merchant of Dreams, Louis B. Mayer, MGM and the Secret Hollywood*, p. 70.

Carey's the kind of guy . . . *Lawrence Journal World*, 2/8/1962, p. 3.

You would be working with . . . *What Happens Next: A Hisotry of American Screen-writing*, p. 126.

The only thing . . . Personal quote taken from wwwimdb.com.

Fine! That'll add some . . . *Thalberg: The Last tycoon and the World of MGM*, p. 67.

Chapter Fifteen: The Rest of 'Em
Our office has nothing to do . . . *The Los Angeles Times*, 11/27/1924, p. A7.

I believe the entire field of . . . *The Los Angeles Times*, 8/24/1924, p. B22.

Mr. Charles Christie, finding . . . *Dog Fancier, Volumes 31–32*, November, 1922, p. 9.

I'd be with Doug Fairbanks . . . *New York Times*, 3/9/1971, p. 40.

Well, we carried on . . . *The Parade's Gone By*, p. 110.

There were 213 cannon . . . *The Los Angeles Times*, 8/24/1924, p. B37.

Close and sealed forever . . . *The Los Angeles Times*, 10/1/1925, p. A7.

Chapter Sixteen: The Gang's All Here
The greatest public . . . *New York Times*, 1/2/1927, p. X7.

It is on the sets . . . *The Los Angeles Times*, 1/10/1926, p. C35.

Chapter Seventeen: Let's Go On With the Show!
. . . the title 'Academy of . . . *A Historical Study of the Academy of Motion Pictures Arts and Sciences (1927–1947)*, p. 37.

If we producing workers, . . . *A Historical Study of the Academy of Motion Pictures Arts and Sciences (1927–1947)*, pp. 38–39.

The academy has been . . . *The Los Angeles Times*, 9/23/1928, p. 26.

Chapter Eighteen: Scholars, Tough Guys and Bishops
As is the case with . . . *The Los Angeles Times*, 9/18/1927, p. B7.

The membership clings . . . *New York Times*, 6/17/1928, p. 102.

How can I compete with . . . *New York Magazine*, 8/29/1988, p. 20.

Movies aren't made . . . *The Leading Man of MGM*, p. 36.

No more epics for me . . . *Without Lying down: Frances Marion and the Powerful Women of Early Hollywood*, p. 332.

The world of art is poorer . . . *Thalberg, Life and Legend*, p. 297.

Credit you give yourself . . . *Hollywood Dreams Made Real IrvingThalberg and the Rise of MGM*, p. 6.

To the Memory of . . . *Irving Thalberg: Boy Wonder to Producer Prince*, p. 377.

It is impossible now for any . . . *The Los Angeles Times*, 6/25/1931, p. A4.

. . . always a credit to his . . . *The Los Angeles Times*, 5/4/1939, p. A4.

I've never felt better . . . *Douglas Fairbanks (Vance)*, p. 306.

Chapter Nineteen: Three Men and a Lady
While other authors gave . . . www.taylorology.com (Motion Picture July 1921 the
    Literary Dynamo by Barbara Beach).
[DeMille] held her hand . . . *My Secret Mother, Lorna Moon*, p. 23.
He will take advice from . . . *The Los Angeles Times*, 4/6/1042, p. A4.
So our first talkie was . . . *I Blow My Own Horn*, p. 215.
Look, this guy's got locks . . . *The Speed of Sound: Hollywood and the Talkie Revolution
    1926–1930*, p. 211.
I enjoyed an all-talkihg picture . . . *Spokane Daily Chronicle*, 9/7/1929, p. 3.
At home, Dad was strict. . . . www.silentsaregolden.com/articles/
    frednibloarticle.html.
Dear Sam—It is only in time . . . *American Silent Film, Discovering Marginalized
    Voices*, p. 233.
not the llittle fellows . . . *The Los Angeles Times*, 8/14/1927, p. 15.

Chapter Twenty: Mad Hatters, Macho Men and Mexican Divorces
It's my commercial instinct . . . *The Los Angeles Times*, 3/22/1936, p. C1.
. . . everything depends on . . . *The Los Angeles Times*, 9/18/1921, p. H113.
I feel like the face on the . . . *Life* Magazine, 9/30/1940, p. 63.
. . . essentially half the . . . *Box Office Magazine*, October 1997, p. 16.
Among his intimate friends . . . *City of Nets: A Portrait of Hollywood in the
    1940s*, p. 4.
To my wife, Margaret . . . *The Los Angeles Times*, 2/1/1951, p. 18.
. . . The motion-picture is . . . *The Los Angeles Times*, 9/23/1928, p. 26.
. . . improved sharpness . . . *The Los Angeles Times*, 6/7/1931, p. C9.
To Arthur Ball, in . . . Quote received from Ball's grandson, Kevin Ball via email
    dated 6/12/2010.
North Hollywood is destined . . . *The Los Angeles Times*, 6/3/1928, p. F8.
Los Angeles is the best . . . *The Los Angeles Times*, 8/18/1929, p. D2.

Chapter Twenty-One: Businessmen, Artists and Mediators
The Don'ts and Be Carefuls . . . http://teaching.arts.usyd.edu.au/history/
    hsty3080/3rdYr3080/3080site/don'ts:2fbe%20carefuls.
1. No picture shall be . . . www.wikipedia.org/wiki/Hays_code.
Activity in the motion picture . . . *The Los Angeles Times*, 11/4/1932, p. A2.
Our present property . . . *The Los Angeles Times*, 11/30/1927, p. A1.
All the agreements connected . . . *The Los Angeles Times*, 9/30/1930, p. 15.
I can give you a closeup . . . *The American Theatrical Film: Stages in Development*,
    p. 235.
The court ruled that the part . . . *The Los Angeles Times*, 6/28/1946, p. 2.
Some of us walk the earth . . . *The Los Angeles Times*, 3/21/1956, p. 2.

Chapter Twenty-Two: Mogul to Mogul

Spare nothing, neither . . . *Lion of Hollywood: The Life and Lelgend of Louis. B. Mayer,* p. 111.

going to be more active . . . *MGM, When The Lion Roars,* p. 282.

Mr. Motion Picture is Gone . . . ww.time.com.

Within a year things were . . . *I Blow My Own Horn,* p. 221.

. . . at long last I knew how . . . *I Blow My Own Horn,* p. 243.

You're never broke if you . . . www.jesse-l-lasky.com.

Well, since they have worked . . . *I Blow My Own Horn,* p. 177.

Mother...went back to the city . . . *Hollywood Be Thy Name, The Warner Brothers Story,* pp. 153–154.

The motion picture industry . . . *Hollywood Be Thy Name, The Warner Brothers Story,* p. 256.

Chapter Twenty-Three: Ancient Slaves, Bad Facelifts and Broken Towel Bars

Better do another historical . . . *World Film Directors, Volume I: 1890–1945,* p. 217.

The old tycoon of celluloid . . . *Cecil B. DeMille: A Life in Art,* p. 374.

Before you were born . . . *My Secret Mother Lorna Moon,* p. 55.

One thing I have always . . . *World Film Directors, Volume I: 1890–1945,* p. 216.

I don't claim that a good set . . . *The Los Angeles Times,* 5/22/1932, p. B6.

Come on up and get it . . . *Scotland Daily Record,* 11/12/2008.

. . . [Lloyd] likes to take a . . . *Time* Magazine, 9/16/1940.

When I went into the Army . . . *The Tuscaloosa News,* 4/15/1953, p. 13.

. . . a film should not be judged . . . www.franklloydfilms.com.

Sound film will leave . . . *British film Institute Film Classics, Voume I,* p. 96.

Television motion pictures . . . *The Los Angeles Times,* 2/13/1930, p. 2.

It was as much the face . . . *Marilyn Monroe: A Life of the Actress,* p. 22.

A producer in a movie . . . *Kentucky New Era,* 1025/1947, p. 3.

The fun had gone out of . . . *The Tuscaloosa News,* 8/6/1963, p. 33.

Chapter Twenty-Four: Pretzels, Lawyers and Potentates

Any work that varies . . . *The Los Angeles Times,* 10/7/1928, p. C27.

We knew they were . . . *Without Lying Down, Francis Marion and The Powerful Women of Hollywood,* p. 375.

Despite all the help . . . *Eighty Odd Years in Hollywood, Memoir of a Career in Film and Television,* p. 222.

Somebody get the . . . *Eighty Odd Years in Hollywood, Memoir of a Career in Film and Television,* p. 61.

. . . has participated in four . . . *Pittsburgh Post-Gazette,* 3/17/1947, p. 14.

"Any talk about my being . . . *New York Times,* 2/6/1932, p. 17.

It has been amazing to me . . . www.haroldlloyd.com.

One of the greatest . . . *The Los Angeles Times*, 3/24/1929, p. C11.
The Screen Guild . . . *New York Times*, 5/1/1932, p. X5.
Those who challenge the . . . *The Los Angeles Times*, 10/22/1933, p. 7.

Chapter Twenty-Five: Last Founders Standing
Talk to me all you want about . . . *Hollywood Be Thy Name, The Warner Brothers Story*,
    p. 146.
The only good thing . . . *Hollywood Be Thy Name, The Warner Brothers Story*, p. 207.
[Jack] stepped close to . . . *Hollywood Be Thy Name, The Warner Brothers Story*, p. 312.
I left the screen . . . *Silent Stars*, p. 52.
Will Douglas ever . . . *Love, Laughter and Tears, My Hollywood Story*, p. 128.
No, I'd get drunk and lose it . . . *World Film Directors, Volume I: 1890–1945*, p. 1153.
For the last five years . . . *The Los Angeles Times*, 3/16/1946, p. 8.
They were all marvelous . . . *The Men Who Made the Movies*, p. 52.
. . . sit on my porch and . . . *World Film Directors, Volume I: 1890–1945*, p. 1159.
I just did my job . . . *New York Times*, 1/2/1981, p. D7.
In the limitless reaches . . . *The Los Angeles Times*, 9/25/1955, p. G2.

Debra Ann Pawlak has been a movie lover ever since she can remember and likes the fact that she shares a birthday with film great, Carole Lombard. She writes from southeastern Michigan where she lives with her husband, Michael. She has authored a book about her hometown, Farmington, for Arcadia Publishing's Making of America Series, as well as a children's book detailing the life of the legendary Bruce Lee. In addition, she completed an in-depth profile of March King John Philip Sousa, which was recorded and released on a children's CD by Allegro Music. Her work has also appeared in several publications such as *Chicken Soup for the Soul*, *The Writer*, *Aviation History* and *Michigan History Magazine*. She has two grown children, Rachel, who lives in Denver with her fiancé, Jon, and Jonathon, who lives in Michigan with his wife, Stacey.